A Slow Life but a Good Life

A Slow Life but a Good Life

Stories from the South Carolina Mountains

John M. Coggeshall

ISBN 978-1-63804-196-2

Published by Clemson University Press.
For information about Clemson University Press, please visit our website at www.clemson.edu/press.

Design by Mars O'Keefe.

Cover Photo: A. G. Gantt Grocery Store, "People and Places – Pickens Area" Digital Collections file, Pickens County Library System.

Dedication

This book is dedicated to all my students – those I knew as a graduate assistant at Southern Illinois University (Edwardsville) and those I taught at Southern Illinois University (Carbondale), at Graham and Centralia Correctional Centers (Illinois), at Radford University (Virginia), at Clemson University (South Carolina), and at Charles University (Prague, Czech Republic). Over the past six decades you have frustrated me, perplexed me, entertained me, surprised me, educated me, challenged me, befriended me, thrilled me, and inspired me. Above all, you have given me a life-long career that I love.

Contents

List of Figures

Acknowledgements

This book is the third of a trilogy of volumes that stemmed from the same research project. Sometime in the late summer of 2006, I was invited by Tom Swayngham and Greg Lucas, both with the South Carolina Department of Natural Resources (DNR), to document the lives and stories of the "old timers" who had lived in the Jocassee and upper Keowee valleys of Pickens and Oconee Counties, South Carolina. Tom and Greg also provided me with an initial list of contacts, and they invited a retired DNR biologist, Sam Stokes, to help me meet these folks. Sam and I enjoyed many trips together in my first year of research, and he introduced me to some amazing people. Unfortunately, Sam passed away on June 24, 2019.

Both Tom and Greg have demonstrated incredible patience as their initial hopes for a collection of stories from the old timers has morphed into two "prequels": *Liberia, South Carolina* (about an enclave of descendants of formerly enslaved African Americans in upper Pickens County [UNC Press, 2018]) and then *Something in These Hills: The Culture of Family Land in Southern Appalachia* (about the deep emotional relationship that inhabitants have toward family land [UNC Press, 2022]). Now comes this book: a collection of mountain stories that I thought were too good to leave on a cutting room floor. Of course, a better way to think about the goal of this book would be to respect the lives of the people who shared the stories with me by bringing these wonderful stories to a wider audience by means of this book.

Fieldwork formally began in the early fall of 2006, with the bulk of my interviews taking place in 2008 and 2009 but continuing into 2012. I would like to thank the eighty-nine men and women of Greenville, Pickens, and Oconee Counties who volunteered their time and memories for the stories that enliven this book. While all of you may not be quoted in this book, I sincerely enjoyed having the opportunity to meet you and to listen to your perspectives.

During the fieldwork for this book, twenty-eight individuals passed away. I would like to remember and thank Albert Aiken, Sam and Leecie Baker, Bill Batson, Brown Bowie, Lloyd Cannon, Georgia Chapman, Lester Chapman, Dock and Alice Crowe, Fred Garrett Sr., Don Gravely, Roger Gravely, Blanche Burgess Hannah, Barbora Holcombe, Gerald Holcombe, Jefferson "J. D." McGowens, Oliver "Hub" Orr, Albert "A. C." Owens, Grover Owens, Robert Perry, Ann Poulos, Charles Powell, Edgar Smith, Sara Snow, Pauline Thrift, Laura Townes, and Odessa Williams. It was a great pleasure having had the opportunity to sit and talk with you.

The Harry Hampton Memorial Wildlife Fund, partnered with the South Carolina DNR, provided $9,500, and the Clemson University Research Investment Fund Program added another $6,000 to support the Jocassee Gorges Cultural History Project, under which I interviewed the mountain residents. Almost all of this money paid the Clemson University graduate and undergraduate students who transcribed the interview tapes, and I am grateful to the professionalism and patience shown by all of them. During the course of ten years, forty-six students helped to transcribe the interviews.

Friends and colleagues have read various drafts of chapters and/or the entire manuscript, and I am grateful for the thoughtful and helpful suggestions from Meredith Walker and Cindy Roper. I also appreciate the comments from the two anonymous reviewers for this manuscript. I also wish to thank the Pickens County (South Carolina) Public Library, for permission to publish selected historic photos from their on-line collection. Finally, I would like to thank John McCloud, rights director for the University of North Carolina Press, for allowing me to reprint portions of an introductory chapter from my *Something in These Hills* book.

Thanks to Alison Mero, director of Clemson University Press, for encouraging me to submit my original manuscript to them, and to Andrew Dorkin, acquisitions editor at the Press, for guiding me through the initial submission process. Thanks to my current student, Mars O'Keefe, (an intern with the Press), who helped me with photograph selection and the book cover design. Special thanks also to Erin Maher, copy editor, for catching all my initial errors and inconsistencies, and to Amber DeDerick, for compiling the index. I appreciate the patience of my undergrad volunteers, Juliette Fleck, Emma Ohrt, and especially Ivy Tarver, as they helped me proofread the final copy.

Finally, once again I want to thank my wife, Cathy Robison, for giving me the time, space, and love, to see this book through to completion.

Chapter One:

"It Was Just a Slow Life, but It Was a Good Life": Stories from the South Carolina Mountains

The man, nearly a century old, sat in a comfortable armchair in his living room one February afternoon, talking about his childhood in the company of his middle-aged niece Elizabeth and myself, as I interviewed him for a project on life in the South Carolina mountains before Duke Power (now Duke Energy) had flooded some river valleys behind hydroelectric dams. "It was just a slow life, but it was a good life," David Nelson stated slowly, as he stared out his living room window across his family property in the beautiful Eastatoee Valley in upper Pickens County, South Carolina. His statement remained with me, even years later, after I had completed two other books on the upper part of the state.[1] To me, the sentence perfectly captured the essence of a time before the internet, before television, and even before the widespread use of telephones. Radios and newspapers were the principal media in Mr. Nelson's childhood. In the context of the conversation, Mr. Nelson had explained to us, "Well, anytime [back then] you run across somebody, you never did say 'Hi' then keep going; you stopped and had a talk, and found out what was going on. . . . They'd stop in the road and just stand there and talk. . . . Had plenty of time to visit."

Picture a gathering of men clad in worn overalls, sitting around a wood stove in the back of a neighborhood grocery store, telling stories about past exploits, some of them even relatively true; several children, about ten years

1 John M. Coggeshall, *Liberia, South Carolina: An African American Appalachian Community* (Chapel Hill: University of North Carolina Press, 2018); and John M. Coggeshall, *Something in These Hills: The Culture of Family Land in Southern Appalachia* (Chapel Hill: University of North Carolina Press, 2022).

old, whittle and listen intently behind the men. Or picture a gray-haired mother and her adult daughter, sitting in the shade of a side porch off the kitchen as the sun declines behind the mountains, snapping beans for canning and talking about the county's school funding plans; the woman's daughter and her female cousin hold the bucket of beans and sit on the steps below, listening quietly. Outside a church on a Sunday morning after services, neighbors gather; the men talk of the weather and county politics, their wives talk of children and school policies, and their children listen for a few moments and then scatter to play before being called back for the journey home. It was during times like these, and countless others, that information was exchanged and critiqued, community morals were criticized and reinforced, and social relationships were created and strengthened. Before the overwhelming onslaught of rapid forms of media and transportation, people in upper South Carolina, like much of the South and like many communities worldwide, relied to a great extent on oral communication and the social links created by conversation.

Capturing a little of the richness of this conversation is the subject of this book. While interviewing residents in upper South Carolina for a project on the importance of family land in the southern Appalachians,[2] I heard many interesting stories about life and people, in both the past and present, and I felt those stories deserved their own volume. At the same time, the stories needed an explanation of the "slow life" that they described, and so a brief overview of life in the upper part of South Carolina through various periods is also included. Finally, in the telling of these stories, readers will note interesting words, unusual turns of phrase, and nonstandard sentence structures that also need some explanation. This book, then, presents stories of the "good life" in the mountain counties of South Carolina, extending about a century into the past, told in the "slow" manner of proper Southern speech. Readers are invited to sit at the feet of the narrators, take a sip of their "co-cola" or their "shine," and slow their lives down and listen.

Organization

This volume is the third of a series of books about the upper part of South Carolina, specifically the northern portions of Oconee, Pickens, and Greenville Counties. Contacted by the South Carolina Department of Natural Resources (DNR) in August 2006, I was invited to collect stories from the older Euro-American residents of the Jocassee Gorges region in upper Oconee and Pickens Counties before the residents had passed away. Early in my research, I discovered in upper Pickens County a small enclave of descendants of freed slaves still living on land obtained right after the Civil War, and I felt the oral history of the community called Liberia needed to be preserved and

---

2 Coggeshall, *Something in These Hills.*

Figure 1: Country Road, Upper Pickens County.
Photo by John M. Coggeshall.

presented. Over the next several years, as I expanded the research area into upper Greenville County, I began to notice that some mountain residents spoke about their family land in a way unfamiliar to me and yet characteristic of the southern Appalachians. Describing this sentiment became the focus of my second book on the region.[3]

Left on the cutting room floor, so to speak, were dozens of stories and observations about myriad topics, shaped largely by the questions I had asked. During the interviews, I often began by asking people to describe their family history and their own life. Many folks often included stories from their lives in the mountains, dating back nearly to the beginning of the twentieth century. After a discussion of the geographical and historical context of the area in Chapter One, and after the second chapter on the dialect in which the stories are told, I introduce the stories, arranged largely by arbitrary topics. Stories in Chapter Three describe the challenges and benefits of rural life in upper South Carolina. Chapter Four presents stories about obtaining food (primarily through hunting and fishing) and food preparation and storage, because I had asked people about traditional uses of land. Since I have always been interested in folklore, I often asked about folk cures, and I have some stories about health care practices common in the Appalachians in Chapter Five. Many people talked about the cultural importance of churches, community stores, and small-town life as locations for these stories, and stories about these places appear in Chapter Six. As part of their autobiographical comments, some people described their school years, and these stories in Chapter Seven range

3 Coggeshall, *Liberia*; and Coggeshall, *Something in These Hills*.

from episodes in one-room schoolhouses to more modern (but still rural) schools. I also enjoyed asking couples how they met, and thus I collected stories of courtship encompassing nearly a century; these stories constitute Chapter Eight. Another topic I asked about was "local character" stories, and some of these anecdotes appear in Chapter Nine. The book concludes with a few words about the people and their stories in Chapter Ten.

Methods[4]

For the initial Jocassee Gorges research project, I first cleared the plan through the appropriate university review process and then contacted possible contributors, asking to speak with them in a place of their choice, at a time of their choice, and with whomever else they wanted to be present. Friends often suggested other possible contributors. For every interview, I always introduced myself as a professor from Clemson University (a title that carries some prestige in the area) and then described the research project in a brief and appropriate way. I always left a note for additional contact and sometimes also a business card. I did not try to disguise my upper-middle-class status, Euro-American ethnicity, and Midwestern origin (revealed by my accent); instead, I utilized my identity to seek further explanations of the questions I sought. Residents relished the idea of explaining their perspectives to me; several times, locals enjoyed teasing me with "you're not from around here, are you," as they tried to explain their favorite foods, common local expressions, or the cultural significance of land.

Establishing rapport, or a sense of trust between researcher and informant, required a set of skills ideally shared by all fieldworkers. While I did not disguise my obvious ethnicity, education, employer, or accent, I tried at all times to express interest and empathy in the presented points of view. For example, after I introduced myself, my university position, and the project to a local married couple (one spouse with a high school education, the other with a seventh-grade level) living far into the mountains, and after the interview had been underway for some time, the husband told me that I was unlike those Clemson "doctors" because, like "these people that live in the subdivisions, they don't associate with us poor people too much. [But it seems] . . . like you're kind of down home a little bit"; he then touched me on the shoulder, perhaps symbolically including me in the "local" group.

About seventeen African Americans and about seventy-two Euro-Americans were interviewed, for a total of about 144 hours of digital recordings (see Appendix One for brief informant biographies). No self-identified Native Americans were interviewed, and my contacts do not include people who

4 Much of this information has appeared in Coggeshall, *Something in These Hills*, and is reprinted with permission of the University of North Carolina Press.

live farther north into contemporary Cherokee lands nor farther east into contemporary Catawba lands (the region's two federally recognized tribes). Informants ranged in education from at least one with a doctoral degree to some with perhaps a third-grade level. Interviews ranged from thirty minutes to several hours, and participants may have been asked for follow-up interviews as well. People were always told that they need not answer any question about which they felt uncomfortable, and they had the right to ask that the recorder be turned off at any time. Transcripts of every interview were done by paid undergraduates, double-checked against the original interviews by me, and then returned to every participant by mail. In a few instances, informants (or their descendants) thanked me for the return of the transcript and then I asked for and was granted a follow-up interview.

All contributors had been promised anonymity during the interview sessions, in keeping with the best practices of anthropological research. Pseudonyms were selected from a random list of first names and then a separate random list of family names, with care to avoid common family names in the region. Pseudonyms were alphabetized in the chronological order I interviewed people, using the alphabet at least three times. I used the same pseudonyms for relatives (e.g., a mother and son or two siblings), especially if it was important to note the kin tie. On the other hand, distant relatives with the same family name were given different pseudonyms, to indicate an unrecognized family relationship. If published accounts (such as local histories) provided real names, then those real names were included here as well, but not matched to my anonymous interviews, even if the same person was involved. In all other instances with living individuals, pseudonyms were used. As mentioned earlier, I have published two previous books on the area, and I have consistently kept the same pseudonyms for the same people across all three books.[5] In other words, the person known by the pseudonym of "Peter Abney" is the same human being in all three books. At the same time, I have tried to eliminate as much repetition between books as possible, but a few of these stories (or excerpts from them) may have appeared in my earlier works.

While scholars referenced in secondary sources are distinguished with their professional attributions, informants are quoted only by pseudonyms. Readers may refer to Appendix One for brief biographies of the informants. I have tried to keep the biographical facts to a minimum, allowing readers to have enough context to understand the source of the perspectives being quoted, while simultaneously trying to prevent the identification of any informants by local readers.

5 However, there is one exception. In writing this book, I discovered that I had used the same pseudonym twice for unrelated people, and so "George Tanner" in this book is the same as "George Taylor" in my previous one.

Interviews were conducted in a variety of settings. Most of the interviews were held in private homes or (weather permitting) on a back porch or gazebo; one interview was at a camping site at Devil's Fork State Park in Oconee County. For the first several interviews I was accompanied by a locally well-known and retired DNR biologist, Sam Stokes, who introduced me and vouched for my credentials. Many interviews were held between childhood friends (now adults) or with both spouses simultaneously, which often made for enjoyable discussions of their lives together. Several times multiple generations contributed – a mother and her young adult son, a father and his adult son and daughter-in-law, a niece and her elderly uncle, another niece and her aunt, and parents and an adult daughter. During one interview I met with several siblings, a niece, and her own daughter – three generations around a kitchen table in the home of the ancestral fourth generation.

Given the current postmodern perspective about the complex impact of the flow of globalized capital on local residents, and given the enhanced awareness by scholars of the influences of class, ethnicity, race, education, gender, and urban/rural residency on the accumulation and manipulation of this globalized capital, many contemporary researchers have argued that it no longer makes sense to separate "insiders" from "outsiders" in a simplistic dichotomy. Because of this, I will use the term "inhabitant" to describe locals with multigenerational ties to land in the study area, while I reserve the term "resident" to describe those without those deeper ties.[6] Almost all of the stories included in this book are from inhabitants unless otherwise indicated.

The stories might appear to be a random assortment of anecdotes, and that is due partly to the questions I asked of the inhabitants, and partly to the necessity of arranging the stories into some logical order (albeit my own logical order). For these interviews, my general topic of investigation was the oral history of the Liberia Community and/or the cultural meaning of land to inhabitants. Thus, stories about traditional curing, school days, or married couples were often merely part of establishing rapport and were not asked of everyone nor pursued with equal detail for all. I did not ask many questions about gardening and farming, two very common activities, partly because I felt I had already covered these topics in earlier works.[7] I did ask questions about "interesting characters," though, and stories about rural life were elicited by my asking about early childhood memories, often to initiate the interviews. In effect, what this collection of stories represents are anecdotes that have not been published previously, but that I felt were

6 See Coggeshall, *Something in These Hills*, for a more detailed discussion.

7 See Coggeshall, *Something in These Hills*; and John M. Coggeshall, *Carolina Piedmont Country* (Jackson: University Press of Mississippi, 1995).

too interesting to discard. In some ways, I feel that it is more respectful to continue to present the voices of my informants in this volume, even if those voices "strayed" from the first two research topics.

In this volume I intended for readers to hear the voices of the storytellers as best as possible. However, this goal presented challenges. I did not analyze the communicative events to the degree that other scholars have done. Quotations have been edited for length but otherwise have not been corrected for grammar. Sometimes brackets are used to add a word or letter to render the quote more easily understandable. But I am not a linguistic anthropologist and did not wish to transcribe the interviews in the International Phonetic Alphabet (for example) so that readers could "hear," and scholars could examine, the dialect as actually spoken. In other words, the words are those actually uttered, but the pronunciations have been standardized by accepted spellings. For example, some older folks pronounced the fruit of oak trees as "ake-urns" (adopting an older British form; see Appendix Two), but in the transcripts the word is rendered with the standard spelling. After the first several interviews were transcribed, I tried to retain as much dialectical pronunciation as possible, but when I returned the transcripts my informants were embarrassed by how they "sounded" on paper, and they asked me to correct the dialectical spellings and redo the transcripts (which I did). Ultimately, for most of the transcripts I compromised, retaining some dialectical pronunciations such as "chimley" (for chimney) or "knowed" (for knew) and explaining to my informants that it was important for accuracy; no one asked for further corrections. In order to keep the transcripts legible, though, I did not include the aspiration before "it" (common among older speakers) or drop the "g" for participles ("comin'" for "coming"), since this latter construction is common in standard English as well.

Although these decisions may seem arbitrary and unscientific to more serious linguistic scholars, it is important to remember that my initial intention in collecting these stories was to document the oral history of an African American freedom colony and then to explore the cultural significance of land in the area; I did not set out to describe or to study regional dialects. But as I interviewed more and more inhabitants, and as I heard more and more stories that were tangential to my research questions, I decided to save the stories and preserve some of the dialect discussion for this book. Some nonstandard pronunciations and grammatical structures are discussed more completely in Chapter Two and in Appendix Two.

Readers might also disagree with my choices of "interesting" linguistic features to examine. There already exists a voluminous amount of scholarly research on Appalachian dialects and their historical, social, economic, and linguistic relationships to other American English dialects, and so I have decided to focus on a selective number of specific features already identified by scholars and that do appear in the stories: "a-prefixing" ("It's a-coming up rain"), "existential 'there/they'" ("They's going to be trouble"), and the "personal dative" ("I'm going to take me a bath"). I also heard a distinction between older folks who reported speech with the verb "say," taking special care to add the verb multiple times, and younger speakers who often used "like" instead of "say." Several times, during the telling of stories, a speaker would shape his/her sentence in an unusual way; I also investigate this. Finally, during my interviews, sometimes I heard familiar words used in unusual ways; upon further examination, I found them to be archaisms preserved in Appalachian dialects. For example, as one of my undergraduate transcribers worked on an interview, she asked me where a Pickens County woman had been raised. To describe the trunk of her car, the woman had called it a "boot," a term still used in England, although the speaker had never traveled outside of her county. A few of these expressions are discussed as well.

Interview quotes might be modified further by eliminating interjected statements by other speakers or by myself, focusing instead only on the sentences of the intended speaker. For example, while I might be interviewing two people simultaneously, all three of us might interject comments or statements, sometimes all at the same time. But I do not wish to burden my audience with reading complicated transcriptions. Instead, if another speaker (including myself) interjected a comment during a story, then this is indicated by ellipses in the quote, in order to focus only on the targeted speaker and to make the stories more readable for an audience.

I have tried to present the views of my informants throughout the book and to keep my own voice in the background. If a comment on a story or theme needs to be made, or support for a point needs to be provided, I have placed those remarks in chapter footnotes. I want readers to experience as much as possible the words and thoughts of the people of upper South Carolina.

Environmental Background[8]

The study area in upper South Carolina preserves one of the most beautiful areas in the southeastern US.[9] At the very edge of the Blue Ridge

8 Much of the environmental and historical information has appeared in Coggeshall, *Something in These Hills*, and is reprinted with permission of the University of North Carolina Press.

9 Butch Clay, *Chattooga River Sourcebook: A Comprehensive Guide to the River and Its Natural and Human History* (Birmingham, AL: Chattooga River Publishing, 1995), 7.

Mountains, cold mountain rivers and streams carve deep gorges through igneous or metamorphic rock and tumble over cliffs, creating spectacular waterfalls. Boulder-strewn rivers like the Horsepasture, Whitewater, Toxaway, and Chattooga (much of the setting for the *Deliverance* film) gather together onto the Piedmont and flow toward the Atlantic. Protruding above the trees are occasional outcrops of granitic rock, with sheer, steeply curving sides and romanticized names like "Table Rock," "Bald Rock," "Glassy Mountain," and "Caesar's Head."

Fueling these rivers is a tremendous amount of rainfall. As moisture-laden clouds drift into the US interior from the Gulf of Mexico, the southern Appalachians intercept the clouds and compel them to release moisture before climbing over the mountains.[10] Consequently, the heaviest moisture falls on the southeastern slopes of the highest peaks. Other than the rainforest of the Pacific Northwest, the southeastern Appalachians receive some of the highest rainfall amounts in the continental US. For example, Transylvania County, North Carolina (the major headwater collecting area for the rivers), "*averages* an astonishing eighty-six inches of rain each year, an amount that nearly classifies it as a rainforest."[11]

Because of this rainfall, the southern Appalachians support a tremendous amount of biodiversity.[12] Cove forests abound in the cool, moist, rarely frozen valleys on the mountain slopes.[13] Hardwoods include species of oaks, hickory, and (historically) American chestnut trees, along with species of hemlock and tulip poplar.[14] Subcanopy species include mountain laurel (locally called "ivy") and rhododendron.[15] Along the ground grow numerous plant species, including ginseng and yellowroot, traditionally prized for medicinal purposes.[16]

Besides plants, the region's abundant rainfall supports a tremendous diversity of wildlife, some rare and/or endemic, some common, and some reintroduced. Fish include native brook trout and non-native rainbow and brown species in the cool mountain streams and colder lakes, along with bass in the warmer waters.[17] Reptiles include venomous snakes such

---

10 Jennifer Frick-Ruppert, *Mountain Nature: A Seasonal Natural History of the Southern Appalachians* (Chapel Hill: University of North Carolina Press, 2010), 5–6.

11 Frick-Ruppert, *Mountain Nature*, 5–6; quote on 6, italics in original.

12 Frick-Ruppert, *Mountain Nature*, 7.

13 Scott Weidensaul, *Mountains of the Heart: A Natural History of the Appalachians* (Golden, CO: Fulcrum Publishing, 1994), 53.

14 Robert Benson, *Cultural Resources Overview of the Sumter National Forest* (Athens, GA: Southeastern Archaeological Services, 2006), 17–18.

15 Frick-Ruppert, *Mountain Nature*, 78–79.

16 Frick-Ruppert, *Mountain Nature*, 75–76.

17 Weidensaul, *Mountains of the Heart*, 71–73.

as copperheads and timber rattlers; the steep, narrow, moist valleys create dozens of ecological "islands," sheltering a world-renowned number of different salamander species. Relying heavily on the acorn (and historically, the chestnut) crops are black bears, with hunting competition from bobcats, coyotes, and (perhaps) mountain lions. Elk have been reintroduced to the Great Smoky Mountains National Park, and occasionally wander outside park boundaries.[18]

Historical Setting

By the early eighteenth century, the Cherokee occupied the northeastern part of today's South Carolina. Large towns occupied the major floodplains, such as those along the Keowee and Big Eastatoee Rivers. As British settlements pushed inland from the coast, the Crown established forts among the Cherokee, in order to secure their cooperation in wars against first the French and then the colonists. Although relatively short-lived, Fort Prince George, in the upper Keowee River valley, overlooked the largest Cherokee Lower Town, Keowee. By the end of the American Revolutionary War, however, both had been abandoned.[19]

With the removal of the Cherokee after the 1780s, the area opened for American colonial settlement.[20] Originally large tracts of land went to land speculators, to Revolutionary War veterans, and then to the Euro-American pioneers; their descendants "became the Appalachian gentry" by the early nineteenth century. Later came the small farmers, "for whom acquiring land, however marginal, was a form of upward mobility."[21] As folklorist Ted Olson noted, the traditional culture that evolved in the Blue Ridge area was a syncretism of several distinctive Old World cultures that by necessity were tailored to a New World environment, with additional cultural information about wilderness survival borrowed from the Native Americans. By the early nineteenth century, "a distinctive Blue Ridge culture survived among those who remained behind."[22]

For the first Euro-American settlers, "the surrounding forest was much

---

18 See Frick-Ruppert, *Mountain Nature*; and Weidensaul, *Mountains of the Heart*, for a more complete ecological and biological inventory.

19 James Mooney, *"Myths of the Cherokee" and "Sacred Formulas of the Cherokees"* (Nashville: Charles and Randy Elder, Publishers, 1982).

20 Clay, *Chattooga River Sourcebook*, 22–23; although see Claudia Hembree, *Jocassee Valley* (Pickens, SC: Hiott Printing, 2003), 20.

21 Allen Batteau, "The Contradictions of a Kinship Community," in *Holding On to the Land and the Lord: Kinship, Ritual, Land Tenure, and Social Policy in the Rural South*, ed. Robert Hall and Carol Stack, Southern Anthropological Society Proceedings, No. 15 (Athens: University of Georgia Press, 1982), 26.

22 Ted Olson, *Blue Ridge Folklife* (Jackson: University Press of Mississippi, 1998), 30.

more than board feet on the stump. The mountain woodlands were a living matrix of plants, animals, and shared memories – a critical if not vital part of mountain life and culture."[23] The abundance of free-flowing water allowed "small family farms to flourish independently without the aid of any earthly power and encouraged a sense of stubborn autonomy among the farming folk who settled there."[24] Those who lived outside the major river valleys carved out farms in the remaining floodplains, free-ranged their livestock through the hills, and transformed much of their corn crop into "runs" of moonshine.[25]

After the Civil War, freed African Americans settled in small pockets throughout the South, including the southern Appalachians, farming and laboring. Existing with whites in an uneasy symbiotic relationship requiring tact and caution, blacks often worked in the same fields and drank from the same dippers as their white neighbors, yet simultaneously lived in fear of physical harassment and in relative poverty of resources. Segregated black schools received inadequate funding and outdated textbooks into the 1960s. Throughout the region, African Americans recall with vivid terror episodes of white gangs beating black youth, gunfire aimed at black houses, lynchings, and arson. Simultaneously, some white neighbors remained supportive, or at least indifferent, to the presence of black residents.[26]

By the early twentieth century, cotton mills had become significant employers in most of the upper Piedmont towns, drawing white mountain folk from the hills and valleys into electrified homes on paved streets, with better schools and secure wages. Jobs remained segregated by Jim Crow laws, and the best jobs and wages went to whites, while blacks were relegated to segregated neighborhoods and loaded and unloaded wagons and trucks, cleaned bathrooms, or swept floors. Black cooks and nannies cared for white households, often enabling both white spouses to work.[27]

As wage-labor capitalism siphoned more folks from self-sufficient farms, valleys like Jocassee transformed into tourist destinations. Hotels brought in outsiders with new ideas.[28] "Collectively these summer people helped change

---

23 Donald Davis, "Living on the Land: Blue Ridge Life and Culture," in *Homeplace Geography: Essays for Appalachia* (Macon, GA: Mercer University Press, 2006), 153.

24 David Fischer, *Albion's Seed: Four British Folkways in America* (New York: Oxford University Press, 1989), 638.

25 Dennis Duncan, ed., *An Informal History of Mountain Rest, South Carolina* (Taylors, SC: Faith Printing Company, 1984), 4.

26 Coggeshall, *Liberia*.

27 Coggeshall, *Carolina Piedmont Country*; Joseph Gauzens, *Salem: Twice a Town* (Pickens, SC: Hiott Printing Company, 1993), 164; Pearl Smith McFall, *It Happened in Pickens County* (Pickens, SC: Sentinel Press, 1959), 146; Clay, *Chattooga River Sourcebook*, 24–25.

28 Gauzens, *Salem*, 28.

the valley from a wintertime ghost town to a summertime paradise," a former resident recalled.[29] Eventually, modernization penetrated even the deepest mountain coves, bringing electric lights, refrigerators, radios, televisions, and broadened horizons.[30]

By the early twentieth century, timber companies expanded, providing mountaineers with another entry point into the larger capitalist market. One of those companies, Crescent Land and Timber, was a fully owned subsidiary of Duke Power (today Duke Energy), a company with an eye for much greater development. Targeting the Keowee River and its tumbling mountain tributaries, Crescent Land and Timber (Duke Power) began a major push in the early 1960s to buy as much land as possible in order to construct an interconnected series of hydroelectric lakes.[31] During the flooding of the valleys, crews collected footage for an upcoming Hollywood film, *Deliverance*, based on James Dickey's novel by the same name. Some of the scenes were filmed on the Chattooga River, but the scenes depicting the moving of a church house, the exhumation of bodies in a cemetery, the bulldozing and dynamiting for dam construction, and the dammed river water inundating standing trees were all filmed at the construction of the Lake Jocassee Dam or the subsequent flooding of Jocassee Valley in South Carolina.

By the 1990s, Duke Power (later Duke Energy) began reselling the former hillsides (now lake shores) to private real estate development companies, who eagerly constructed a series of gated and exclusive communities along the lakeshores and in the mountain coves.[32] New settlements also have integrated formerly isolated mountain communities into general American society, undermining more traditional ways.[33]

By the end of that decade, most of the prime real estate along the shores of Lake Keowee had been either developed or purchased. The Duke Energy Company then decided to begin divesting itself of the undeveloped and less economically valuable lands higher up in the mountains around Lake Jocassee. Eagerly purchased by the states, the wilderness property formed the core of Gorges State Park in North Carolina and the adjoining Mountain Bridge Wilderness Area of South Carolina, enclosing the upper reaches of the Horsepasture and Toxaway Rivers or the "Jocassee Gorges." Today, this

29 Hembree, *Jocassee Valley*, 5.

30 Hembree, *Jocassee Valley*, 110.

31 Alice Badenoch, *Keowee Key: The Origins of a Community* (Seneca, SC: Jay's Printing Company, 1989), 17; John Lane, *Chattooga: Descending into the Myth of Deliverance River* (Athens: University of Georgia Press, 2004), 31.

32 Lane, *Chattooga*, 32.

33 Joshua Blackwell, *"Used to Be a Rough Place in Them Hills": Moonshine, the Dark Corner, and the New South* (Bloomington, IN: AuthorHouse, 2009), 98.

expansive area of mountain wilderness ties federal, state, and private land into a prime recreation area.

Conclusion

The picture of heavily forested mountains carved by tumbling, rocky streams sets the stage for the stories in the following chapters. Some inhabitants I have interviewed grew up in homes so isolated that they remember traveling miles by foot or by mule to the nearest road. Subsistence farming, supplemented by fishing and hunting, supported many families into the 1960s. Social activities revolved around extended family gatherings, small churches, or country stores well into the twentieth century. Some inhabitants fought the boredom of rural isolation through high school activities like small-town football games and cruising down Main Street. Many of these experiences would be common to small-town life across the United States, but they are presented here from upper South Carolina. Imagine the Blue Ridge Mountains; the rolling foothills; the valleys of pastures and corn fields; the tree lines delimiting streams and rivers; the steeples of Christian churches rising near groves of oak trees shading small cemeteries; and the wood frame, brick, and trailer homes of the inhabitants. Now listen to the voices of those who live there.

Chapter Two

"Just Straight-up Country": The Dialects of the Stories

The dialects spoken in southern Appalachia have been examined by numerous individuals from a variety of backgrounds; for example, there are over eight hundred items in the annotated bibliography on Appalachian English maintained by the University of South Carolina's "Appalachian English" website.[1] Moreover, our understanding of the relationship between these dialects and that of Standard English has varied over the decades, highly dependent on the relationship of Appalachian residents, and the region itself, with larger American society. Are the residents "our contemporary ancestors," who speak virtually Chaucerian or Shakespearean English? Or are the residents of southern Appalachia "yesterday's people," speaking a grammatically improper dialect reflecting the backwardness and underdeveloped nature of the region itself? What are the economic, political, and social consequences of these markers?[2] How have linguistic scholars characterized the dialects of the region, and what special features mark the dialects of the region today?

For some standard English speakers, the Appalachian dialects reflect speakers of lower socioeconomic status. "Those with a southern accent [an area greater than but including the southern Appalachians] are placed

1 See the website: https://appalachian-english.library.sc.edu/index.html, accessed July 3, 2024.

2 Michael Montgomery, "English Language," in *High Mountains Rising: Appalachia in Time and Place*, ed. Richard Straw and H. Tyler Blethen (Urbana: University of Illinois Press, 2004), 149–50; John M. Coggeshall, *Something in These Hills: The Culture of Family Land in Southern Appalachia* (Chapel Hill: University of North Carolina Press, 2022), 4–13.

at a disadvantage in communicating with persons outside the region," communications scholar Stephen A. Smith argued.[3] Linguist Jennifer Cramer noted that residents of Louisville, Kentucky, viewed Appalachian speech "as incorrect, nonstandard, informal, and uneducated; yet [also] somewhat pleasant."[4] As linguist Michael Montgomery observed, the speech became stigmatized by its association with "lower-status speakers from less prosperous parts of the country," and now reinforces those stereotypes.[5] According to Montgomery, today the dialects have little prestige except among country-western singers, stock car racers, and a few other groups.[6]

For the "imperfections" of Appalachian dialects, historian David Hackett Fischer blamed "the oral culture of the backcountry," created by settlers from northern Britain, southern Scotland, and northern Ireland, for their "actual antipathy to fixed schemes of grammar, orthography and punctuation."[7] Appalachian scholar Cratis Williams suggested that "the mountaineer's habit of speaking with a half-open mouth and fixed chin thrust slightly forward has no doubt contributed to the perpetuation of an archaic semidiphthong (or vowel and a half)" in rhyming words such as "flour" and "power" with "flar" and "par."[8]

In contrast, other writers at various periods equated Appalachian dialects with English dialects centuries old, in attempts to demonstrate the cultural (sometimes racial) "purity" of the region "in order to counter a prevailing national perception of Appalachia as a deprived region having little culture and an unflattering, often violent history,"[9] among other reasons. For example, scholar Lester Berrey attributed the linguistic characteristics of Appalachian dialects to a "survival of earlier English" rather than to a "degradation of language."[10] Epitomizing this romanticized ideal, educator John C. Campbell

---

3 Stephen A. Smith, *Myth, Media, and the Southern Mind* (Fayetteville: University of Arkansas Press, 1985), 103.

4 Jennifer Cramer, "Perceptions of Appalachian English in Kentucky," *Journal of Appalachian Studies* 24, no. 1 (2018): 61.

5 Montgomery, "English Language," 159.

6 Montgomery, "English Language," 159.

7 David Hackett Fischer, *Albion's Seed: Four British Folkways in America* (New York: Oxford University Press, 1989), 721.

8 Cratis Williams, "The R in Mountain Speech," in *Southern Mountain Speech*, ed. Jim Wayne Miller and Loyal Jones (Berea, KY: Berea College Press, 1992), 11.

9 Michael Montgomery, "The Scotch-Irish Element in Appalachian English: How Broad? How Deep?," in *Ulster and North America: Transatlantic Perspectives on the Scotch-Irish*, ed. H. Tyler Blethen and Curtis Wood jr. (Tuscaloosa: University of Alabama Press, 1997), 190.

10 Lester V. Berrey, "Southern Mountain Dialect," *American Speech* 15, no. 1 (1940): 45.

wrote of western North Carolina: "One may, in a conversation of a few minutes, hear expressions from Chaucer, Spencer, or Shakespeare."[11] Fifty years later, Cratis Williams described the isolated Appalachian dialect as "the oldest living English dialect, older than the speech of Shakespeare, closer to the speech of Chaucer."[12]

"While such a claim may have a certain romantic charm," linguists Walt Wolfram and Donna Christian cautioned, "it is, unfortunately, too simplistic and categorical to be meaningful."[13] Spoken languages constantly change, which contradicts "the simplistic notion that there is an undefiled version of 16th-century English in the backwoods hollows."[14] Still, linguists such as Wolfram agreed that "some of the language characteristics found in Appalachia represent remnants of an earlier period in the English language," persisting in Appalachia even after disappearing in other regions.[15]

In contrast to (and sometimes alongside) the "Elizabethan/Chaucerian survival" hypothesis is that the Appalachian dialects owe much to the English dialects of northern England, southern Scotland, and northern Ireland. One of the earlier voices in support of this hypothesis was that of Appalachian scholar Cratis Williams. In many of his articles, Williams argued that the dialect of Appalachia owed much to a Scots-Irish influence.[16] According to Williams, the Scots spoke a nonstandard variety of eighteenth-century English, carried their old-fashioned dialect to northern Ireland, and then brought it "with little change . . . to the American back country. . . . That is the basic speech of the mountain people today."[17] In his footsteps followed historian David Hackett Fischer, who noted that a "flow of English-speaking people from the borders of North Britain and northern Ireland [came] to the Appalachian backcountry mostly during the half-century from 1718 to 1775," creating Appalachian culture.[18] Thus, according to Fischer, the Appalachian dialect comes from dialects spoken in northern England, lowland Scotland, and northern Ireland.[19]

---

11 John C. Campbell, *The Southern Highlander and His Homeland* (New York: Russell Sage Foundation, 1921; reprinted Lexington: University Press of Kentucky, 1969), 144.

12 Cratis Williams, "Appalachian Speech," *The North Carolina Historical Review* 55, no. 2 (1978): 174.

13 Walt Wolfram and Donna Christian, *Appalachian Speech* (Arlington, VA: Center for Applied Linguistics, 1976), 161.

14 Walt Wolfram, "Is There an 'Appalachian English'?," *Appalachian Journal* 11, no. 3 (1984): 218.

15 Wolfram, "'Appalachian English'?," 217; see also Wolfram and Christian, *Appalachian Speech*, 4.

16 For example, see Williams, "The R in Mountain Speech," 9.

17 Cratis Williams, "Subtlety in Mountain Speech," in *Southern Mountain Speech*, 57.

18 Fischer, *Albion's Seed*, 6.

19 Fischer, *Albion's Seed*, 654; Williams, "'Appalachian Speech'?," 174.

Other Appalachian scholars are more cautious about the extent of the Scots-Irish influence. For example, while linguist Michael Montgomery identified some vocabulary terms from a Scots-Irish influence (e.g., "evening" for afternoon and "you-all" and "you'uns" for you [Pl.]),[20] he perceived this influence as less in vocabulary and more in grammar – an influence that is "broad and deep."[21] This influence differentiates Appalachian dialects from those in the Deep South and creates a distinctive regional dialect.[22]

As one of the major contemporary scholars of Appalachian dialects, Montgomery has described the Appalachian "dialect" as continually changing, demographically diverse, and of multiple origins.[23] "The speech of the Upper South, particularly the southern hills and mountains, derives largely from the colonial settlements in Pennsylvania. It was carried, by the Scotch-Irish, English, and Germans, westward across Pennsylvania, then southwestward down into Virginia, North Carolina, [and] South Carolina."[24] While Montgomery recognized influences from both North Midland and South Midland English varieties,[25] he also credited African languages in the South as "the deepest and most persistent influence of all."[26] Based on his years of research, Montgomery concluded that the dialects of Appalachia are much more "colonial" than "Elizabethan,"[27] containing some elements that were "quite fashionable British usage two hundred years ago."[28]

As Wolfram and Christian observed, when compared to standard English, Appalachian English "is more advanced in some areas and slower to change in others," as is typical in languages.[29] "Appalachia is a region settled at different periods in different places under different circumstances," Montgomery noted.[30]

20 Montgomery, "Scotch-Irish Element," 195–96; Michael Montgomery, "Voices of My Ancestors: A Personal Search for the Language of the Scotch-Irish," *American Speech* 80, no. 4 (2005): 341–65; see also Michael Ellis, "On the Use of Dialect as Evidence: *Albion's Seed* in Appalachia," *Appalachian Journal* 19, no. 3 (1992): 289.

21 Montgomery, "English Language," 154; compare Ellis, "Dialect as Evidence," 291.

22 Montgomery, "English Language," 154; see also Montgomery, "Scotch-Irish Element," 201.

23 Montgomery, "English Language."

24 Michael Montgomery, "The Southern Accent—Alive and Well," *Southern Cultures* (1993): 55.

25 Montgomery, "English Language," 151.

26 Montgomery, "Southern Accent," 56.

27 Montgomery, "English Language," 152–53.

28 Montgomery, "Southern Accent," 56; Cratis Williams, "Vowels and Diphthongs in Mountain Speech," in *Southern Mountain Speech*, 13.

29 Wolfram and Christian, *Appalachian Speech*, 161.

30 Michael Montgomery, "The Historical Background and Nature of the Englishes of Appalachia," in *Talking Appalachian: Voice, Identity, and Community*, ed.

As a result of all these transatlantic influences, "it is the unique combination of linguistic features which sets Appalachian English apart from other varieties of American English and which complicates attempts to establish direct connections with a specific British regional variety."[31] In fact, despite language change, it is this cluster of unique features "which combine to set this variety [of English] apart from other varieties, so that the dialect is alive and well."[32]

While many scholars have invested a lot of time and printer ink (or typewriter ribbons) in differentiating an Appalachian dialect from other historic varieties of English, most scholars also recognize a significant amount of linguistic overlap between the geographical boundaries of various American English dialects. For example, Wolfram observed that the Appalachian "dialect" has no distinctive boundary differentiating between "Southern" and "Southern Appalachian" English.[33] Citing the Linguistic Atlas of America, Montgomery located Appalachian English in the "Midlands" dialect, with the southern Appalachians more in the "South Midlands."[34] Linguist Allison Burkette described the linguistic streams contributing to Appalachian English as "a constellation of features and ideas," making it difficult to sort out "Appalachian" from "Southern" or even "Appalachian sub-regional" dialects.[35] And, as Montgomery asserted above, African languages provided a significant contribution as well, adding the stretching of vowels to create the "Southern drawl."[36]

Further complicating the distinctiveness of an Appalachian dialect is that dialects overlap socially. For example, lower classes typically speak more stigmatized varieties of dialects; however, this trend might be counterbalanced by local positive values given to that same dialect,[37] thus explaining locals' teasing my occasional misunderstanding of their pronunciations with "you're not from around here, are you?" Dialects might also vary by education, by residence, by gender, and by age.[38] Speech might also vary by context – listeners would expect a traditional story to contain

---

Amy Clark and Nancy Hayward (Lexington: University Press of Kentucky, 2013), 49.

31 Ellis, "Dialect as Evidence," 291.

32 Wolfram and Christian, *Appalachian Speech*, 162.

33 Wolfram, "'Appalachian English'?," 217; see also Montgomery, "Southern Accent," 52.

34 Montgomery, "Historical Background," 36–37.

35 Allison Burkette, "Linguistic and Object-Based Stance-Taking in Appalachian Interviews," *Language in Society* 45, no. 3 (2016): 337.

36 Montgomery, "Southern Accent," 56.

37 Wolfram, "'Appalachian English'?," 219–20.

38 Wolfram, "'Appalachian English'?," 221–22; Wolfram and Christian, *Appalachian Speech*, 162.

"traditional" linguistic elements, for example.[39] In fact, Montgomery argues for "the designation Appalachian *Englishes*."[40]

Although not a professional linguist, I have noticed some of the sociolinguistic variations identified by Wolfram in the stories I have collected, and I will highlight two: a generational difference in reported speech and the use of poetic elements in the narration of traditional stories. I have also detected a tendency by speakers with better educations to use more standard English forms (although this has not been quantified), and I have noticed that those with less education are quite aware of their "improper" dialects. I have heard some differences between speakers from the Piedmont and those raised in more isolated communities farther into the mountains, but the differences are (I think) mostly in vocabulary. I also think I have heard some distinctions between Black Appalachian English and White Appalachian English, although how much of this difference might be attributable to segregated schools or more recent media is difficult to tell but would be interesting to explore.[41]

Inhabitants themselves are quite aware that the standard English dialect differs from what Pickens County resident Peter Abney described as "the mountain language here." College student Jason Taylor's mother's family spoke "proper English," he reported, but his father's side spoke "just straight up country." As Douglas Edison explained, "I know what correct is, but I don't say it correct. That's just the way people talked around here." "We just speak our own little dialect, how we like to talk, I guess," Margaret York explained; "we might know better but we still talk the same way, so I call that just country." "It was the way that we was brought up," Peter Abney acknowledged. "No wonder I can't speak English," Theodore Franklin reported that a friend joked; "I never heard it spoken until I went [to college]!"

Ryan Trask, having an advanced professional degree, described the far northern South Carolina accent as "more like what you'll hear in western North Carolina or in the mountains all the way up the [Appalachian] chain." Daniel Hall, also with an advanced professional degree and echoing the stereotyped "archaic" hypotheses, argued that this "mountain language" "was really Elizabethan English." Denise Craig attributed the "heavy R sound" in her mountain accent to a Scots-Irish origin, producing such pronunciations as "far" or "tar" for "fire" and "tire." Theodore Franklin described his dialect as a "mixture of Old, Middle, and whatever the next form of English is . . . because you get the archaic words that people use," such as "holp" or "zink"

---

39 Wolfram, "'Appalachian English'?," 223; see also Ellen Johnson, "Yet Again: The Midland Dialect," *American Speech* 69, no. 4 (1994): 428, on social variations within dialects.

40 Montgomery, "Historical Background," 49.

41 See Walt Wolfram, "African American Speech in Southern Appalachia," in Clark and Hayward, *Talking Appalachian*.

for “help” or “sink,” he explained.

Occasionally, the accent created problems for inhabitants. For example, Peter Abney, a professional contractor, rented a machine from Powell Brothers Construction Company for a particular job, but when he explained over the phone to the homeowner to whom to make out the check, she thought he said “Pile Brothers” and made the check out that way. “It went on through,” Mr. Abney explained, most likely because “I reckon it hit another mountain man somewhere.” As a girl, Stephanie Jamison was teased by her classmates in Easley schools for adopting her grandmother’s “mountain” accent. “And I used to come home and cry and cry because they made fun of me talking,” she continued. In fact, Ms. Jamison admitted, “they wanted to put me in Speech [Therapy] when I was in elementary school, because of the way I talked. They thought I had a speech impediment, and it wasn’t. It was mountain.”

On the other hand, the accent also might have benefits. For example, Stephanie Jamison, while visiting her mother’s relatives in New York, was invited by her school friend to “Show and Tell” at the grade school, “to hear my southern drawl.” Denise Craig provided another example: “When my daddy was in World War II,” he was stationed in California, and “he got so many free meals because people would invite him to their homes just to hear him talk. So he kind of made the most of that!”

Many inhabitants recognize the existence of regional dialects even within state boundaries. “Well, the accents in this little sliver of South Carolina [the mountains] are much different than the Piedmont, much different than the Midlands, much different than the Low Country,” Ryan Trask observed. Jason Taylor remembered a summer church camp that drew high school students from all over South Carolina, and the participants spent one evening comparing accents. “We definitely said things different,” Taylor recalled, despite the fact they were all from the same state. “And . . . the people from the cities,” Taylor added, “they talked less Southern. Like it wasn’t as bad of an accent.” Taylor joked that his urbane college friends from the state capital in Columbia “think I talk ‘hick.’ And I’m like, I mean, ‘We’re all from South Carolina, guys.’” Raised in upper Oconee County, Denise Voight conceded that she spoke with a Southern accent but she was not “from way up in the mountains where they talk funny,” nor did she admit to having a “brogue” like some of her former college friends “from Charleston [South Carolina]. You could hardly understand them,” she remarked.

When Elizabeth Nelson was a college student at a small North Carolina liberal arts school about five decades ago, she admitted that “I was teased a number of times by kids because I had such a pronounced Southern mountain way of talking, the drawl and everything. . . . So I purposely changed the way I spoke. . . . I did it as a means of self-preservation so people wouldn’t make fun of me! . . . [But] the older I get, the more I appreciate all these differences in speech. . . . And it has to do with where you're from and your ancestors." The college friends of Donna Trask, several decades younger than Ms. Nelson's colleagues, teased her about phrases she used, such as "hose pipe" (rather than "hose"), "license tag" (rather than "plate"), and "fixing to" (rather than "getting ready to").

Ralph Glenn described code switching among his current mountain dialect, that from his family home in coastal South Carolina, and even from his time spent in the military:

> My grandparents spoke Low Country Geechee dialect. . . . And then I learned to do that. . . . If I go across the creek over here [at his home in the mountains] and talk to [my neighbor], I will speak his dialect of mountain English. If I go down to Beaufort [coastal South Carolina] and run up on one of my cousins down there, I'll speak Geechee English. . . . And . . . it does not happen deliberately. I mean, it's somewhat like getting off the airport in Germany and when I walk up to the counter I know to speak German, what little I know. . . . And I don't have to think to do that.

Having served in the Air Force, James Edwards had to modify his speech pattern into more standard English, but "I've gone back" to the original upper Pickens County accent, he acknowledged. "It's said that most people in the South speak about three languages," Mr. Edwards continued; "we know how to speak, especially you know those of us with education, we speak educated English, and then we . . . can get down and dirty and speak redneck with the best of them, or, and then this everyday idiomatic speech" shared "amongst ourselves." In an insightful expression of dialect relativism, Douglas Edison added: "But I have heared [that] correct English was whatever you was used to in your community."

Despite the various linguistic streams that have shaped the dialects of the southern Appalachians, despite the demographic variations of those dialects, and despite the influences of media and education on modifying "improper" dialects,[42] linguists agree that as long as dialects retain an ability to differentiate "us" from "them," and as long as that distinction is important to preserve, distinctive Appalachian dialects will persist.[43] As Montgomery observed, Appalachian English has symbolic value, and it designates "a region in the mind as much as in reality."[44] "To sound local is to belong" to a place,

42 Smith, *Myth*, 149; Montgomery, "Southern Accent," 58.

43 Wolfram, "'Appalachian English'?," 222; Paul E. Reed, "The Importance of Rootedness in the Study of Appalachian English: Case Study Evidence for a Proposed Rootedness Metric," *American Speech* 95, no. 2 (2020): 222.

44 Montgomery, "English Language," 159.

linguist Paul E. Reed wrote, "and such belonging is of prime importance to residents."[45] Speakers with a strong attachment to place, regardless of educational level, gender, and generation, will demonstrate more local speech features.[46] "The words, sounds, and grammar patterns of Appalachia continue to conjure strong reactions among speakers who carry heritage in their mouths."[47] Appalachian English, Montgomery concluded, will persist, preserving some archaic but also innovative features, because the dialect provides a cultural cohesion and continuity that creates and supports a collective regional identity, despite pressure to conform.[48] "There is still an objective basis for the designation 'Appalachian English,'" Wolfram asserted,[49] and so I will also use that designation in this volume.

Context of Storytelling

Numerous authors have described the cultural importance of storytelling in Southern culture.[50] Montgomery, citing anthropologist Anita Puckett, argued that mountain speakers often preserve "rhetorical uses of the language in personal interaction, such as in narrating or recounting personal experiences."[51] Arising from a theoretical movement in anthropology, linguistics, and especially folklore in the early 1970s, scholars have shifted their focus from types of stories or themes in stories to the context of storytelling.[52]

I experienced an example of cultural awkwardness of collecting stories out of their appropriate cultural context. On my first meeting with Ryan Trask in August 2009, he pointed out a small walnut tree growing out of a divide between stones in his front walkway. He then told a story about his young son cracking walnuts in that spot one time, and how one walnut escaped processing and took root, and now the little tree stood about four feet tall, making for physical evidence upon which to base a delightful family story. Several days later, on a return visit, I asked Trask to repeat the story so

---

45 Reed, "Importance of Rootedness," 204.

46 Reed, "Importance of Rootedness," 221.

47 Amy Clark and Nancy Hayward, "Introduction," in Clark and Hayward, *Talking Appalachian*, 19.

48 Montgomery, "English Language," 161; see also Montgomery, "Southern Accent," 50, 64, on the Southern dialect in general.

49 Wolfram, "'Appalachian English'?," 224.

50 See for example Smith, *Myth*, 145–46; Wilbur J. Cash, *The Mind of the South* (New York: Alfred A. Knopf, 1941), 51.

51 Montgomery, "English Language," 157; Anita Puckett, *Seldom Ask, Never Tell: Labor and Discourse in Appalachia* (New York: Oxford University Press, 2000).

52 See for example Robert A. Georges, "Toward an Understanding of Storytelling Events," *Journal of American Folklore* 82, no. 326 (1969): 313–28.

I could record it. Trask hesitated a little and then explained, "I don't think about telling stories in that format. I feel like I ought to just happen by it [the tree], explain the tree to you, [and] tell you about the tree." In fact, he did not repeat the story, but instead elaborated on why the tree is important to him.

With a little hyperbole, scholar Cratis Williams believed that a mountaineer is "a natural actor with an innate sense of timing, pause, facial expression, and dramatic punctuation."[53] I was fortunate to witness one such event early in my fieldwork. On a bright, sunny morning in late January 2007, I was invited by a local colleague to interview two friends (and distant relations): Robert Davidson and Douglas Edison. We met at Mr. Edison's home in upper Pickens County, in a glassed-in shelter behind his house, with a built-in bathroom and comfortable seating area. As Mr. Edison served us coffee, I listened for over two hours as the men told stories about local characters. Almost perfectly, Mr. Davidson met Williams's definition of a storyteller. Like a compelling actor, he varied his tone, his timing, and his facial expressions to entertain and inform his audience; in fact, he even switched into what Angelina Oberdan (a Clemson poet and colleague) described as iambic pentameter as he related his narratives (see below). We stayed for over two hours.

Because of the nature of my research projects, though, I observed relatively few such storytelling events and instead primarily collected narratives during the course of interviewing individuals, couples, or friends about other research topics (the importance of family land or the oral history of the Liberia community).[54] Williams, though, offered some examples of typical storytelling contexts: "In the crossroads store, at the filling station, or on the courthouse square, the mountaineer finds time to talk. His values fixed, his judgments hardened early in his life to dogmatic pronouncements, his likes and dislikes sometimes violently differentiated, he talks easily and authoritatively on almost any subject proposed to him."[55] Elizabeth Nelson provided another type of context: "It's wonderful to be able to get out and walk with your neighbors up and down the valley, and then, you know, I meet other neighbors who are walking and we stand and talk with them. Or we'll find somebody out in their yard and go talk with them and, it's just a wonderful way to keep in touch and visit with them."

Brian Alexander's father owned a small business in downtown Pickens, and as a child in the 1970s he would ride his bicycle to town and listen to the

53 Cratis Williams, "Metaphor in Mountain Speech," in *Southern Mountain Speech*, 37.

54 See Coggeshall, *Something in These Hills*; and Coggeshall, *Liberia*.

55 Williams, "Metaphor," 38. See also George Hicks, *Appalachian Valley* (New York: Holt, Rinehart and Winston, 1976), 84–87; and Joseph S. Hall, *Smokey Mountain Folks and Their Lore* (Asheville, NC: Cataloochee Press, 1960), 7, on stores as locations for storytelling.

Figure 2: Family on a porch.
Sims Collection, Digital Collections files, Pickens County Library System.

men in the hardware store and barber shop "tell jokes and tell stories." As a little girl, Claudia Alexander remembered that when relatives would come to visit, "women folk that were married could sit and talk. Little ears were not allowed [because] we might hear what the women folk were talking about. So we were to go play outside but some of us was sneaking around trying to listen and learn." When I asked Mrs. Alexander what she wanted to learn about, she replied, "Probably about women having babies and stuff like that." She added that "that was not discussed" until a young woman was married or a "good-sized teenager."

As a boy, Ryan Trask remembered the same precautions. His storytelling relatives would say, "'You kids get out of here!' You know they'd lower their voices and I remember we'd sneak around through the hall and crawl back through the dining room with all the lights off and see if you could sneak around the corner or listen through the vents to try to hear the details." Trask equated his transition to being included in adult male conversations to a "rite of passage." Eventually the men "might tell you a joke that previously you could only see the men standing over by the grill telling, and then they let you in on it later."

Families also told stories as entertainment. Claudia Alexander and her relatives "would sit around our living room and . . . they would share events that happened in their life." Mrs. Alexander's father was "a great storyteller," because, she reasoned, "it comes in the Irish descent." In a later interview,

Mrs. Alexander elaborated:

> I can remember it being dark and cousins would come to the house and we couldn't get three stations [on TV]. . . . And so what they would do instead of having any old TV on then was, they would sit around a house full of cousins and Daddy and all and they would start telling them tales. . . . I can remember the room being dim and the room full of people and him telling all them stories. Yeah – I grew up with a rich environment as far as like storytelling.

"Thank goodness I was born without cable TV or anything," Ryan Trask exclaimed,

> because everybody [his extended family] gathered together out on the screen porch or you know in the yard or down by the pool and just visited. And told stories and tales and jokes and "remember this, remember that." And when you grow up the way they did . . . there's a lot of stories that are much better than anything that's come from a Hollywood screenwriters' guild. . . . And as kids I remember just being fascinated. I remember falling asleep on the floor at night when they'd gather inside for supper just listening. . . . And they'd go on for hours and hours.

"We'd go to our grandparents on Sunday and on holidays," Donna Trask recalled, "and there was a table in the dining room where all the adults would sit and the kids sit somewhere else. And they'd never leave! They'd sit and they'd talk and they'd tell stories." Because of the propensity to sit and visit for long periods of time, ending a conversation was also difficult. Margaret York described some family friends from Ohio who tried to leave a local's residence at night, but the hostess kept saying, "'Oh, just stay on with us awhile, John!' He said he didn't want to insult them so he set back down," but eventually got "so sleepy" until he finally left.

Family stories also functioned as life lessons. For example, Ryan Trask remembered a story his grandmother told "until the day she died" about her first cousin, killed on one of the final days of World War II. Trask explained, "It was one of those stories that you had to listen to and you had to understand and appreciate it." James Edwards explained that

> a favorite part of our life was, as kids, being allowed to sit out on summer evenings on the porch with our uncles and aunts and cousins and grandparents, listening to them tell about the family history. The tales and events, and of course, as kids we were encouraged to listen and not butt in but allow the grown-ups to talk. . . . That's still some of my fondest memories.

> Sometimes there'd be music, but most times they'd just be talking. A lot of folks say, "Well, sitting on the front porch, that's wasting time; that's doing nothing." But to a Southerner, sitting on the porch is doing something. I mean, that's productive.

As Ryan Trask ages, he finds it more difficult to recall details from family stories he heard "around the dinner table on Sunday" and, as he later elaborated, "every Saturday and Sunday of my life from the time I was born until I'd say . . . when my granddaddy died." Then Trask reflected, "And I really need to go back and write a lot of stuff down, 'cause there's just some fascinating and I think important stories that I want my kids to be burdened with!" On the other hand, Trask explained that because his wife and her sister live close to their mother, the extended family still gathers together to tell stories. "And I see my daughter who's just all ears, who's listening and [who] . . . soaks it in," Trask explained; "I hope some of that carries on and that people just don't have memories of what's on television."

Selected Characteristics of the Appalachian Dialect

In a general description of the Appalachian dialect (South Midlands, more precisely), many linguistic aspects could be explored. The ones discussed in the following pages are those that struck me (a resident in the area for over thirty years) as interesting or unusual, especially as I collected information for my previous two books. Although born in Boston, I learned to speak in the St. Louis, Missouri, area under guidance from parents and grandparents originally from that city; thus, I hear a distinct difference between speakers in my childhood home from inhabitants in my current home in Upstate South Carolina. I am not a linguistic anthropologist, and so much of the subsequent analysis and discussion might appear superficial and informal rather than detailed and academic to professional language experts. Nevertheless, my intention is to present some of the noticeable characteristics that will appear in the stories in subsequent chapters, so that readers regardless of educational background might enjoy both the narratives and the dialects in which they are presented.

"History" as an Entity

As I interviewed inhabitants, I noticed that they spoke about history in a manner that seemed slightly different from that of mainstream American culture. To many whom I interviewed, "history" was an entity. For example, Margaret York was describing the different valuations in antiques and other materials between her grandchildren and her husband and herself, who collected such objects for resale: "They [her grandchildren] grew up in different times with telephones, computers, televisions, all the electronical goods. And anything that was made *back behind that*, not many of them are very interested in it" (emphasis added). Notice that in this sentence, Mrs. York used a preposition indicating a spatial relationship between items in chronological order, as if they were blocks of entities.

Similarly, other inhabitants described "history" as almost tangible. For example, Harry Edison described the adventures of a neighbor, who had been in the US Navy and watched from a nearby ship as the Doolittle Raid took off in April 1942.[56] "He saw those planes take off to take that flight, so this man, boy, he saw some history now, didn't he?" Similarly, many inhabitants described places as "having a lot of history." It is as if "history" is a tangible substance that might envelop things or people.

If history is a tangible entity, and if places or people possess history, then to legitimate a story about those places or people, the speaker might feel obligated to show any listeners those actual people or places, to grant the right to talk about those people or places. For example, Robert Davidson had been telling his audience (two other men and myself) about old roads in the mountains: "It [a particular road] went around there and it come right up that steep hill. I can go show you right where it's at today." Peter Abney described some of the first buildings he constructed as a contractor: "I can easily carry you right to them houses today," he stated.[57] When interviewing James York and his wife in early April 2008, we were interrupted by a phone call from a friend of his, Brian Alexander. Mr. and Mrs. York eventually transferred the phone to me, and Mr. Alexander proceeded to tell me his family story, along with describing artifacts he possessed that would support his story. Several weeks later I interviewed Brian and Claudia Alexander in their home. Almost immediately after I had been welcomed into the home, Mr. Alexander proceeded to show me, with great intensity, seriousness, and rapidity, various family heirlooms that demonstrated his family's Confederate ancestry and his locally well-known surname. In fact, I wrote in my field notes that Mr. Alexander seemed almost frantic in his desire to establish his authority to tell his family's story to me even before the interview had formally begun.[58]

It has been difficult to document this idea in the literature, but I may have found some hints. Historian David Fischer argued that the oral culture of the Scots/British borderlands and the American backcountry "placed an

56 The Doolittle Raid was launched in April 1942, to send American bombers against mainland Japan in retaliation for Pearl Harbor and to boost American morale. While little damage was done, the raid did improve American spirits.

57 In this sentence, Abney uses "carry" as a verb meaning "to take." This usage is very common locally.

58 See also Puckett, *Seldom Ask, Never Tell*, 347.

exceptionally high value on speaking the truth. . . . This oral culture also put a high value on memory, which was often strong in proportion to the weakness of the written word." The backcountry's oral culture "gave great importance to experience, memory, testimony and truth-telling," Fischer concluded.[59] Appalachian scholar Cratis Williams described mountain people as telling elaborate stories, "but at the same time they have a scrupulous regard for the exact detail and the actual fact."[60]

But how does one establish the right to tell the truth, and to prove the veracity of one's story? "In southern society," communication scholar Stephen Smith argued, "the spoken word (any spoken word) becomes a cultural password that allows the speaker to enter the shared social reality as well as the particular conversation with other Southerners."[61] Linguistic anthropologist Anita Puckett discovered in her eastern Kentucky communities that "having physical proof and being able to tell the story are both ways of enacting an authoritative stance, which is then layered with these ideas of 'local' and 'mountain' and 'strong' in order to create a nuanced social identity." "Once the physical link between the speaker, object, and interlocutor is established, proof of something has been established and then the conversation can move to objects not present," Puckett continued. "Whether immediately present or merely invoked, physical objects can be powerful tools" for creating an identity in a conversation.[62]

Digression in Storytelling

Since the nineteenth century, linguist Catherine Evans Davies remarked, digression has been a noted component of Southern storytelling.[63] After I moved to the South (i.e., South Carolina) in 1988, "getting off the subject" (digression) in storytelling was one of the first linguistic patterns I noticed among Southern-born colleagues. Although often frustrating to those unused to the linguistic device, digression may serve important sociolinguistic functions. Davies explains: "Digression may in fact be a crucial element of regional as well as individual storytelling style, expected by an audience that prizes anticipation, that has been 'taught' by regional conventions and the individual storyteller's cues to anticipate delayed gratification." Digression allows for "an associative process with a meditative quality" and "a cultural

---

59 Fischer, *Albion's Seed*, 720, 721.

60 Cratiș Williams, "Rhythm and Melody in Mountain Speech," in *Southern Mountain Speech*, 18.

61 Smith, *Myth*, 145–46.

62 Puckett, *Seldom Ask, Never Tell*, 345, 348.

63 Catherine Evans Davies, "'We Digress': Kathryn Tucker Windham and Southern Storytelling Style," *Storytelling, Self, Society: An Interdisciplinary Journal of Storytelling Studies* 4 (2008): 167–68.

value placed on the extended process of storytelling." Listeners have the benefit of being socialized into a tradition as well as experiencing "a rich and complex experience of entertainment." Consequently, linear storytelling "is potentially intrusive and even insulting to the intelligence of the listener, for whom, presumably, part of the aesthetic pleasure of the discourse is derived from the cognitive ability of making the connections." For the speaker, the perspective "would involve respecting the autonomy and cultural knowledge of the listener, and the listener's ability to find the necessary links to create coherence." Davies argues that the genre may be traced back to an Irish oral tradition, but it may not have a specific name.[64]

Meter in Storytelling

Early in my research, as I double-checked the transcript of Robert Davidson before returning it to him, I noticed that he used an unusual sentence structure when telling a story. In describing a fight between two individuals, Davidson said "Back down he'd go" instead of "He got knocked down again" or something similar. I allowed a colleague of mine, Angelina Oberdan (a poet), to listen to the tape; with a surprised expression, she looked at me and said something like, "You realize he's speaking in iambic pentameter!" She explained that when he spoke in normal conversation, Davidson did not use metered speech; he did so only when he launched into a story.

At that moment, I reflected on the field experience from which the stories came. My Department of Natural Resources (DNR) contact, Sam Stokes, had introduced me to Douglas Edison, who took us out to his enclosed gazebo behind his house, where we sat in the warm January sunshine and drank coffee, awaiting Mr. Edison's friend and distant relative, Robert Davidson. After Mr. Davidson arrived and introduced himself to me, he soon regaled his audience with stories about his past. As he told the stories, he utilized lyrical phrases, as Oberdan had recognized. Then, as I re-listened to the stories on the recording and remembered Mr. Davidson's animated face and the poetic sound of his voice, I realized that the man was an expert storyteller. Despite having very little formal education, Mr. Davidson used the same techniques that Homer, Virgil, Chaucer, and countless other bards had used for millennia to capture and hold audiences raised within a tradition of orally presented narratives. Whether aware of his abilities or not, Robert Davidson used oral skills he had learned in his mountain upbringing to capture and hold an audience's attention.

But is Robert Davidson a unique raconteur or an expert in a well-established cultural tradition? Is there documented evidence for the use of metered speech in storytelling in Appalachian culture? Brenda Kendrick, born

---

64 Davies, "'We Digress,'" 170, 176, 176, 177, 178.

and raised in Oconee County, suggested that "if you've ever heard any people that are actually back in the mountains talk, there's a certain cadence to how they say it – their words." Perhaps it is possible to argue that some of the earlier descriptions of Appalachian dialects as "Elizabethan" or "Shakespearean" may have alluded to this tendency by mountain storytellers to utilize metered speech when narrating, but without examples provided by the scholars, it is difficult to understand what specific features these authors are indicating. Cratis Williams mentioned the "traditional pitch, intonation, melody patterns, inflection, and rhythm" of mountain speech, without providing additional details.[65] In another essay, however, Williams elaborated on this point, arguing that various factors in mountain speech produce "metrical patterns similar to those found in traditional nursery rhymes, riddles, ballads, and folk songs," ultimately creating in mountain speech "a poetic quality similar to that of folk epics and the quaint reliques [*sic*] of primitive people."[66] "In reciting personal experiences or telling what they have been witness to," Williams continued, mountain people "display qualities which belong to the best of oral literature," including "figures of speech, trenchant epigrams, compound oaths, and superlative phrases."[67]

Fortunately, in my fieldwork I have been able to record some examples of Williams's "metrical patterns" and "superlative phrases." As mentioned above, Robert Davidson provided some of the best ones. In one story, for instance, Davidson described his grandfather and another man tearing down abandoned houses in the area:

> But my granddaddy and [another man] tore a house down in the Rocky Bottom. And I don't know whe're it was the Roark Powell house way up there under the mountain or whe're it was the Bob Powell house down there under the old lake. But anyhow they tore one of them down and hauled it to the Cane Break *in a one horse wagon and a club footed mule.*

Later in that same conversation, Davidson related anecdotes about some local characters who had been drinking together and eventually got into a fight:

> Claude – he got mouthy. . . . Said that old Deal, he could tell old Deal wasn't liking it too good and said he kept on. Said directly they got into it, sure enough. Claude was a big old fellow, too; old Claude [last name] was a big fella, pretty big fella. He said directly old Deal hauled off and hit old Claude [pause; chuckles] and said he hit the ground [pause; chuckles] and he said about the time he got up he hit him again; *back down he'd go* [emphasis

65 Williams, "Appalachian Speech," 174.

66 Williams, "Rhythm and Melody," 17.

67 Williams, "Rhythm and Melody," 18.

> added]. And he said every time Claude'd hit him Deal would jump straight up, just jump straight up and pop his feet together and fart! [audience laughter] And he said he'd jump up and pop his feet together and fart! [audience laughter] And said directly he reached down and jerked up a big old root about that [big] in the ground, sitting out there in the road, said he grabbed up a big old root, said he didn't know how in the world he got that thing out of the ground. Said he jerked that thing up and he hit Claude [last name] and said that was the end of it.

In a follow-up interview about a month later, Robert Davidson provided one of the most lyrical sentences I have ever heard as he described the challenges of his childhood deep in the coves of upper Pickens County:

> I can remember, I went to school with the boys that was, lived in the Arch Bottom. They walked out of the Arch Bottom to the Rocky Bottom schoolhouse. And I was a-going – I went to school with them. Okay, they left there, a lot of people left there a-walking, *with a young'un on the hip, and a sack on the back, and not a dime in the pocket*. Not knowing where they was a-gonna go.

Lyricism also appeared in a story by Jeffrey Donnelly as he told about childhood pranks:

> People, like somebody coming home at night or something, they knew they'd be drinking and they had an old foot log they had to walk across, a log with it hewn off on the top. And they'd get out there with a saw and saw underneath it; they'd get out over the creek, the log would break and *into the creek he would go!*

It is possible that storytelling is diminishing as a popular form of mountain entertainment, perhaps due to the isolation of families in individual homes watching individual screens bearing customized electronic images and sounds, as some of my informants had feared. It is also possible that the improvisational narrative skills necessary to create lyrical sentences as one tells a story might also be diminishing. But at the same time, it is hoped by my informants that the instructional and entertainment values of good storytelling will persist.

Reported Speech in Storytelling

Another interesting feature of Appalachian stories is the way that inhabitants report the speech of others. The standard English verb for doing so would be "say," as the first examples below demonstrate. However, first appearing in the literature in the late 1980s and early 1990s were discussions of a new verb for reported speech: "be like" (as in "He's like, 'You need to stop that'"), gradually replacing "go" (as in "He goes, 'You need to stop that'") among younger speakers.[68] According to scholars, the more recent usage has several postulated origins.[69] Evolving from a meaning of "similar,"[70] the verb may stem from a convergence between White English Vernacular and Black English Vernacular or from middle-class teens;[71] by the early 1990s the verb was strongly associated with California "Valley Girls."[72]Since youth culture was more unified and required more interactive conversations, linguists Suzanne Romaine and Deborah Lange argued, the verb predominated there.[73]

Scholars also differ on the gendered use of "be like," with Romaine and Lange suggesting that females initially utilized the verb more frequently because of an interactional, emotional, and nonconfrontational speaking style.[74] Linguists Carl Blyth Jr., Sigrid Recktenwald, and Jenny Wang observed that "be like" is more versatile than "go" or "say," because it might indicate direct speech or "a thought, a state of mind, or inner monologue and therefore may be interpreted as never having been uttered."[75] As my fieldwork examples below demonstrate, by the late twentieth century, "be like" had entered the mainstream of southern Appalachian young adults regardless of gender but remained mostly outside of the dialects of older informants.[76] In fact, since "be like" is found in Appalachian speech, scholars Kirk Hazen, Jaime Flesher, and Erin Simmons use this example to dispute the idea that Appalachia "is an isolated speech community with an old-fashioned dialect."[77]

As the scholarly literature has demonstrated, for older residents, it is characteristic of regional speech patterns to use the verb "say," but in a curiously repetitive manner. For example, Robert Davidson (born in the

---

68 The first scholarly documentation of "be like" for reported speech is an editorial note by Ronald Butters in *American Speech* 57 (1982): 149.

69 Carl Blyth Jr., Sigrid Recktenwald, and Jenny Wang, "I'm Like, 'Say What?!': A New Quotative in American Oral Narrative," *American Speech* 65, no. 3 (1990): 215–27; Suzanne Romaine and Deborah Lange, "The Use of *Like* as a Marker of Reported Speech and Thought: A Case of Grammaticalization in Progress," *American Speech* 66, no. 3 (1991): 227–79.

70 Romaine and Lange, "Use of *Like*," 245.

71 Blyth, Recktenwald, and Wang, "I'm Like," 216; Romaine and Lange, "Use of *Like*," 236.

72 Romaine and Lange, "Use of *Like*," 225.

73 Romaine and Lange, "Use of *Like*," 268–69.

74 Blyth, Recktenwald, and Wang, "I'm Like," 221; Romaine and Lange, "Use of *Like*," 228, 269; female style from 269.

75 Blyth, Recktenwald, and Wang, "I'm Like," 222.

76 See also Kathleen Ferrara and Barbara Bell, "Sociolinguistic Variation and Discourse Function of Constructed Dialogue Introducers: The Case of *Be + Like*," *American Speech* 70, no. 3 (1995): 270–71; see also Kirk Hazen, Jaime Flesher, and Erin Simmons, "The Appalachian Range: The Limits of Language Variation in West Virginia," in Clark and Hayward, *Talking Appalachian*, 67.

77 Hazen, Flesher, and Simmons, "Appalachian Range," 67.

early twentieth century) told a story about working on a construction job in Pickens County:

> I was working over here on this big bridge down here and we lacked about two spans of being done. And boss man come up to me and he told me, he said, "Now listen, [Robert]," he says, "now we're gonna leave here as quick as we can get these handrails poured"; says "we're gonna leave here and go to Alabama." And he said, "if you want to go with us," says, "now you're well welcome to go." Said, "I'd like to take you with me to Alabama."

Anne Flowers, also born in the early twentieth century (and a distant relative of Mr. Davidson), told a story of the matriarch of a moonshining family who had been apprehended by the sheriff with a suspicious trunk-load of half-gallon fruit jars:

> And so they's a-trying her. And she talked looong and slow. Said that judge asked her, says "What was you doing? What was you gonna do with all them fruit jars you had in your car?" Said she said, "I was gonna can 'maters in 'em." Said he said, "'Maters?" Says, "What's a 'mater?" Said she said, "Surely to God, you know what a 'mater is!"[78]

Harry Edison, born in the early 1950s, also used the verb "say" in this story about a local man shooting a skunk in his house:

> But she came in here one morning on her way out, she asked my mother, she says "Alma" (that's my mother's name was Alma), she says, "Alma," says "do you smell anything?" And Momma says, "Yeah, I smell polecat" [skunk]. . . . She says, "I thought so." She says, "I went up there to check on Aunt Emily"; she said, "J. D.[79] had shot a skunk, shot a polecat in his kitchen!"

In contrast to these older speakers, informants born in the late twentieth century (college students at the time of the interviews) often used "like" to report speech. For example, Jason Taylor was describing "country words" that his family typically said:

> That's a big thing we always say: "We're going to town and get something." I said that one day and my sister's like, "Man, we get that from my grandma 'cause people just don't say, 'We're going to town.'" And I was like, "Really?" I was like, "I thought that was a common thing you said."

Taylor's friend and same-aged college student Kayla Radcliffe described

---

78 A "'mater" is a tomato.

79 See other stories about J. D. Chappell in Chapter Nine.

a frustrating situation where her father wanted her to come home from college and process a deer he had killed:

> Last year, I've got exams and my dad calls me and is like, "Hey, I need you to come up and cut this deer up for me." I'm like, "Dad, I can't. I go to school, I can't." And he's like, "Well, I don't know when I'm gonna do it." I'm like, "You used to do it all the time!"

Amy Driver, about two decades older than Taylor and Radcliffe but not raised in the South, also used the verb as she described the start of her family's rafting company in upper Oconee County:

> And they [her parents and friends] canoed here on the Chattooga. . . . And he [her father] just was like, "You know, this might be a good thing." . . . And they [family friends] came down, and they ran Section 4 [part of the river]. . . . And the guys were like, "What do you think?" and they were like, "Well, if you don't do it, we will."

In addition to the differences between generations in verbs used to describe reported speech (supported by the scholarly literature), it is also interesting to note the great care older speakers take to report, and to report multiple times, the designated speech and speakers in their stories. Notice how the older speakers frequently repeat the verb "say," as if to emphasize the quote and the speaker with exaggerated clarity. Perhaps this linguistic habit relates to the critical importance of reporting facts and "truth" in Appalachian speech, as described earlier.

Personal Dative Insertion

My department chair, originally from Oregon, recoiled in mock horror when her five-year-old daughter announced one evening in their home that she was "going to take me a bath." The girl's father, raised in Pickens County, saw absolutely nothing incorrect in his daughter's speech. To standard English speakers, the insertion of the personal dative ("me") in that sentence is unnecessary and marks the sentence as regional speech. However, this construction is another well-established feature of Appalachian Englishes. For example, some linguists argue that the construction originated from general standard British English,[80] while other scholars identify the construction as emerging from southern British English.[81] The common

---

80 Wolfram and Christian, *Appalachian Speech*, 121; Michael Montgomery, "Scotch-Irish Element," 202–4; Montgomery, "Historical Background," 46.

81 Jim Wood, Raffaella Zanuttini, Laurence Horn, and Jason Zentz, "Dative Country: Markedness and Geographical Variation in Southern Dative Constructions, *American Speech* 95, no. 1 (2020): 3–45; Gert Webelhuth and Clare Dannenberg,

construction occurred multiple times in my interviews, across genders and generations.

For example, Ryan Trask, a Pickens County resident with an advanced university degree, described his childhood interest in clogging: "If there was a clogging contest as a kid, I was going to enter it, 'cause I could win me ten dollars." Peter Abney used the first-person plural form as he described a friend and himself seizing an opportunity for work: "Boy, me and Mr. [friend] grabbed us a paintbrush and we went after it." Margaret York used a second-person pronoun as a dative in this story about smoking "rabbit tobacco"[82] and coffee grounds as a youngster to emulate adult smoking: "But you took a brown paper bag and you cut you out a square in it and get them coffee grounds. . . . You'd roll them things up." Anne Flowers used the same construction as she teased me about visiting Salley, South Carolina, for the annual Chitlin Festival, after I admitted I had never tried chitlins:[83] "You ought to go down there and try you some!" thus generating laughter in the group gathered in her living room.

Other Appalachian English Constructions

As mentioned earlier, the English dialects spoken in Appalachia have numerous grammatical features that distinguish them from standard American English dialects. Rather than review the extant literature and provide examples for each feature, I will just list them (since they might appear in subsequent stories) in a random order and provide a citation or two for those who might want to pursue the features in greater linguistic or historical detail.

Double Modals: From King James's colony of Ulster in Northern Ireland came thousands of Scots to the American colonies, having first come from Scotland to Ireland.[84] These settlers brought distinctive linguistic features with them, including double (or multiple) modals. Like many other Appalachian features, double modals also entered Black English Vernacular.[85] Double (multiple) modals (and their negations) combine two modals together where in standard English one would suffice: "I might could do that," rather than "I

"Southern American English Personal Datives: The Theoretical Significance of Dialectical Variation," *American Speech* 81, no. 1 (2006): 31–55.

82 This could be *Pseudognaphalium obtusifolium* and not related at all to real tobacco, *Nicotiana* sp.

83 Pig intestines, typically chopped and fried.

84 Montgomery, "Voices," 342; Margaret Mishoe and Michael Montgomery, "The Pragmatics of Multiple Modal Variation in North and South Carolina," *American Speech* 69, no. 1 (1994): 19–20; see also Ellis, "Dialect as Evidence," 290; Wolfram and Christian, *Appalachian Speech*, 90–94.

85 Mishoe and Montgomery, "Pragmatics," 19–20.

could do that" or "I might do that." Linguist Steven Coats observed that while double modals might occur throughout the US, they were most common, and most often deemed acceptable, in the southeastern states.[86] Linguists Margaret Mishoe and Michael Montgomery further analyze multiple modals, finding that the feature most frequently occurs in one-on-one conversations and in situations of "face-saving" in conversations.[87]

Existential "They": Another Scots-Irish import to Appalachian Englishes is "existential they." At first I transcribed sentences like "They's coming up a cloud" as "There's," assuming the R had been dropped by the speaker. However, according to linguists, the intended word is actually "they," and the feature is described as "existential they." For example, in the following sentence, a well-educated speaker (describing her childhood on a Pickens County farm) initially uses "existential they" but then corrects herself: "You know it's a wonder we hadn't been sick from that because they – there's no telling what they put on the peanuts."

According to Montgomery,[88] this construction stems from Scots-Irish dialects, originally inherited from Scotland and then brought by Scots-Irish settlers to Appalachia and that it is not a derivation of existential "there,"[89] although Wolfram and Christian suggest that "there" may have evolved to "they," but probably did not.[90]

A-prefixing: In another distinctive Appalachian speech feature, the prefix "a" is attached to certain verb forms indicating potential action: "I'm a-fixing to go." Wolfram and Christian identified this feature as a remnant of an earlier period in the English language;[91] more specifically, Montgomery traces the evolution of the feature to Early Middle English, originating with a preposition ("on" or "at") + a gerund, then transforming into the "a" prefix + a participle (still preserved in standard English words such as "afire" or "afloat").[92] Eventually, the feature persisted in southern British English,[93]

86 Steven Coats, "Naturalistic Double Modals in North America," *American Speech* 99, no. 1 (2024): 47–77.

87 Mishoe and Montgomery, "Pragmatics," 6.

88 Montgomery, "Scotch-Irish Element," 202–4; Montgomery, "Historical Background," 45–46; see also Ellis, "Dialect as Evidence," 290.

89 Michael Montgomery, "Notes on the Development of Existential *They*," *American Speech* 81, no. 2 (2006): 132–45.

90 Wolfram and Christian, *Appalachian Speech*, 124–25.

91 Wolfram and Christian, *Appalachian Speech*, 69–70; Clark and Hayward, "Introduction," 16, citing Walt Wolfram, "Sociolinguistic Assumptions, Labels, and Change," *Appalachian Journal* 11 (1984): 217.

92 Michael Montgomery, "Historical and Comparative Perspectives on A-Prefixing in the English of Appalachia," *American Speech* 84, no. 1 (2009): 5–26.

93 Montgomery, "Scotch-Irish Element," 202–4.

with ties to Scots-Irish dialects.[94] Montgomery added that this construction has not been current "in Ireland, Scotland, or northern Britain over the past five centuries."[95] By the nineteenth century in the United States, the feature came to be seen as improper, but today is still common in the Appalachians and in areas settled by those from the region, especially where the feature marks "the property of vernacularity"[96] or "rurality"[97] for speakers.

Because of graduate school interests, I was somewhat familiar with both Middle English and modern German. I had remembered that German marks past participles with "ge-," and that past participles appeared as "y-" in Middle English, as in the fragment "Sumer is icumen in," from AD 1250. At a conference in the late 1990s, I had asked Montgomery whether this Middle English/Germanic connection explained the a-prefixing in Appalachian English, but he instead provided the argument in the articles cited earlier. However, in a footnote in a more recent article,[98] Montgomery proposed that the a-prefix on past participles may have a different source than that on other participles. Paralleling my original hypothesis, Montgomery suggested that the Appalachian "a-" attached to past participles may stem from Middle English and ultimately from Old English and West Germanic "ge-," the indicator of past participles.

Atypical Aspirations: Quite distinctive in the speech of older mountain inhabitants is an aspiration (a puff of air) before the initial vowel in "it," so that the word sounds like "hyit." Because I knew this feature to be characteristic of the dialect (although at the time I did not know its history), I initially added the aspiration in the transcripts I returned to my first several informants. But, since Douglas Edison asked me to remove it and spell his pronunciation of the word in standard English form, I did not transcribe later examples. However, both my undergraduate transcribers and I heard the aspiration numerous times, especially in older speakers. Wolfram and Christian identified this feature as an earlier remnant of English dialects.[99] Although the aspiration was common in Old and Middle English, Montgomery stated, "hit" had already become nonstandard English in England by the seventeenth century.[100]

94 Montgomery, "Historical Background," 46.

95 Montgomery, "Scotch-Irish Element," 205; see also 267n24.

96 Montgomery, "Historical and Comparative Perspectives," "improper" 7, "common" 6, vernacular mark 10.

97 Allison Burquette and Lamont Antieau, "A-prefixing in Linguistic Atlas Project Data," *American Speech* 97, no. 2 (2022): 167–96.

98 Montgomery, "Historical and Comparative Perspectives," 11; see also 24n6.

99 Wolfram and Christian, *Appalachian Speech*, 57–58; Wolfram, "'Appalachian English'?," 217.

100 Montgomery, "Voices of My Ancestors," 361; see also Montgomery, "Scotch-Irish Element," 202–4.

Another form of aspiration I heard but did not transcribe occurred in some Appalachian English words beginning with W. Linguist Joseph Hall argued that these words preserved an Old English initial aspiration, persisting into Middle English, and currently heard in words like "what," "wheat," "wheel," "when," "where," and "whip" in Appalachian speech.[101] Thus, to many inhabitants, these words would sound like "hwhat" or "hwhere." In student class papers I have graded at Clemson University, I can frequently tell the local educational backgrounds of a few of my students, who occasionally misspell "were" as "where": I think they spell the word like they hear it pronounced, still with that aspiration, but "correctly" placed after the W (since the writer would recognize *hwere as an incorrect contemporary English spelling).

Vowel Homophony: Another very well-documented linguistic feature heard throughout my interviews (and during my residence in the South) is vowel leveling or homophony, between the E and I sounds in words like "pin/pen," the O and I sounds as in "boil/bile," or the A and I sounds as in "far/fire."[102] This is another linguistic feature that I initially tried to document in transcripts but was asked to remove and did. However, some of my undergraduate transcribers occasionally wrote "steel" when the speaker was discussing a homemade alcohol-producing apparatus, for example, and in Peter Abney's story earlier, the nonlocal speaker heard "Pile Brothers" rather than "Powell Brothers." I once heard an inhabitant joke that one knew the occupations of the Three Wise Men (they were firemen) because the Bible said they "came from afar."[103] One of my Clemson colleagues from the Miami area told me that, driving her young daughter to school years ago, she was surprised to hear her daughter say, "Look, Momma, a house on a 'heel.'" As a professor at Clemson, I can tell who may be from the area when students sometimes spell "sense" as "since," just as they hear the word pronounced locally.

Atypical Vocabulary Terms: Peter Abney, at the time a retired contractor, told a story about a confusion over several very common words that have a slightly different meaning in the South in general and the Southern Appalachians in particular:

> I done a lot of work in Keowee Key [lakeside retirement community], and here in the South after twelve o'clock during

101 Joseph S. Hall, "The Phonetics of Great Smoky Mountain Speech," *American Speech* 17, no. 2 (1942): 105.

102 See for example Henry Alexander, "Early American Pronunciation and Syntax," *American Speech* 1, no. 3 (1925): 141–48; see also Montgomery, "Southern Accent," "Voices of My Ancestors," and "Historical Background"; and Williams, "Vowels and Diphthongs."

103 Coggeshall, *Carolina Piedmont Country*, 63.

> the day, us mountain people that's the evening with us. . . . And this lady had contracted – had called a plumber about meeting her right after "dinner." So she goes to town . . . and don't come back till about four o'clock. And he had a note on her door: "You promised me you'd be here." And she called me and told me and said "Hey, look. That guy, now I told him 'right after dinner' and I know that guy didn't have his dinner before four o'clock." And I said, "No, ma'am, you're wrong." I said, "That guy had his dinner at . . . twelve o'clock. The evening started at one o'clock and he was here." And then she broke out in the biggest laugh and says, "Law, I forgot my raisin'!" Said, "I was raised that way on a farm." Said, "We called it dinner on a farm." . . . It's just the way we talk.

Elizabeth Nelson, although college educated, admitted that "I still have to translate in my mind when I hear people using those terms even till today. . . . It's like somebody translating into a different language." Appendix Two lists many more typical words and their local meanings.

Conclusion

While scholars acknowledge the myriad variations in dialects spoken in the mountains between east Tennessee and northern Georgia, and the additional variations by gender, age, education, ethnicity, and even context, English speakers from this region and from other places in the United States still recognize a difference in the way people from the Southern Appalachians speak. Moreover, this difference (or these differences) helps to distinguish a regional identity as well, and thus the dialect (or dialects) continues to have social meaning by both inhabitants and others. It is this dialect, to a greater or lesser degree, that animates the stories in the following chapters, giving the words life, nuance, and spirit.

Chapter Three

"People Had Good Times Back Then": Stories of Rural Life

Whether told in standard English or in mountain dialects, stories of rural life encapsulate periods of time in inhabitants' lives that help readers to occupy in imagination a different place in a different time. Stories of local activities help us to visualize life in the region from before the Great Depression through the early twenty-first century. Because of the nature of the interviews, some regions and neighborhoods are discussed more than others, and some topics are discussed more than others. I have also tried to focus on the stories themselves rather than on themes or concepts. The stories are arranged in what I thought might be a logical order, but there will be overlap between topics, and of course many topics are not covered that might be of interest to an audience. Readers are invited to pull up a chair, prop up their feet, sip their sweet tea or their moonshine, and relax.

The Great Depression

As a prelude to a general description of rural life in the mountain region of South Carolina, several older inhabitants remembered the Great Depression and its impact on the lives of their own families as well as on the entire area. For example, Robert Davidson observed:

> He [my father] . . . was in pretty good shape till that Depression hit and when the Depression hit he lost it all. But that was in 1929. . . . We was living up there in the Rocky Bottom, up on that hill there. . . . Well, when they went broke and they left up there and there was people left up there with a young'un on

> the hip, a sack on their back, and not a dime in their pocket going the other way. They was going back up around Bluefield, West Virginia. They was going to Kentucky. They was a-going everywhere. And that's the way they left, a lot of them left here walking. We never did know what ever happened to them or nothing else a-tall about it, but that's the way a lot of them left.

Joseph Yeats recalled:

> During the Depression a kid had to fight to survive. If you had a toy you had to fight to keep it; somebody would take it away from you. It was something else. We, in 1933 both my mother and dad lost their jobs and we didn't have anything. My granddad lived over in [community name], Georgia. He had a farm and he had chickens and he had a cow, milk cow. So we went over there, 'cause no food at home. So we went over there and lived out of his garden and off the farm one whole summer and then up till the cold weather. [Eventually I] got into the mill and got a little bit of work and [name], the supervisor over the Preparation [unclear word] Department down there, tried to take care of my mother. He sent word that he'd try to give her [work] at least two days a week. So we came back to Judson [Mill, Greenville area] and that petered out pretty soon.

Later in his interview, Mr. Yeats added a memory from his time in the Judson Mill Community:

> During that Depression Judson [Mill] Number Two was this side of West Greenville a little bit. But the train would stop this side of West Greenville before going into Greenville and kick all the hobos off. Make them get off the train. And they would come across that mill village just in droves begging for food. Do *anything* for food, you know. And that was a daily thing for a long time.

After Mr. Yeats and his family left the Judson Mill community,

> We was hungry again and found out she [my mother] was pregnant with her third child. Things were rough. . . . I had a[n] uncle that was a mechanic. His job continued on pretty good and he found out we were in real dire straits and he would bring us food. . . . Yeah, we would cry. . . . A lot of mornings we – my sister and I would have maybe a half cup of coffee and a biscuit crumbled in it, and on good days a spoon of sugar in it. That was breakfast. That was it. . . . My dad during the Depression he made the remark, "If this thing ever gets old, we're going to a farm to raise our own food. And we'll have a garden." So he was able to get a job at Slater [Mill, northern Greenville County] in

Figure 3: Family listening to radio, 1941.
Clemson's Cooperative Extension Photographs, Special Collections,
Clemson University Libraries.

> 1939. The first of '39. So the first day of March of '39 we moved to the farm. We rented a place. And for two summers now he loaned me out to a farmer to teach me to farm. My thirteenth, fourteenth year I spent the entire summer with a neighbor, no money involved. He'd take me home on Saturday night and pick me up on Sunday night and I'd farm for him, work with him. And then my third year I had to put a crop in. My dad made me start farming. So then we had vegetables and everything. I entered the Navy then when I was – I finished high school in '44 and went in the Navy in '45. I was at Bikini [Atoll] with the atomic bomb test.[1]

For families already on the farm, Depression life was difficult but tolerable. Elizabeth Nelson asked her parents to describe their lives at that time:

> And they said, well, it didn't affect them that much because they were mostly self-sufficient. They had a milk cow for milk. They had their own mules for plowing, so they had their own vegetables. They had the fruits. And they grew pigs and then my dad would hunt for rabbits and squirrels, so there was very little they had to buy. You know, they bought flour, and sugar,

1 The first two tests took place in 1946.

> and coffee, and salt and pepper. And that was basically all they needed at the store. And they didn't have to have most of those things. It's amazing how self-sufficient you can be when you start to think about it. . . . So you learned to survive without the money and the things money bought.

James Edwards had a similar experience:

> When I was growing up at the tail-end of the Depression (I was born in 1938), of course my family did not know that there really had been a Depression because there was no change when the Depression came in what they were living before. . . I mean we had none of the modern conveniences that we can think of, like, of course no electricity, no running water, plumbing, telephones, TV; of course we did have radios. . . . It was our primary entertainment. We pretty much had our little home, farms of raising our – keeping our cows for our milk and raising hogs for our meat and chickens, of course, for eggs. Every little homestead would have those as necessities, and a little garden patch where we grew our vegetables. And special treats were reserved for, like Christmas when you might get oranges or bananas or something as a special treat.

General Rural Life

Having been raised during the Depression or by parents who had experienced those times, many inhabitants emphasized how that period had shaped the characteristics of self-reliance and group cooperation that they argued typified the region's core values today. For example, Elizabeth Nelson described the general characteristics of her neighborhood, and neighbors, in upper Pickens County:

> But there's always been a very strong sense of community here. . . . Whenever a neighbor had a problem, needed something done, they called him [her father] and he always went and helped them for nothing, just because he wanted to be a good neighbor. And we've had other neighbors come and help us. And, to me, that connotes a very strong community when you can call upon your neighbors in time of need.

When I asked her to describe the general characteristics of mountain people, she explained that these traits were due to

> the way people had to live to survive. They had to be very no nonsense, hardworking, worked all the time to survive. It was a rural mountain community and there were no luxuries. But,

> if they didn't have their sense of humor to get by, where would they have been? The sense of humor helps lighten the load and make[s] life more bearable, you know?[2]

In Nelson's Eastatoee Valley mountain community, her neighbor Ralph Glenn elaborated on the characteristics of mountain people in general:

> Because everybody around you couldn't afford to pay somebody else to do it, if they wanted it done, they either got help from their neighbors, in many cases they did, or they did it themselves, or it didn't get done. And I guess that's the definition of self-reliance, to a large extent. But I don't ever remember seeing a contractor up here. . . . That's a very prominent characteristic of the people that lived up here. They didn't have anybody to do things for them. They didn't have the money to afford to pay somebody to do things for them. And so they did without, or relied on themselves or relied on their neighbors.

Elizabeth Nelson described her own childhood (in the late 1950s and '60s) and that of her mother's life in the Eastatoee Valley:

> My mother worked *hard*. She worked as hard as any man that I've ever known. She did all this cooking from scratch. She took care of the garden. She planted, she weeded, she harvested, she canned, she froze, and cooked. She took care of the farm animals, 'cause my dad was on the road with his job all the time. We had cows, and a mule, pigs, and chickens, and dogs, and cats. She took care of the kids; didn't have too much time to take care of the house; took care of the yards. Good heavens! And when my uncle and my dad retired . . . he and my uncle had a herd of about fifty cattle at one time. . . . When the cows would break out she would go, with our help, and get them back in. So my mom was a very strong lady, very hard working. It was hard on her. I'm sure; very hard. . . . She was very physically strong, as well as emotionally and mentally.

Living about ten miles away from Eastatoee Valley, retired couple Anne and Joshua Flowers described their early married life in the Holly Springs area in northern Pickens County. Mrs. Flowers said: "People had good times back then. They say it's hard times, well it was pretty hard but people had good times, and they enjoyed theirselves." Her husband added: "Didn't have no money but they enjoyed theirselves." In an interview several years later, the couple's daughter Alice Flowers and her niece Stephanie Jamison remembered the elder Flowers' lives. "I mean we lived poor, but we didn't know it," Alice Flowers recalled; "because everybody around us was in about the same shape. There were some people that were better off, but nobody knew that, you

2 For examples of mountain humor, see Chapter Nine.

know. . . . But whatever Dad killed or caught, fish or –" "Bear," interjected Ms. Jamison, and Ms. Flowers agreed. Then Jamison added, "Or turtle." Ms. Flowers agreed that "turtle was one of his favorites. And groundhog, coon –" I interjected, "Possums, I think your mom talked about" from her earlier interview. Ms. Jamison quickly added, "Squirrels," and then Ms. Flowers summarized:

> I mean, that's what we ate. You know and people ask me if I would ever eat it again and I said if I got hungry enough I would. You know because you just – you have to make the best of the situation. And Momma said there was one time that she didn't have something to cook and she was out there digging potatoes that might have been left over in the garden. And somebody showed up with some wild meat that they didn't want to cook. And so she went in and made gravy and biscuits and meat, and those potatoes. So, the only time I've ever been hungry is when I chose to be, you know, dieting or doing whatever.

In the Cane Break region of far northern Pickens County, Robert Davidson described his early childhood:

> Most of them people back there lived pretty good over what they lived. That country was cleared up back them days; there was a lot of fields in there. And they had to fence the corn, they fenced it off, fenced the house and the corn fields off and the cattle and the hogs and things run on the outside. And they'd kill a hog anytime they wanted to. And they had corn. They lived – cornbread and that's about all they knowed; the cornbread and milk. They had, most of them had a cow. . . . And they pickled a lot of stuff. . . . They pickled beans. They pickled corn. They canned corn. They didn't have much to can with. If they didn't have more cans to put it in then they pickled it. . . . I remember Grandpa and them having as much as two barrels of kraut, and a barrel of pickle beans and all that stuff. . . . They tell me they worked from the time they got big enough to work.

Gregory Clayton described the same area at about the same time:

> There wasn't too many people living there then. We was . . . two miles there, from the neighbor's house. And there was a lot of fish; we had fish. I mean we had a good place to fish, and hunt. We . . . didn't even know there was a [game] season on anything. Whenever we needed something to eat, we'd just get it. We figured that's what it's put there for, anyway – to eat when we needed something to eat on. We done a lot of fishing. We farmed; we had – all the time we had hogs, and chickens, and cows. Always kept two milk cows, raised calves all the time.

> Wasn't too much stuff to buy. . . . Buy flour and salt and stuff like that. Didn't cost too much to buy groceries. I remember the first time I may have went courting. I wasn't old enough to get – to have a car then. I rode my mule and carried my rifle three miles – went a-courting. One thing about a mule, if you go courting on a mule, you don't have to have a light [at night]. You, how you start back home you just get on its back and turn it loose, and it knows its way home. It'll go all the way home.

Just a valley away, in Rocky Bottom, Daniel Hall would spend the summers there with his parents, having come from the city of Pickens to escape tuberculosis and to seek cooler summer temperatures:

> And the mountain folks would keep you in produce, too. They had farm gardens and that sort of thing, and the ladies would pick fresh blackberries when they were in, and they'd pick huckleberries and blueberries. . . . They'd come around with a gallon lard bucket, or a half-gallon lard bucket, and sell you produce like that. And we had chickens, we had our own garden, we had apple trees, and that sort of thing. . . . You'd get your eggs and save some hens, and the "coloreds" would cook those. But they had to bring ice up once a week or twice a week, and you had an ice box. An ice box was a big, thick-walled sort of box that was lined with, with metal and you'd put the ice down in there. . . . Buy it at Pickens, at the ice house at Pickens. . . . And we'd cook with kerosene. We had kerosene lamps. . . . You could see at night! . . . When the war [World War II] was over, or toward the end of the war, Dad was so proud. He bought a radio, portable radio. . . . He was so happy he got that radio. And he said, "Gonna bring it up there, and we're gonna play the radio up there." Well, when he got up there, radio didn't work [because of the steep mountain terrain]. The only place the radio worked was out in the middle of a lake, in a boat!

Before the 1950s, radios were the principal means by which information traveled, especially in the mountains, but they might not always have been reliable, as Ryan Trask reported:

> So my great-grandaddy had a country store at Mile Creek [Pickens County] and it was the gathering spot for that whole region through there. And they were all farmers and so the weather was critically important, no irrigation or anything. And [a neighbor] apparently one day said, "Well," he said, "I heard –" and he gave him a weather report. He said, "That's what I heard on the radio." He said, "Well, you can't pay any attention to that thing. It's just a cheap radio anyway!"

Colleen Zimmermann had married into a Southern urban family, but then the couple moved to rural northeastern Pickens County in the 1950s. "And one thing that was kind of interesting, there were no phones here when we moved up," Mrs. Zimmermann mentioned. "And my husband was an attorney, and he felt as though he needed to have a phone, so he talked to the phone company. And they said if we would get everybody on this road to agree to have a phone, that they would put a line in. And everybody had to agree to have two phones, and so we did, and they did."

Benjamin Craig, having married into an upper Pickens County family, had discussed older times with his neighbors: "And one thing [a neighbor] . . . used to talk about too was that everybody was on the party line on the telephone." His wife interrupted: "*When* they got the phone up here. It was like big . . . and when they got the electricity. Grandma, in town [Pickens city], they had electricity forever. She had a [indoor] bathroom, you know?" Mr. Craig then continued: "But if you got a phone call, you had to be careful what you said," and his wife added, "Because everybody would answer, you know." "They would probably stay and listen," Mr. Craig speculated, and his wife confirmed: "They did! 'Cause Grandma would say, especially Aunt [Cate] out here at the end of the road, she'd say, 'Now you know Aunt [Cate]'s going to be listening whenever you answer the phone.' So we couldn't tell any secrets. But most people would pick up the phone [and eavesdrop on other conversations] just because there wasn't that much to do up here!"

Even today, "the cell phones don't work here" in our valley, Mr. Craig explained. "Like my brother came up, he had a Sirius satellite radio and he said, 'Oh, I can pick it up anywhere.' And he was showing me this new car and he turned it on and he said it doesn't work here because we're kind of wedged into the mountains!"

Elizabeth Nelson, neighbor to the Craigs, "was about four years old when we got our first television! And we loved that. . . . It's 'Howdy Doody Time!' . . . . And then there was the 'Little Rascals' after that.[3] I *loved* cartoons. . . . Greenville was the only one [channel] we could get and it's the only one that I can still get clearly; 100 percent clearly, although I suppose that will change with digital. I can get three [channels] now!"

Harry Edison told a story about his grandfather, a former moonshiner who had been captured and jailed in Spartanburg County decades earlier. Toward the end of his life the elder gentleman lived with Edison and his family, and "we'd be sitting there watching TV; . . . he'd be happy watching TV, the next thing they say, 'This is Channel 7 Spartanburg.' . . . He said 'Shah! Turn that thing, I don't want to watch that!' . . . So he doesn't like [anything

3 *The Howdy Doody Show* was a children's TV show from 1947 to 1960. *The Little Rascals* was originally a series of short films entitled *Our Gang*, filmed between 1922 and 1944 and later aired on TV as *The Little Rascals*.

from] Spartanburg" because of his former incarceration in that city.

Over in Oconee County, Brenda Kendrick remembered the life-changing introduction of electricity to her rural home:

> I didn't have to do my homework by lamplight anymore, with electricity. Then of course, Mom got a washing machine, and a 'lectric stove, and a refrigerator – well, we had an ice box before then. The guy with ice would come once or twice a week, and we had this big ice box sitting out on the back porch. He'd bring his ice and put it in and then we got electricity, and you know, you get the modern things, and it's just totally, seemed like it just – we got a TV, you know, all the things that a child now, you think, "You didn't have a TV? I mean, this is the Dark Ages? When was – when were you born?" It's hard to make children of this generation understand that it just, you know, how it was back then. You didn't miss it because you'd never had it. We didn't have a TV to sit and stare at every day. We were out playing in the yard, or playing games, or whatever. Or working, picking cotton.

Garvin Bradshaw and his youngest sister, Claudia, grew up in northern Oconee County, near the border with North Carolina, in a tiny house their father had constructed by himself. Their life was challenging, Mr. Bradshaw recalled: "If you lived in the mountains, you lived hard. Daddy'd get up in the morning, go feed his mules, feed his hogs, while Momma cooked breakfast, and time he got the breakfast done, he'd come back in 'cause he'd be in the field at daylight a-plowing."

At one point in his interviews, Mr. Bradshaw elaborated:

> I was borned [*sic*] over here on top of the hill. . . . My daddy he built this li'l old shack down here – . . . two room shack what he moved in to. And he raised cotton and he cleaned that new ground off down there and he raised corn; he had a hog, had a mule. And wasn't no running water in the house, carried it from a spring. No outhouse and no inside outhouse; it was all on the outside. Go feed the hog and go down on a real cold morning and build you a big fire, get your water good and hot and knock a hog in the head and clean it. Have something to eat. Then maybe have to get up and go down to the wash branch [small creek]. . . . You just have an iron pot down there; you go down to the branch and put you a battling board across there to wash your clothes on. And heat the water in the pot and wash them in a tub like I got hanging out there on the building. Then they'd put it on that battling bench and take a board and beat them clothes, beat the dirt out of them. And they'd hang them on a line and let them dry. And every morning out there, we'd, for a living we'd cut locust posts,

> break ivy. . . . And he [his father] used to trap a whole lot. He'd go catch muskrats, minks, and he'd bring them to the house and skin them, stretch them on a board.

Claudia, the youngest child in the family, added:

> We had a farm, and I can remember walking behind my momma going down to the barn to milk the cows. And I was just a little girl. And I can remember just walking behind her. She said, "Be careful, watch out for snakes; now you gotta walk right in my steps." Because there was grass on both sides so I was a little kid and I'm trying to stay in her footprints 'cause I'm scared of snakes. But we'd go down to the barn and she'd milk the cow. We had chickens, farmed everything; my father farmed everything. Farmers had a big family back then; everybody pulled their weight. We all got out and pitched in, even as (I was a little kid) I can remember trying to pick up potatoes. He [my father] would plow them up, and our job was to pick up the potatoes. I can remember it in the fall, like when the stalks, the corn stalks are dead you know, and they'd cut them down. And you'd have to pile them to burn trying to get the fields ready, you know, like for spring time. 'Cause when spring time come, you know everything was getting ready to be re-plowed; the ground turned under. . . . We canned everything. When I say "we" my mom did. Back then I told you people would swap work. I can remember one of my aunts would come up there and out on the front porch they would have this big tin tub full of apples, and the women would sit around the big tub of apples peeling apples and getting them ready. And then they would cook them down. They'd make homemade applesauce and they'd can it. Or they'd all sit outside 'cause it was very hot – we had no air conditioning. And my mom had one wood heater in the kitchen, and she got a[n] electric stove I think when I was ten or eleven, but she wouldn't never get rid of a wood stove. But she would can and it would be, oh blazing hot outside in the summertime but she'd have the wood stove going so hot you'd think you was gonna die. And she'd be canning, cold packing, you know in the big black pots, you know putting the jars in it. But she actually would can sausage; . . . I can remember being a little girl and trying to help out. Couldn't do a whole lot but I would help out. I could do good breaking beans or washing stuff. I can remember her being at the kitchen table and having the old crank sausage grinder and they would grind sausage.

For entertainment, the Bradshaw family had to improvise, as the oldest son, Garvin, recalled:

> Well, we didn't have a radio. We had to walk through a trail way, and we'd walk over to [a neighbor's house], and he's the only one had one in this country. And we'd walk over there and listen to the Grand Ole Opry on Saturday night. . . . Finally, we finally got one. Well, we'd get out here, and we'd get up enough wood to last us till midnight and sit up and listen to the Grand Ole Opry. Then that antenna [?] come along, television come along. Then we had it made then, boy. We got electricity in '66, I believe it was. . . . Then we had something – we got a refrigerator; we had ice in it!

"Oh, my momma . . . made my dresses," Claudia Alexander recalled, and continued:

> And she had an old sewing machine that was the pedal kind and she would sew like my dresses. And she would take the bed in the living room and lay material on the bed and she would take either brown paper bags or newspaper and she would put my dress on top of that and make her own patterns. She could sew anything she wanted to, but she knew – mountain people's clever, and they would have to use their ingenuity. My brothers could rig up anything and tinker on a car or lawnmower or whatever little contraption. . . . They had to depend on theirselves because they didn't have money to go to town to have somebody work on stuff so they would rig up something.

Even after some of her older siblings had married and moved out of her parental home, Mrs. Alexander recollected,

> we were just like a big clan, you know. We'd just pop in on each other. And I can remember growing up and it's just like my brothers would always come down there [to the parents' house]. . . . And Momma would get up and cook breakfast . . . and she always had coffee. It was like they all came together at Momma and Daddy's house to have their coffee, or if they wanted something to eat, they were welcome to eat. . . . They checked on the parents to make sure they were okay even though they're married, even though they're going off to their jobs.

These family connections continued even after death. "Old people (when their loved ones died) they brought them home, not a funeral home," Claudia Alexander explained, and continued:

> So when my daddy died, my momma had him brought home. . . . She wanted him brought home and even that little house, as little as it was (they had to take the front door off to get his casket in) but he was brought home and it was in January. ... 'Cause that was a[n] old tradition. Before my momma died just three

> and a half years ago I had this talk with her. I said, "Momma, I know how you feel but would it be alright when that time comes to have a visitation at the funeral home?" . . . And she did give in and say it would be okay.

Individuals living in the small towns had more amenities earlier in time, and so sometimes viewed their rural cousins with slight disdain. Moreover, inhabitants born and/or raised in the rural neighborhoods far from any incorporated village were quite aware of how they were viewed by the more "sophisticated" townsfolk. Because of their isolation, rural residents were often the butt of jokes. For example, Joseph Yeats told me and a gathering of his neighbors:

> I'll tell you something that happened to me. I was serving on a Navy cruiser over in the Mediterranean [in the late 1940s]. And somebody come up with an old World Atlas. And they looked Dacusville up, you know; they knew I was from Dacusville. It said, "Population sixteen." From then on [whenever] I'd get a letter [from home], you know, they'd say, "How's the other fifteen doing?"

"Those city students [in high school], they kind of looked down on us little country students," one man related, and explained:

> See, we had no, anything out in the world to teach us, I mean like the television or the telephone or the radio or anything like that. And they did. And they knew things that we didn't know. . . . They got the paper. We didn't even get a paper. And knew nothing. Our mail route came three times a week when I was a child. . . . And our mailbox was over there on that side of the road. And we had a little footlog. . . . My daddy and the neighbors on the other side got together and cut some big trees and just let them fall over across the river. And we had that to cross to get to our mailbox. When . . . it rained a lot and the water rose, we didn't get any mail because we couldn't get to the mailbox.

"Now when I was younger," Peter Abney confessed,

> we always felt like the town people felt a little bit better than we were, so that was alright with us. . . . It used to be: "Oh, you live back up there in the sticks." And you accepted that. But now here I am [an] old man and they say: "Oh, you live back up there where that valuable property is!" . . . [As a contractor], I used to buy a lot from Greenville. This guy come up here . . . [and] asked me, said, "Do you get your newspaper the same day I'd get mine." . . . [I replied:] "No, it comes in next week; it'll

> be new stuff." And I said, "The television program you want to watch tonight," I said, "it'll come up to my house tomorrow night!"

Another time, Mr. Abney was in a hurry for an appointment and speeding through a county seat:

> And the police stopped me. And I pulled out my driver['s] license and he just looked at them and he said, "Where in the 'H' is Sunset, South Carolina?" I said, "That's a little old mountain post office back in above Pickens." I said, "We don't never get out from up there too much." And he just slowly handed me back my license and said, "Well, feller, if you ever do come through this way, slow it down." And I took off; he didn't fine me! He thought I was from *way* back in there.

As a child, Denise Craig had the benefit of two grandmothers, one who lived in the city of Pickens and one who lived in the mountains. "From what Momma said," Mrs. Craig explained, "the mountain people were more ignorant and folksy and then the town people were more sophisticated, I guess. And I could compare my two grandmas, you know." Mrs. Craig then elaborated:

> Well, Grandma [Kate] . . . lived in town and she was a town person! She . . . had a yard and a garden. I mean, her garden was flowers. And she was into decorating and that. And Grandma [Cindy] was into her canning and her vegetable garden and her chickens and her cows and her guineas.[4] She really wasn't into flowers or decorating. It was just simple, even though Grandpa had a good job. He was a superintendent or something at the mills. He wore a suit and a hat to work.

But, Mrs. Craig continued; even the city grandmother "had twenty-something acres between Easley and Pickens and a barn and cows and my goat. I had a goat, and it ate our laundry so therefore, my goat had to go! And my rooster jumped on her and . . . then I went out to look for my rooster and I had to find out I had eaten it [for Sunday dinner] and that was horrible. It was a traumatic experience for me!"

A retired city-dwelling professional whose family vacationed in the mountains tried to demonstrate the transition between country and city folks with this anecdote, which also demarcates a subtle class distinction between Christian denominations:

> When the fellows first came in the mountains, . . . the old mountain men said, . . . I had three things: I had an axe, a Bible, and a gun. A wife and a gun. Four things. He says I got

4 Domesticated birds (*Numida meleagris*).

> in there and he says I chopped me some land out there and a little square, and soon as I got all that chopped up, here come the Baptists walking in there. And . . . pretty soon there got to be a trail. And he said soon as there got to be a trail, said here come the Methodists. And said the trail got wider and wider and they built a road and he said here come the Presbyterians. And said it got so populated up there and wide up there, they got railroad track in there and the Pullman cars came in there, and here come the Episcopalians!

In more recent decades, with paved roads, ubiquitous automobiles, and improved communications, the boundaries between rural and small town life have blurred. University college student Forrest Sanders described his weekends:

> Like when I was in high school and middle school, growing up, every Saturday we would work outside in the yard, whether it was cutting grass, cutting down a tree that had gone dead, or just work in the workshop on some project that he [his father] had at the time. Saturdays were work. And I love to do that; I'm not a big fan of just sitting around all day. . . . Every Sunday we were in church. . . . When I was younger we would just walk to church, since we were right there in town. In the summer and fall we would walk to church and walk to high school football games on Friday evenings. But, let's see, most Sundays we'd go to church, we'd come home, Mom would cook lunch – she always cooks a big lunch for Sunday. I still go home a lot on Sundays and eat, just because it's twenty minutes down the road. Great meal, my mom's a great cook. Sunday afternoons my dad would normally take a nap, my mom would take a nap, then we'd go back to church on Sunday nights. Eat a small dinner, and just kind of get ready for the week ahead.

Sanders's friend and fellow university classmate Jason Taylor described his general life in the country:

> A lot of people say there's nothing to do in the country. I mean we'd always go on picnics, just walking around. . . . Me and my sister would ride our bikes and she got us into the habit of like, you know, picking up cans and stuff on the side of the road. Like, we were doing like Adopt-A-Highway but it wasn't even. It was just volunteer. And I just liked it 'cause it was so relaxed. And I don't know. We'd go on vacations a lot too to different cities and I've never liked just living in the cities. I like the country life where you can just, if you get fed up with the things that are going on, you can just walk outside, do whatever you want. . . . You know, in the country you just go out in someone's backyard.

> One of my, a friend of mine I made in middle school, he lived on like a three-hundred-acre farm, so we were always camping, spending time out there. We would – I *love* exploring. I just do that all the time. No purpose in mind. We like to find creeks and follow them, see where they lead. That's one of our big things. I don't know, just the whole atmosphere of the country is great.

Now that family farms have largely (but not entirely) disappeared, and now that transportation has significantly improved, employment for young adults has changed dramatically. University student Kayla Radcliffe described the jobs she and her friends did:

> Some of them had jobs at the Mall in Greenville. I'm like, how do you drive all the way to Greenville every day? And then some of them had jobs at McDonald's, lots of them as cashiers at Bi-Lo and Ingles [grocery stores]. Like when you go to Bi-Lo or Ingles, it's always a high school girl or boy checking you out. That's just where they go, and fast food, stuff like that.

Less frequently, teens could find employment at some of the region's gated communities, as Radcliffe explained:

> For the actual company The Cliffs [gated community], they had actual applications. Knowing somebody would help your chances of getting a job, but for jobs like I had, with an independent person, you did have to know somebody; they don't just advertise, and say, you know, I need help. Not a lot of them [her friends] worked there, because like I said 'cause of the distance, and they needed very few people. Most of the people they hired, they didn't want them to be younger; they wanted them to be older. And I think I knew one girl who worked at The Cliffs, and she was like a waitress at one of the restaurants, and they have like the club house restaurant, and she was a waitress. Maybe those kind of jobs they'd hire high schoolers. They didn't like to – I never saw younger people there.

Another group seeking employment in the South Carolina mountains are Spanish speakers from a variety of Latin American national origins, creating neighborhoods and communities throughout the area. Small bakeries and bodegas may be seen, and roadside signs in both Spanish and English announce their presence. While most participants did not discuss Hispanics in great detail, while I did not interview anyone of Hispanic origin (due to the nature of my research questions), and while I did not specifically ask about this group, a few inhabitants did mention them.

For example, Kayla Radcliffe's father worked for one of the gated communities as a landscape manager, and so he hired a lot of Spanish speakers. Radcliffe continued:

> There was one guy (his name was [José]) and my daddy worked with him for like eight years, and he's Mexican. And it's almost one of those times where you're almost positive that he's illegal, but he has all the documentation, and just, you know he didn't get it. But – and it's very sad because he has like five children, right? And a wife. . . . But he'd come to pick up his paycheck from my dad, 'cause he helped him out a lot. Like every time my dad has an extra odd job, [José] comes to him and is like, "I'll help." And I guess my dad saw where he lived or something, but whenever we have extra deer meat or something, Dad's like, "Oh yeah, take that, we're not gonna use it." And it just depends on how well he knows the person, but [sighs] I don't know. I always found that really interesting, that my dad knew that they needed something, so like if we weren't going to eat something, he's just like "Here." And [José] was always like, "Oh wow, thank you, thank you, thank you, thank you." And they're always so grateful. . . . I read these signs about presidential candidates that are like, "Stop immigration, no amnesty, kick 'em all out," and I'm like, you know, look at them. They're not bad people, they work hard, and they're thankful, so I mean, I don't know, it makes issues a little bit harder to deal with.

When I asked a follow-up question about her father working with Hispanics, Radcliffe described her father's growing awareness and sensitivity:

> Honestly, I think it was a really good thing for him to work with them, because I think I mentioned before there are racist tendencies, and I think he saw that they are hard workers. That's something that most [local] people they'll respect; if you're a hard worker, whether you're Mexican or black or whatever, they'll respect you. So I think that was good for him. But he found something really interesting. Like when I started taking Spanish classes in school, he'd be like, "Teach me Spanish, teach me Spanish! I'm trying to talk with my workers." And they'll teach him words sometimes, but mostly it's like really amusing ones. . . . 'Cause the workers would play jokes on the high-ups, the ones that thought they were better kind of people, the ones who would be working directly with Jim Anthony[5] or something and would kind of patronize them. My dad told me a story once with these Mexican workers and this guy, this big – he may have been an executive or something, came up to them, "*Hola, amigos*, how's it going?" And they called him a very derogatory term in Spanish, and he thought it was hilarious; he thought it was his own little nickname, but they were calling him "faggot." . . . And they thought it was *hilarious*, because he couldn't understand them, but they told my dad later, they were like, "Yeah, that's not

5 A well-known regional developer. See John M. Coggeshall, *Something in These Hills: The Culture of Family Land in Southern Appalachia* (Chapel Hill: University of North Carolina Press, 2022), 49–50, 124, for details.

a good word to be using to call someone." But he never – he tries to keep a little bit of separation, simply because he's their boss. . . . But he does have personal interactions with them.

Farming

Of course, one of the most common labor activities in the region was farming, especially on smaller, relatively self-sufficient farms prior to World War II.[6] One of my oldest informants, Anne Flowers, described her early life before the First World War:

> When we got married, we moved in the house with his [my husband's] grandpa and granny. . . . And then we moved out yonder . . . and we farmed. We had, growed cotton, and corn, wheat – we had our meal, our flour at home – we didn't have to buy. We raised our hogs, and had a cow, and had our chickens. And we just had to buy, you know, like coffee and sugar – stuff like that. So we just lived at home. . . . We never went hungry and we never went cold.

Cynthia Niles described that same life: "That's the way you had to live back then. You had to make your own living. And then, we picked cotton for our school clothes and things like that. I mean . . . you wasn't poor, you was just like the rest of them – you didn't have anything! But nobody didn't. We was all in the same boat." Niles's friend Patrick O'Connell added: "But everybody was happy."

In upper Oconee County, John Summers recalled, "we used to raise hogs right in there, me and my daddy did. We raised hogs. We had cows . . . out here behind us up here. We used to have, this field used to come on out closer to the house. We'd plant that whole field in a garden. We had one of the biggest gardens. Yeah. We raised a lot of what we eat." Douglas Edison described his early farm life back in the hills:

> But the old farmers up in there, they had a lot of food. They'd make molasses, you know. What kept them going was them, they called them smokehouses. . . . But now that smokehouse was just about full when fall come, you know, of cured hams and deer meat. And I can remember my dad had a big old keg made out of wood, and he'd fill it full of molasses. And it had a plug; you'd pull it out and catch it in a smaller container, and then by [the] time it got on the table you know it was in a pitcher. . . . We would strip the – the blades was called fodder. Strip it off, then we'd cut it, cut the heads off, for the seed, and run it through [a

6 John M. Coggeshall, *Carolina Piedmont Country* (Jackson: University Press of Mississippi, 1996), 181–88.

> mill]. Old mule pulled a mill around and around and mashed the juice out, and boy the yellow jackets would come after that juice. And you'd run it – my dad had a little pipe he would run from the mill down to the – they call it [an] evaporator, and it had sections. And as it come down through them sections, the last one is where the molasses come out. . . . Had a big old fire under it. And you had to know what you was doing. If you cooked it too long, it'd be too thick. And if you didn't cook it long enough it wasn't right.

Families assisted each other in planting, cultivating, and harvesting, and the large numbers of children provided additional labor. A retired Pickens County employee remembered that "we would hoe cotton and stuff like that. And Daddy . . . said, 'Well, if y'all,' said, 'we'll get out here and we'll hoe the cotton until noontime.' . . . Saturday morning and then we'd get a quarter. . . . We'd get a quarter each, and he'd take us to Easley. We'd go to that theater down there, and we'd get one bag of popcorn and a Coke each. And then we had ten cents left for a comic book!"

When children were drafted as farm laborers, especially when unsupervised, the desired outcome might not always be assured. Julie Jackson recalled a time when her father had asked her to plant peanuts; she complied, but with the least amount of effort. Carrie Jackson, her mother, added: "And when they [the peanut plants] come up, they all come up in one place!" Ms. Jackson then explained: "Well, they come up about this wide in one row. We planted one row. . . . But we ate all we could eat! You know it's a wonder we hadn't been sick from that because they – there's no telling what they put on the peanuts."

One topic I have always been interested in is the well-documented Anglo-American folk tradition of planting crops by the signs of the zodiac or on specific dates;[7] the *Old Farmer's Almanac* listed monthly phases of the moon and the zodiac signs, to help rural farmers determine the optimal times for planting.[8] For example, Brenda Kendrick remembered:

> My daddy always planted watermelon on the first day of May. . . . That's how he planted his crops is by the almanac every year. My oldest sister, her husband – her in-laws did that. I think the older generation that's how they planted was by the almanac – the people that I knew. They say it works. I don't know. When I was younger I know my daddy did, but when I was doing a garden I just planted when I got a chance! . . . This is just the way they'd always done it and this is the way it was done. I guess I never questioned it because that's how it was always done. . . . My daddy (and I guess my grandparents did the same thing) went by that

7 Coggeshall, *Carolina Piedmont Country,* 181–88.
8 The *Old Farmer's Almanac* still lists these lunar and solar events.

almanac just like a Bible.

As mentioned earlier, livestock (especially pigs and chickens) had been a common part of most upper South Carolina farms. Typically, stock roamed freely, feasting on materials in the natural environment, especially acorns and (in earlier times) chestnuts for hogs. In upper Pickens County, Douglas Edison took his father back to his old homeplace, and his father described traditional ways of raising hogs:

> He said I think right over there is where I had my hog lot. He said that every spring they would have a bunch of hogs and they'd take them over there, keep them in this little pen, in a little poled (he built it out of poles), and he'd keep them there till they took up. Then they'd turn them out and they'd go back that fall and butcher them. And he said hogs that had got fed on acorns, that their lard never would congeal; it'd always pour.

In more recent times, cattle (and other livestock) were fenced into pastures, but curious children sometimes ventured into places they should not go, as Denise Craig recalled:

> Grandpa kept his cows on this side of the road. And so the cows were back up on the mountain and so we just didn't go back there. . . . My cousin and I went back there one time. And we didn't get far, and we heard – Grandpa had a bell on the bull and we heard – you couldn't see up through the trees, you know – but we heard [slow] ding, ding. And then it was [fast] ding, ding, ding, ding! And then it got faster and we ran. And that bull came out of the trees, you know. And I went feet first but my cousin went head first [through the fence] and she ripped her little shirt. . . . So we were glad he did have that bell on [JMC: Yeah!] the bull.

Contemporary college student Jason Taylor has noticed changes to the upper South Carolina landscape; he was also fortunate enough to observe the butchering process, much more frequently used in past generations. The process definitely had an impact on him and his friend:

> But I've always been interested in the farms in Dacusville 'cause none of them seemed like really big like active kind of like they're selling a lot kind of farms. They're just kind of like people just have these farms just for the heck of it. I don't know; they have cattle. They raise cattle; . . . they're not beef cattle. I think they may just breed them. I'm not really sure because they hardly ever, I think maybe thirty, forty years ago they might have been more operational 'cause I remember the first time I did see them kill a cow, though. . . . It wasn't just for like any purpose like they're going to sell it. The cow just kept on getting out of the fence, and they're, "Ah, well, let's shoot it." So they shot it, put it up on a front

> loader and they just skinned it and gutted it and everything. It was me, my friend that lives there, and another friend. We were just two of us we'd never seen anything like that. We were just like amazed, blown out of our mind. And they let us see like the whole process of the thing being cut up and we were just like "Wooooow!"

Small-Town Life

As an attempt to understand what life had been like a generation ago, I sometimes asked people about life in small towns as they were growing up. Such information provided a balance to descriptions of rural life and also afforded a glimpse into the county seats or markets where community or commercial business was conducted.

Some of my informants were from Oconee County, and they recalled descriptions of the small towns there. For example, Mike Davidson described the closest small town to where he had been raised:

> When I was a kid growing up, . . . Salem used to have a Gulf [gasoline] station, the Exxon station, two pool rooms. Clyde Talley had a grocery store. He had a man that worked in the meat department, another guy worked in the produce department, and one or two boys bagging groceries and another guy that delivered. That's how busy the store was. . . . And Geneva Green had a café there; there was another café on the other end of town, and there was two pool rooms. Look at it now. You got one filling station in town and a junk store on the other end. Now, you do have the Dollar General, but I mean, it's nothing to what it was thirty years ago. Thirty years ago Salem was – and a barber shop. First job I ever had I shined shoes, fifteen cents. I give him a nickel, I think, and I kept the dime.

John Summers, also in Oconee County, described his visits to Seneca, the county's largest community:

> My aunt worked down at Behrens store for years and years down there on [a] back street. . . . I'd go down there and spend time with him [first cousin]. We'd go to the movies on Saturday evening while she was working, you know. . . . She'd give us money to go to the movies and get us a bag of popcorn and a Coke-Cola or something. . . . It was a real big deal for us. It was a treat.

Traveling to town was a major event in the weekly schedules of most rural inhabitants. Nancy Daniels described her childhood visits:

> Now we'd go to McDonald's. That was a big thing for us on Saturday night. But we drove all the way to Berea [Greenville County]. That was the only McDonald's around . . . at that time.

Figure 4: Main Street, Pickens.
People and Places - Pickens Area, Digital Collections file, Pickens County Library System.

> But we would go over there. We thought that was great. And we would eat like hot dogs at . . . a café in town. As far as eating at a restaurant, I was in the tenth grade. We were at the beach one year and I didn't even know how to order a salad or anything.

Peter Abney, Ms. Daniels's father, remembered an even more momentous occasion on a trip to town:

> The first red light I remember ever going in Pickens County was at Liberty. And we went down there, one Sunday afternoon; my granddaddy lived on the other side of Liberty. But Daddy stopped with us and let us watch that red light work. We wasn't by ourselves; the street was lined up with people watching that red light! I mean, hey – that was new to us, you see.

Many inhabitants described life in downtown Pickens, the county seat, in their childhoods of about fifty years ago. Harry Edison recalled: "Oh man, see, Easley and Greenville's taken over the business that Pickens had, mostly. . . . Those streets, especially on Saturday, the streets of Pickens were lined, you know, people just lined up on both sides of the streets and they had different kinds of stores, you know, clothing stores, hardware stores."

Jesse Alexander owned a small business in Pickens, and he provided a somewhat more detailed picture:

> Everybody came to town from the country on Saturday. They . . . would come in on wagons and old granny women would be sitting in a straight-back chair riding backwards. I've seen them go by the barber shop fifty, sixty years ago, coming into town, and they'd park behind the stores and the men would go to the

Figure 5: J. M. Reece Barber Shop.
People and Places - Pickens Area, Digital Collections file, Pickens County Library System.

> barber shop and the street corner to get all the news, you know. . . . Matheney – he ran a silent motion picture show right there below the hardware. . . . But Gary Hyatt, the local paper editor, said that Sonny Katz . . . said, "Gary, I don't have to pay to see the movies" (they lived overhead); he said, "I've got a knothole in my bedroom about this big," and says, "I can watch every one of those movies." It was in the adjoining place where he could see right down there. I thought that was funny.

The senior barber in the downtown Pickens shop described his patrons and their activities about a century ago:

> For the most part, all men came in there, and they'd bring boys sometimes. You didn't hardly ever see a woman. Now in the late '20s . . . women bobbed their hair, and they didn't have beauty shops and they came in there and got their hair bobbed. And then some of the men didn't like that too good, but the men felt comfortable coming into a barber shop, you know. And if a minister came in the barber would say, "Come in, Preacher So-and-So" real loud to where they wouldn't misspeak – somebody'd tell a dirty joke or something. But most of the time people behaved their selves, but . . . some of them'd get too much to drink – some of the hillbillies. . . . When I first started I'd

> shave all Saturday morning – just one right after another. You'd have farmers who'd come in there, or saw mill people, and they'd get one every week. Your businessmen, . . . they'd get one every day or every other day – a barber shop shave. . . . Most barbers made all their money on Friday afternoon or Saturday. And then you had baths. You had two baths going up there [upper floor of barber shop] all the time. Shine boy had to keep the baths clean – papers and towels and soap. And you got twenty-five cents a bath. You'd put that twenty-five cents in a cigar box, and a lot of times that would pay your rent. . . . You had to have spittoons in a barber shop sixty-five, sixty and seventy years ago. Even barbers would chew tobacco. . . . I was a shine boy; you had to clean those cuspidors. . . . You took a little disinfect[ant] and put in there, and they'd spit in that and throw their stubs in there. And the shine boy had to take and scrub them out and fill them back up.

A generation later, Elizabeth Nelson described her childhood recollections of downtown Pickens as her father took their family into town:

> And every Saturday he would take us to town and we would buy groceries at the little locally owned grocery store . . . on Main Street of Pickens. . . . And I can remember even when I was in my early teens that we would buy three large brown paper grocery bags full of groceries for fifteen dollars, which we thought was a lot then; but that was early 1960s, maybe 1963 or so. And those were good trips and sometimes my mother would go, but usually it was just my dad and us. . . . And I remember as a preschooler loving to go there [local filling station] on Saturday when my dad filled up with gas. And he had a bubble gum machine just inside his front door. And the bubble gum was a penny a piece back then so my dad would give me a penny and I would get my bubble gum. And that was such a treat! . . . There was a Five and Dime on Main Street that I thought was the best store in the world. And of course [an] . . . "upscale" clothing store . . . had glass cases in the center of the store where the little lace hankies and gloves and such resided under the glass. And there was Young's Drug Store down on the end of the block. And they had a soda fountain, which is where I had my very first milkshake! . . . People would come to town to shop on Saturday afternoon and a lot of them would sit in their cars and just watch people walk up and down the street. And if they saw anybody they knew, they would have conversations with them and that's how they visited. . . . I do remember at least one wagon with horses that

> I would sometimes see go down Main Street in the early '50s. . . . And of course, our treat from the grocery store was a bag of candy and, more often than not, my brothers and I ate it before we got home!

Even into the early twenty-first century, college student Jason Taylor related, traveling from the "country" to the "city" was a significant trip. Taylor admitted:

> I mean it wasn't even like we lived far out in the country. We only lived like ten minutes away from Easley and Pickens now. I mean but Easley and Pickens aren't the biggest towns, of course. We probably lived fifteen minutes away at our old house, but it was just like the only time we ever went was to get like groceries. That's the only thing we needed. Or go to Walmart or if my parents decided to take us to the movies once in a blue moon (which that hardly ever happens now). We always rented movies a lot. We didn't have – I was a junior in high school before we had any sort of cable or DirecTV so we had like three channels.

While Saturdays in the small towns were economically and socially significant, holiday celebrations were major social (and economic) events. For example, Harry Edison had fond memories of parades through downtown Pickens:

> And at Christmas time, now that was a big deal. When the Christmas parade in Pickens we'd all go to the Christmas parade. . . . You talk about a crowd of people. I mean the streets would be just jammed. . . . The kids'd go over to the courthouse and get candy. . . . Old Santa he would pitch some off of his sleigh but, you could go over and get a bag of candy and a[n] apple, apple and maybe a pear.

Edison then continued:

> I remember my favorite thing in the old Pickens parade was, there was this place over there I think it was like a junkyard. They had an old car . . . and it didn't have a top on it. . . . And that old car had a bunch of people dressed up like convicts in that thing. And they would be riding down that street and they would kick the clutch out and that thing would rear up and the back bumper would scrape the street. Boy, kids just loved that! . . . But I do remember one amusing incident. One time this old boy I knew, he was on the [prison] gang out there for near nothing, but he could care less. They had him following the horses down the street, you know, scooping up behind

them. And he was waving like he was part of the parade!

Reflections on Transportation

During our discussions of life in earlier decades, inhabitants occasionally referenced methods of travel, especially describing how these methods have changed through time. Most of the oldest inhabitants grew up before automobiles and paved highways were commonplace, and so, because of walking, distances that today seem insignificant were perceived as much greater in the past. For example, Benjamin Craig reported a conversation between Elizabeth Nelson and a much older woman from far back in the mountains. Mr. Craig reported that Ms. Nelson asked the woman if she lived nearby to Eastatoee Valley, and the older woman replied, "Oh, no. I live *waaaay* over in Rocky Bottom," exaggerating the adverb to document a distance of about five miles by road. "I've walked from here [his Oconee County home] many a day and walked all the way up there [to Jocassee Valley – about two or three miles]," John Summers admitted; "walking wasn't nothing for us. That old bicycle, I'd ride that old bicycle up there and just have a good time." When I asked Robert Davidson, a former resident of the mountains, if it took a long time for him and his neighbors to walk to the local community grocery store, he replied:

> Oh, it didn't take long. They could walk down there and back in a day. They'd walk down there and back in a day. My grandma and her sister left early one morning where they lived in the Reedy Cove, and walked to Price's Store, and got what they had to have and got back home, and their daddy had a polecat [skunk]. He was rendering the lard (the grease) out of a polecat. And they thought it was a rabbit. So they was pretty hungry, and they started eating, and they eat nearly all of that polecat and thought they was eating rabbit!

In that same conversation, Davidson also described another form of transportation:

> Yeah, this old man lived over here on Keowee [River]. . . . He bought some land down there in the big bottom. . . . And the old man had a good yoke of cattle up there. And this old man that owned this land was wanting him to move down there 'cause he had that good yoke of cattle to farm with, you know. . . . Well, they decided they gonna move with him. Well, they didn't have nothing to move on. So they went up there and cut down a big white oak, they said a pretty good size white oak, had a lot of limbs on it. Drug it down there at the house and they tied everything they had on that treetop. Got everything they had on that treetop and they pulled that treetop from the Cane Break

> plumb down here . . . at that old house where them people lived.

"People didn't think nothing about walking or even riding in a wagon," Peter Abney remembered; "but when I was a kid, . . . we rode a wagon to plow corn that was about five miles, but you rode in a wagon." David Nelson noted: "Back then there wasn't no cars and stuff. You couldn't get too far from where you was raised just a-walking. . . . Horseback was about the best way you had of traveling. . . . You had a wagon, you could pull it with a horse." Then his niece Elizabeth added: "Yeah, and you didn't have to buy gas for him, either!"

Garvin Bradshaw remembered horse-drawn wagons:

> People used to raise cotton and they'd haul the cotton in two horse wagons from here to Walhalla [Oconee County seat] – dirt road. . . . And they'd tie their oxens [*sic*] and stuff and the horses to hitching posts in town just like that right there [in his yard]. And they said if they'd hauled it in the wintertime and it was real cold, they'd heat a big rock and lay it in the front of the wagon where they could stay warm by that rock. That rock'll hold heat all day. And they heated rocks to stay warm by.

The first automobiles in the area made quite an impression on the mountaineers. Robert Davidson explained:

> My daddy was the first man ever drove a car in as far as over the mountain and into the Reedy Cove [northern Pickens County]. He went up, drove an old Buick up the Beasley Mountain up yonder and went into the Reedy Cove. The first car that my great-granddaddy ever saw. He never had saw a car. . . . It was an old Buick. Yeah, an old Buick he had. And he drove that old Buick car up the mountain. And it had to be dry weather; they couldn't've got in there. In wet weather, you didn't dare to get up through there with a car.

The combination of wet weather, dirt roads, and inebriated drivers made for some likely mishaps, as Elaine Parker remembered:

> And my daddy, he always, he'd take a little nip. And he'd wait till he was about half high before [he visited his parents in the country]. . . . My momma wouldn't be with us. I guess she'd say, "Well, I got so many kids, he'd take them out there, kill them. That'd be one less mouth to feed!" She wouldn't go with us up there 'cause Daddy'd be drinking. But we was kids, we didn't care. Just to get to go somewhere, we didn't care whether our dad was drunk or what. And he wanted to go to Grandpa's. He'd take us up to Grandpa's and we knew we was going to have some fun! It didn't make no difference to us. And I think a lot of times that's why we got stuck up there. He'd drive off in the ditch or something like that 'cause he [was] about half high! But it still was fun.

Since few people had automobiles prior to the 1950s, and yet purchasing groceries in town was frequently a necessity, obtaining transportation from isolated country homes to town grocery stores presented a challenge. John Summers described a common solution:

> The mailman come by. You could set your clock by it. And if you wanted anything from the store, he'd bring it; you'd tell him, leave a note in the mailbox for him to bring it. And he'd stop at the store and get whatever you need, bring it, then you'd pay him. . . . Lot of people didn't have no way of going. . . . You needed sugar, or flour, or whatever you needed. He'd bring it. Just leave his money in the mailbox. And you didn't have to have stamps. If you wanted to mail a postcard, put your card in there and drop a penny on it. . . . I can remember when you could lay down in that road [in front of his house] and go to sleep! I mean there wasn't no traffic. If you seen somebody at night they was somebody sick going out to the doctor. . . . It had to be a real emergency if you seen anybody at night go out. Seeing lights on that road at night, they's something wrong.

Garvin Bradshaw described a similar practice from Oconee County:

> We walked from here to Salem [Oconee County, about three miles one way] and tote our groceries back. And a lot of times, my momma would send by the mailman. So like if he went around today, well she'd take a note out there and he'd bring the groceries back the next day that she wanted. . . . Save them a trip to Salem. And they done that for years and then after awhile there was peddlers started coming through, and they'd have a pickup load of stuff. All sorts of stuff – you could buy your sugar and stuff off it, and coffee. And you don't never see that now but they used to do that.

Sometimes, neighbors provided an informal public transportation system. Douglas Edison remembered: "They was a man lived up there, a Chapman. He always kept a right new car, and he would carry people places. I guess you'd called it a country taxi. He'd carry you anywhere you wanted to go. And he wouldn't charge much, but he'd charge you enough to, you know, he could pay for his car." Daniel Hall recalled a Greyhound bus that "ran from Pickens to Brevard [North Carolina]. It'd run one way, turn around and come back. It brought the mail. And you could get a ride into town and then turn around, come back the other way."

As Robert Davidson had explained earlier, the appearance of never-before-seen modes of transportation sometime shocked mountain dwellers. For example, Margaret York told this story about her grandmother:

> My grandmother said when she was a little girl and they was living up in Cove Creek [Pickens County] up there, . . . she said they had laid the . . . railroad lines or something. But they didn't know nothing about it because they didn't have no communication with the outside world. . . . They didn't know there was no trains coming through there. (They didn't know what a train was, actually.) And she said that train started blowing its whistle when it came through there. And they was all pretty religious people. And she said they thought the Lord was coming back at the End of Time 'cause all that sound come bellowing out of those mountains and they didn't know what in the world it was! Like to scare them to death!

"And I can remember the first airplane I ever seen," Anne Flowers recalled, and elaborated:

> I was just small and me and one of my cousins, standing in the gulley a-playing in the sand up there, and we heared somebody a-hollering. Well, we done heard, you know, they was having a[n] airplane to come for the Third of June [Old Soldiers Day, Pickens – Jefferson Davis's birthday]. So we raised up to look and this man . . . was running down the road a-hollering and a-pointing up, you know. And we looked up and we seed [saw] and heard that plane and boy, we split and in the house we went. . . . Lord! We thought that was the greatest thing that ever had been.

Margaret York admitted that "if we ever heard a plane, everybody run out of their house and look up at the sky to see what it was!"

As children, Garvin Bradshaw and his sister were walking back home from the nearest town, Salem [Oconee County], "and the sun was going down over yonder, and had one of these jet airplanes come across, and they were leaving two" – "Streaks," his sister Claudia Alexander interjected, and Bradshaw continued: "like they was splitting the elements apart. And me and [my sister] thought the End of Time was coming; we split and run! We run home to [a neighbor's] over there, and [he] was out in the yard, and we told him what we seen. Well, [he] said, 'I seen it, too,' but said, 'It's an airplane.' We come to then. It scared us to death, boy."

For those who have lived through the transformation from small, almost independent mountain farms and isolated communities to the times of national social media and global interactions, the former world seems so distant as to be almost unimaginable. In one of our conversations, James and Margaret York reflected on the changes they have seen during their lifetimes: "If you go back seventy years ago," Mr. York recalled, "we didn't have no indoor toilets; everything was outdoor toilets, . . . and going to the spring, and getting your wash wood for your wash pots, wash clothes. I mean everything was just different back then. . . . It was like living in another world then, compared to today. . . . Over the years we've seen a bunch of changes." Margaret York agreed, adding, "It's just a different time all together. They [grandchildren] can't imagine what it was like back then." Fortunately, as the above stories have documented, we can learn about this "different time" through the recorded voices of those who lived through those eras.

Chapter Four

"That Was Good Eating!": Stories of Food Procurement and Food Traditions

Even well into the twentieth century, family farms dominated the landscape of upper South Carolina. Supplementing farm products was protein obtained from fishing the mountain streams or (later) artificial lakes, and from hunting both small and large animals in the surrounding forests and fields. Wild and domesticated plants, fruits, and nuts, whether from personal gardens or neighbor largesse, added to the larders. Skilled cooks (often women) then transformed fruits and vegetables and seasonings and meats and fish into all sorts of meals to feed their frequently large and very hungry families. Since fishing and hunting were both for subsistence and for sport, and since cooking was both functional and enjoyable, inhabitants told many stories about these activities.

Residents, including myself, have noticed that inhabitants often manipulate the dominant economic system by working for wages at jobs (such as construction or lawn maintenance) where hours or days may be flexible.[1] This strategy allows inhabitants to work when they want to and to recreate when they want to, including going fishing (or hunting) at will or in season. For example, when I asked a resident of a gated community about problems she and her husband faced when moving to the area, she replied: "Just that everybody takes off to go hunting and fishing no matter what job they have to do. If it's a nice day out there and they want to go fish, they take

1 John M. Coggeshall, *Something in These Hills: The Culture of Family Land in Southern Appalachia* (Chapel Hill: University of North Carolina Press, 2022), 15–16.

off to go fishing. Or to hunt." For residents, often upper middle class and possessing what they consider a strong work ethic, such "unprofessionalism" strikes them as indicative of slothfulness, whereas inhabitants consider such flexibility in working when they want to as indicative of their individual freedom and a healthy work/life balance.

Fishing[2]

One of my oldest informants, Joshua Flowers, loved to fish, including on the Chattooga River before it was transformed from private to public land, and thus regulated by the federal government:

> I used to go there. I want to confess, I have never ridden down the river. I can't swim as good as a fish. . . . I have caught my limit of rainbow trout in Long Creek down here – ten, twelve-inch rainbows. . . . Yes, you know, you used to could go fish on the river, you could camp on the river right on the riverbank. . . . When they came in and wanted to make it a Wild and Scenic River, that's fine. But I didn't see that much pollution. . . . Now, you know, supposedly you can go fish on the river but you can't camp – you got to camp back so far off the river, and no roads with access to the river; you have to walk in and so forth. But it seems like you'd find just as much, or more litter on the river now than you did then, because of all the increased traffic. . . . Used to have a lot of fun camping on the river, staying two or three days at a time, and catch and eat what you caught, and then come on back out. There's nothing better than catching it right there, cleaning your fish and frying it on a pan, and you know taking some corn meal in and making you some cornbread and stuff like that, and camping out. It was good times. . . . I did that in high school. . . . You know, you'd go with some friends, and we'd go in, fish – most of the time we'd just go in early in the morning, fish all day, and come out at night.

"Well, it hurt me when they dammed that old river [Keowee] up," Mr. Flowers continued, "but we ain't never been able to catch us one nowhere that's as good as the flavor up in, catch and eat out of the Keowee River. . . . After I got up and married, I'd just go over there and hit the river and I didn't see nobody at the river until I found me a few fish. And I'd catch me a mess[3] there and turn around and come back home."

2 See also John M. Coggeshall, *Carolina Piedmont Country* (Jackson: University Press of Mississippi, 1996), 137–38.

3 "Mess" is an older British English usage referring to an amount suitable for a meal. See Appendix Two.

As a teenager, John Summers spent his vacations in much the same way, but exploring the mountain rivers in the Jocassee Valley area:

> Toxaway [River] was a lot warmer than Whitewater [River], 'cause it come out of Lake Toxaway [North Carolina]. . . . Boy it was just slam full of catfish. . . . Wished I had a mess of them right now. . . . And we'd go up there and walk across the mountain, what they call the Jane Owens Hole. It's a two-hour walk to get across the mountain. And we'd go in there and stay two or three days at a time. Camp right there on the river bank. . . . My momma would make me a big old pan of biscuits. And I had canned stuff. I had what I called an old haversack. And she'd pack them biscuits for me. Put them in. I'd take potatoes. Take, had a little old iron frying pan. . . . We'd take that, coffee, and stuff. We kept us a coffee bucket hid back in there. . . . We kept it hidden under an old log back in there. And yeah, we'd go in there and camp two or three days at a time. Sleep on the ground, fish. Man, we'd catch fish. Back then we didn't have Crisco and Wessen oil. We had lard! . . . And boy, put me a little old thing of lard in there to brown my potatoes and fish in. Fix me up a little sack of corn meal flour and pepper and salt in it to roll them in. Boy, it [was] good! We'd catch them catfish about that long and clean them. Man, we'd fry seven or eight frying pans full of them things. You talk about eating; oh, we'd eat up some fish. . . . Not a care in the world. Didn't owe nobody nothing. . . . Lot of times I'd go by myself back in there and stay two or three days. On Friday evening I'd get out of school. Momma come in, she'd fix me up stuff and I'd say, "Well, I'll see you on Sunday." . . . They knew where I was at. It wasn't like I was down yonder in some beer joint somewhere. They . . . knowed that the only thing that could hurt me back in there was a bear or a snake or something. But I took a snake bite kit with me. . . . Built an old lean thing, you know. Covered it up with brush and stuff. And I crawled up under there; . . . just have a big time.

Joseph Yeats had somewhat different childhood memories of fishing with his older relatives:

> We camped out there [in upper Pickens County]. We would cook, catch fish and cook them right where the branch runs into the river. . . . I was fourteen year[s] old. And they would stop off . . . and buy a gallon of liquor on the way up, you know. Well, they'd taught me to drive the summer before. And all day long I'd carry the rifle, the whiskey, and the fish. And when they got through in the evening, and I had to drive them home, I tell you they were pretty high. But they let me drive them home. We'd do that just about once a week for all that summer of '41.

Downstream from the Toxaway and Whitewater Rivers, Charles Watson fished the upper Keowee River before the dam restrained it:

> There used to [be] some of my favorite fishing down in there. . . . You'd go over there during the summer time, use hellgrammites[4] all year, use grasshoppers. Lord, o' mercy! Throw that thing out there, and it'd just go down the current just barely; by the time that thing quit rolling there'd be a fish on it. . . . Usually if you'd fish in a pool that had a good rock bottom in them, you'd catch fish. Wasn't no need to fish in one that just had sand or mud bottom, 'cause wouldn't be nothing in it but carp or sucker, something like that. But if you found one that had a good rock bottom, there'd be some good fish in it. . . . Get your hook just back under a rock, and you can watch it – the water'd be so clear you could just see it. You'd see an old catfish ease his head out from under a rock. He'd sit there and then just all of a sudden he'll run out there and grab that thing. You don't realize how quick he is but he'd grab that bait and run back under that rock before you jerk it, a lot of times. Now them things are good. And eels, you'd catch a few eels.[5]

John Summers also had an eel story that he recalled from his childhood:

> They had an old riverboat in the river there – had to pole that back 'cross the river. I just set my pole, . . . got down there and a big old eel on that thing. . . . That's all a male catfish, that's all a[n] eel is. And I got that thing out there, he just slide and wrapping around my arm, slime everywhere, man, all over my clothes! . . . He [a friend] come running down there and "Here's some sand" and throwed that thing out in the road. . . . A[n] eel – all it is is a male catfish. . . . It looks like a snake. But it's got a catfish head, got the fins. It's a male catfish.

Another traditional way to catch catfish is by hand, called by various names such as "noodling" or "grabbling." One man described the process:

> I've heard my dad talk about that. My brother was in on it. The river got real high over there, and got out of the banks. . . . Well, when the river went back down, there was a pretty good size little stream over there, you know. And they went over there fishing or something or other and seen a fish or two run, you know, went under a rock. One of them reached up in there and *got* him; "See?" he said, "Works good! Try another'n!" Just got rooting around under them rocks; they got a pile of fish that way.

Other traditional forms of fishing included seining or using baskets (often

4 Larva of the dobsonfly, subfamily Corydalinae.

5 This fish is most likely *Anguilla rostrata* rather than a member of the order Siluriformes.

hand-woven from oak splits) to trap fish. Robert Davidson explained:

> Seining, yeah. But you didn't have to seine, if you didn't – get out there and get you some red worm and get over there in a good hole back in there somewhere on that river and catch you a mess of catfish 'bout any time you wanted. And white suckers used to run that river. . . . You can't hardly catch them in a seine 'cause you gotta get down here where the water'll push your seine back in, and you can't do that 'cause I done tried it. They'll run between your legs and everywhere else and they'll keep a-going right up the river . . . and spawn – that's what they going for and all that. And they could catch them white suckers in there; they'd catch them in a basket. Put a basket in the river, you know, . . . and them white suckers would go right in.

Brian Alexander also used fish baskets:

> I'd set out fish baskets and catch fish in it and I'd go and get in the river and fish in the river and wade and fish hole to hole and all. I'd bring back a mess of old chubs and brim and bass and catfish and all. . . . I'd sit the basket into the river and it had meal cake in it and that would attract them. And you'd have it weighed down and tied where it wouldn't go down the river. And I'd catch some fish in there; mostly fishing what I done. Momma would cook the fish and everything; I kept plenty of fish.

Some local characters used illegal means to catch fish. Mac "Houn' Dawg" Erwin[6] described a method he called "telephone fishing," where the scofflaw connected wires to an old-fashioned hand-crank telephone, submerged the wires into a body of water, and cranked the phone. The electric shock caused the fish to just "boil up" to escape the electric current. Franklin Gravely, a well-known game warden in the region, had tracked several men deep into the backcountry as they telephone-fished illegally. Both men were "bad to drink" and were highly intoxicated. As one man cranked the phone, he pretended to be calling Gravely the game warden. Unknown to him, Gravely by this time had snuck up behind them, and when the culprit called out, "Hello, Franklin," Gravely responded, "I'm right here." "Uh-oh," the criminal replied, "Franklin just answered me!"

Fishing was not exclusively a male activity. Fathers or mothers who were avid fisherfolk sometimes took their daughters with them. Several inhabitant women had stories to tell. For example, as a girl, Deborah Mitchell grew up in Jocassee Valley, and remembered:

---

6 Franklin Gravely (1927–2000) was a game warden in upper South Carolina, and Erwin served under him. The story comes from a video, "Franklin Gravely Remembrance 2021," produced by the South Carolina Department of Natural Resources and loaned to me by Greg Lucas of the department.

> If it started raining up the river, you know, he [my father] could tell if it was raining on which mountains; and if our side of the river was going to be muddy, that was always a good time to go fishing. And so he would send us out to dig up worms, you know, in his Prince Albert tobacco can. And we would go fishing, and sometimes, he would go with us in the river and we would actually – you know, sort of like fly fishermen do today – we would wade down the river. And I remember even as a child turning over rocks and getting hellgrammites. That was fun and crazy. . . . He would take the boys [her brothers] across the mountain to the Toxaway River. There were some campsites over there, and they would go over there and fish and camp, and everything. My sisters and I have said in more recent years . . . we felt left out, because the guys got to go tramp in the woods, and the girls had to stay home with Mommy. Which was okay, except we missed seeing some places, you know, that are now covered by water.

Brenda Kendrick's father sometimes allowed her to accompany him on fishing trips, "and the thing I remember most about when my dad was going, he'd say, 'Now, you know you can't talk.' . . . [And] he'd say, 'Now you have to be quiet when you go fishing; you'll scare the fish.' And I thought, 'They can't hear me!'"

Elizabeth Nelson, as a "fishing girl" in the Eastatoee Valley, had some more awkward moments:

> My dad would take me fishing some times. . . . We were down here, across the road in the bend of the creek one summer. He and I were sitting on the bank on this side and we were fishing with our poles. . . . I caught the big one, a big trout. And it was about to pull me in. And I was pulling back and Daddy'd say, "Do this." And he'd help me pull it back and pull it back. And the thing did come flying out of the water in front of us. And you could see it arch over and go back in. And it got away! . . . The last time we went fishing, he accidently hooked my finger with his hook when he threw it backwards. And then he had to get it out. And I was bleeding and screaming and crying and he wouldn't go fishing with me anymore!

Beth Yeats also had a "one that got away" story. She had been fishing near her home with her mother, and "I'd been trying to catch a bass. I couldn't catch that bass. Well, Mother would catch these old suckers which were full of bones and she said, 'I've got this fish on my line; can you get it out?' I waded out – wasn't just a few weeks before he [my younger brother] was born. I said, 'That's my bass!' and fell right in the river."

When I asked Joan Randall how she had gotten interested in fishing, she replied: "I don't know; get out of work, I guess." I laughed, and she continued:

> I used to fish when I'd go to Grandpa's; he had a corn mill. I'd go to the lake, pond there, and I'd go down there and catch chubs and hornheads.[7] . . . Then after . . . the lake backed up, I guess the kid was still in me and I still like to fish. And I wouldn't clean them; I had to clean them when I was little and young, . . . but up at Jocassee I wouldn't clean them; my husband would do that. He'd eat them, but I didn't. He said carp was good. . . . I cooked them. It cooks pretty, but I didn't eat none of them. That's just me.

Fishing as a sport is not for everyone, as Jeffrey Donnelly acknowledged. "Now my older brother was a fisherman, but I was never much into fishing," Mr. Donnelly confessed; "it was always boring for me, even now. I've went out with my brother on the lake and he'll catch them just as fast as you can pull them in and after an hour or so I'm bored. But he would set out there all day in the hot sun and fish. But that just – that was never something that I really liked."

Hunting[8]

Another major food procurement activity was hunting. Most of the time, hunting was done for subsistence (especially adding meat protein to mountain diets) and less commonly just for sport, at least decades earlier. Joseph Yeats explained: "Daddy was a true sportsman. He wouldn't just shoot something just to be shooting. If he shot it he was going to skin it and he was going to eat it. He didn't care whe'r it was a bear or a squirrel or whatever. If he shot it he was going to eat it." Hunters included both males and females, of all ages. Game included amphibians, reptiles, birds, and small- and large-bodied mammals. Theodore Franklin affirmed that "I've eaten raccoon, squirrel, rabbit, turtle, groundhog; I've never eaten possum. I've never eaten rattlesnake, but I've eaten just about everything else. . . . Until probably twenty-five, well, thirty years ago, deer were rare here. Turkeys were as well. It was mainly squirrels, rabbits, raccoons, possums that people ate."

For many hunters, a significant part of the sport lay in the chase itself, whether on foot or by tracking with dogs. Mike Davidson described his father, Robert Davidson, as being

> good in the woods. . . . Daddy was a good hunter. He was a good shot. Daddy killed two deer the same day several times. Kill bear. Loved to bear hunt. Oh, Daddy just loved to bear hunt. I remember when I was a kid we had beagles. And Daddy would go out there and turn the dogs loose and just lay in bed and listen to them. And then whenever they'd put the rabbit in the

7 Small bait fish of various species.
8 See also Coggeshall, *Carolina Piedmont Country*, 135–37.

> hole, or whatever, he'd get up out of bed and go call his dogs and put them back up. Just to listen to them run. He loved to hear dogs run.

Although raised in a larger community in the early twentieth century, Daniel Hall would accompany his family up to remote northern Pickens County every summer, to escape the heat and communicable diseases. The family had a summer cottage along Sugar Likker Lake:

> The fire department and the police force would come up every year and catch all the turtles in it [the lake]. They had a . . . fish fry and a turtle stew. . . . We'd go around the lake and get the frogs. We didn't gig[9] the frogs; you took a flashlight and you caught the frog, you see? You caught the frog and then you put him in a croaker sack. And then when you got through going around the lake, you would look in your croaker sack and decide which ones you wanted. And you'd knock them on the head, and you'd save those. And the ones that were too small? Throw them back in the lake.

Robert Davidson "seed a man that'd hunt them turtles, could tell which way its head was and everything. And he'd get along with a stick, and he'd . . . get in the river down there and he'd gouge and hunt and gouge – he could tell exactly when he hit a turtle. And he'd get on in there and get him by the tail! But I never did do none of that now." Elizabeth Nelson described how her father occasionally "would catch a mud turtle in the creek and she [my mother] would first pressure cook it because the meat is eternally tough. . . . She would pressure cook it for – it seemed like – half a day and then she would fry it for him. And it was so tough! You would just chew, and chew, and chew. It was good chewing gum. And I ate it one other time when I was a camp counselor. . . . And I finally just had to spit it out because I couldn't even chew it enough to swallow it. I prefer turtles alive!"

While reptiles and amphibians could be hunted by hand, birds such as turkeys required rifles. Nearly hunted to extinction in the region by the early twentieth century, wild turkeys have returned to the mountains in larger numbers in more recent decades, and thus are now hunted in season. Kayla Radcliffe said that her father

> hunts whenever he's not working. He's really big on turkey hunting. . . . Turkey hunting's a lot more of a challenge, 'cause turkeys are pretty challenging. They have extremely good eyesight; you have to be completely silent. You can't hunt in a stand – or I mean, you can, but the more effective way is to sit down on the ground to be at that level with them, so that's a challenge. . . . I can remember growing up – March starts, I don't

---

9 To use a gig, a pointed or barbed spear, to stab fish or frogs.

> see my dad for a month, because he's either working or turkey hunting or I'm asleep. That's the way it is.

Garvin Bradshaw heard his father brag one time that "he went up to the ridge there one morning, that little creek, brought the shot gun in there. Said he called some turkeys up and said they come right down the road, a whole row of them. Said he let them get right where he wanted and said he whistled and he said they just stuck their heads up, like that. And then he said he shot right down through them; said he killed four with one shot!"

The hunting of small and large mammals often required dogs as an essential hunting accessory. As a youngster, Harry Edison remembered his family

> had this one dog, all you had to do was mention hunting and that dog would just get to dancing. . . . We'd go, and that dog would be in front of us and when he'd hear squirrels [snaps fingers] he would just go off the road. And we'd stop, go ahead and shoot the squirrel, get back in and go on. But I'll tell you something you didn't do – if he had went off that road around the curve and you didn't see him and you passed that dog up, that was the end of the hunt. When he came back out he was *mad* that dog was, and he wouldn't do anything but follow the car. He'd just walk around behind the car; he would not get back in front of the car again.

"One of the big topics of discussion on the school bus when I remember riding home in the fall was 'How many squirrels [did] you kill this week?'" Ralph Glenn reported, and continued:

> And there were guys that would kill a hundred, you know, or more! And of course, they'd help to feed their family. And good squirrel meat is actually pretty good. . . . And you can't start hunting squirrels until after the first frost, because they've got these bot fly larvae that grow under their skin; the common name for them is wolves. And, "them squirrels still got wolves; can't hunt them yet." So you don't start hunting them until after the first freeze and those things have erupted and are gone. And I don't know why, it doesn't affect the meat or anything else.[10] It was just the way it was done. And then boy, once the first frost, it was rough on squirrels! And most people didn't hunt with a dog or anything. They'd get out in the woods, and . . . sit down and be real quiet and listen and then move on to the next place.

---

10 Glenn is correct. The flies do not affect the meat, nor do they emerge until after the first frost. See Alabama DCNR, "Squirrel Bot Flies: Fact Versus Fiction," *OutdoorHub*, October 30, 2012, https://www.outdoorhub.com/how-to/2012/10/30/squirrel-bot-flies-fact-versus-fiction/.

> . . . And I still know guys my age that, if they have the time to go out and hunt, they'll come up here and squirrel hunt. It's just what they did.

"And my mother would take the squirrels and stew them; make gravy with them and stew them. We'd eat it over rice," Elizabeth Nelson recalled. Douglas Edison elaborated on squirrel consumption:

> You know, squirrel used to be a delicious dish. Everybody liked squirrel. But now, there's not many people would eat a squirrel. . . . My mother, she would make kind of like chicken and dumplings out of squirrel. Then if they was young and tender she would fry them. Now they was good. And my dad would kill a lot of turkeys, and the breast part, she would slice it like tenderloin and fry it, and now that was something delicious. Fix you some good gravy to go with it.

Girls and women would hunt squirrels as well. For example, Beth Lepre's mother "grew up with my grandfather. He hunted, I guess is how she learned, but she had a little rifle and she would actually squirrel hunt. . . . I remember when we were little she would go and hunt and kill squirrel and then my grandmother would cook them. They were kind of nasty, but she cooked them and we would eat them!" Brenda Kendrick always envied her brother accompanying her father when he went squirrel hunting, until finally,

> when I got big enough, he [my father] would say, "You wanna go with me?" "Well, yeah, of course I wanna go." So I'd bundle up, you know, in the wintertime or whatever. He and I'd go rabbit hunting, squirrel hunting, whatever. I'd carry a gun but I didn't shoot anything, but, you know, I'd get to go along. . . probably until I was early teenager, and then Momma'd say, "You're not supposed to be tagging after him everywhere you go." But he didn't mind. . . . [My sister] wasn't into the outdoor stuff. She liked to work in the yard and the flowers and stuff like that, but she didn't like to get out and tramp through the woods and all that like I did. And I was just – like I say I was just a tomboy, so I was tagging along after him when he'd let me go. . . . They usually just, I can't remember them like going coon hunting or anything like that at night. But you know, rabbit hunting, squirrel hunting, things like that they'd let me tag along sometimes. . . . Coon hunting is at night. They may have done that, but they wouldn't've let me went at night either way, probably.

Denise Craig accompanied her grandfather when he went squirrel hunting, but "that only lasted a little while, because every time he would start to aim at a squirrel I'd say, 'Grandpa! Don't kill the squirrel!' . . . He took me home."

Although not premium or preferred meat, opossums were also hunted. As with other expeditions, opossum hunting was done partly for sport and partly for food procurement. In their joint interview, Shirley Patterson and Pamela Charles remembered that their fathers "used to go possum hunting. . . . He would come to the house and then they would get lost probably sometime and then they would have their little moonshine boozing." In his family interview, Joseph Yeats confessed that he

> had these two pups I just acquired, you know. And I said, "Let's go out there and turn them loose under that tree; we might tree a possum," you know. So we turned them loose, and sure enough they struck [got a scent]. . . . We treed four or five times, but it was bobcat. They would jump out when we approached the tree and run on, you know. We . . . waded the river, got out on the bank over there, and here comes a car, sliding in. Four doors flew open, you know, and four men jumped out. They were all game wardens. . . . I'd never shot a gun. I throwed it up, you know, and he told me who he was, you know, and they loaded us up. . . . And they went on toward Greenville, you know. I said, "Wait a minute." I said, "I got a little money." I said, "Take us back home, I'll pay the fine." So they brought us back home and I paid the fine. They let us out. We went in the house; . . . [my wife] just jumped all over me.

At that point in the interview, Beth Yeats interrupted and exclaimed, "Yeah! He was laughing about getting caught and . . . our money was gone, his shorts was shining, and he was like –" Mr. Yeats then interrupted and explained that his angry wife "took our wedding picture" and slammed it over his head, so that he was wearing it like a collar! Their son then "went through the house, got every picture he could find and hid them. . . . He didn't want me hit anymore." We all laughed at Mr. Yeats's hard-learned lesson.

Hunting raccoons required specialized dogs, and Norman Cleveland described his favorite breed and how to train them:

> Well, I like them Walkers better than any of them. But about any of them, you can get them trained and many times it won't make no difference. You get them trained up; they'll work for you. That's a pleasure for that old dog to get out there and find that with his nose and run it and tree it. That's play, that's just nature for him to do that. But you've got to get him, work with him, get him used to working for you, see. . . . Pet him, take him, and holler at him when he's running. Let him know that you're backing him up.

Once treed, the raccoons will fight the dogs to the death. "And I never will forget one time talking about a coon, about the dogs fighting, something like that," Joseph Yeats recalled, and in the story his father replied: "'Well, son, they're fighting for their life.' And I never thought about it like that. He says, 'It's do or die. . . . That's the reason why they're fighting.' It's kind of hard to swallow, but it was the truth."

As inhabitants have mentioned, deer in the mountain counties are much more plentiful than in decades past, and many people told stories about their favorite deer hunting experiences. Often, hunting began early in life. When Ryan Trask was a young teen, and before he had a driver's license, he and his best friend

> were hunting on the backside of Beasley Mountain [upper Pickens County]. . . . That was thirty years ago. And deer were pretty rare. Bear were pretty rare, you know, turkey. The game was sparse. But we climbed all the way up on top of Beasley, came up the back side and I saw a big doe, big pretty doe, and watched her for awhile. And I knew the deer were in rut [so a male deer would be nearby]. And his daddy told us, he said, "Well, I'll take you back." . . . He said, "I'll get y'all up in the morning and we'll go again." Well, the next morning came and [my friend] and I woke up and it was already daylight, and we said "Uh-oh, we've been had." Well, his daddy changed his mind and he sneaked out about four o'clock that morning and went fishing with his two brothers and left us in bed. So [my friend] and I were just upset as we could be. . . . It was just breaking daylight. So we jumped up, made us a few sandwiches, and packed some water and threw it in the backpack and got our guns. And his sister was still in bed asleep. She was in college at the time. And we got her car and pushed it out their driveway. Knocked it out of gear and pushed it a couple hundred yards to the end of the driveway, cranked it up, and headed up here. Neither one of us had a driver's license. And climbed that mountain ourselves. Came driving all the back roads hoping we wouldn't get caught. And I killed that deer. It was the first buck I'd ever shot. And then we thought, "Oh, my goodness. Now what are we going to do?" And he and I were just wormy and skinny as we could be, and that deer weighed more than the both of us together at the time I believe. But it took us half a day to drag it off of that mountain and get it out of there. And we couldn't dress it because we couldn't get blood in his sister's car! So we, he wanted to go the back roads to be sure we wouldn't get caught coming home, but I said, "We're not going the back roads; we're going to go to Holly Springs Grocery and show this thing off!" So we go over there to Holly Springs, no driver's license. 'Course everybody knows that when we're there. So anyway that was one of my greatest hunting memories made right here, you know.

Kayla Radcliffe went deer hunting with her father a few times, and admitted:

> I killed two deer; it really wasn't that exciting. You sit in the stand for eight hours to see something and shoot it and it takes thirty seconds and you're like, well, it's over. I didn't enjoy it very much. One of my main jobs, though, was cleaning the deer for him. That was like – in the winter, that was my source of income for little things like – it's one of those skills that I don't like to go around telling people, like "Oh yeah, I know how to butcher a deer." It's kind of weird when you tell people that! . . . Because whenever my dad would kill a deer, . . . you have to skin it immediately, or it's best to, because it's hard to skin it after it gets cold. So it'd be twenty degrees outside and I'd have to go outside at night and help my dad skin this deer. And most of the time it would be like a family affair kind of thing 'cause you have to have two people who know what they're doing cutting up the meat, some people running the machine, some people wrapping it, because we didn't like to send our meat to other people. . . . But in the last year, like when I was a senior in high school, it would be the job I'd do. He wouldn't even do it anymore. And it kind of got annoying because he'd just assume I could do it. . . . So he became dependent on me to do that, and I guess it was a useful skill then, but now it's kind of a nuisance, because whenever I'm home and they're doing that, they expect me to help. . . . An interesting thing that growing up butchering the meat has done is I don't like ground meat because I know what goes into it. I've tried to avoid it at all costs, so that's why I don't eat sausage very much. Mostly my mom would use it for roasts, or stew meat, just very little hamburger . . . mostly because it's cheap. You don't have to go out and buy a fifteen-dollar roast, you can just go get one out of the freezer. For hamburgers, you have to; you can't really make hamburgers out of deer meat. But it wasn't like we had it every night. Maybe once a week we'd have something with deer meat in it. . . . It was kind of one of those social status things, like because in high school, it was mostly the guys who went hunting, mostly because the girls didn't know how, and when they did go they – it was kind of, I'm not sure if they were actually excited about it or if they were being excited about it so they could be with the guy. It was kind of a borderline thing. I didn't ever meet any girls who actually were like, "Yeah, I'm totally into hunting." It was mostly a flirty "Yeah, I'll go hunting with you!" kind of thing, and that was when it was annoying. But not a lot of girls did it, just because

> they weren't interested in it. Maybe that's just something we don't like to do. I got bored all the time. That's why I stopped.

When I asked Ms. Radcliffe about an initiation ritual after a hunter (male or female) killed their first deer, she laughed uncomfortably, agreed, and explained:

> It was terrible. It was horrible. It's extremely embarrassing, and every time they pull up the pictures I get extremely embarrassed. You kill the deer, you're out there cleaning it, and my dad totally takes me by surprise, because he's dipped his hand in the blood and smears it all over my face. And I was like, "What did you do that for? That was completely unnecessary!" So yes, there is, and that's what they do, and it's really embarrassing because you have sticky blood all over your face.

Charles Watson stalked larger game:

> Got older, started bear hunting. And bear hunting, you know they cover a lot of ground because a bear that's traveling, . . . if he decides to move he might go twenty-five miles. . . . I remember one – the longest I ever knew – I had one little old female dog, she trailed one [bear] where it'd been gone three days. Now that's – a colder nose I'd never heard of. But she had as much sense as most people did. She could – she knew so much about that animal that when she lost it, she could just raise her head up and look around and maybe see an impression or something there in the leaves, you know a footprint, you know how a bear'll make a depression? And go stick her nose in it and smell it and afterwards just look at the terrain and figure out which way the animal would've went. She might go quarter mile that way and hit him off again, but maybe'd get on a branch [creek] or something where it's damp, could pick a scent. She was – she just was hunted so much, all that come natural to her. . . . Well, a bear would mark his territory. . . . Most of the time it'd be a . . . Virginia pine or a shortleaf pine, up on top of a high knoll. And he'll back up to that tree and reach as high as he can and make a claw mark, and if another bear comes and sees that and if he can't make a claw mark any higher, he knows to get out of there.

Very rarely, Charles Watson reported, extremely large animals hunted humans!

> I remember my grandmother telling me, they used to talk about *her* mother when they lived in there, it was her job to feed the hogs. And back then they let them run loose in the woods, you know; they had acorns and stuff like that. And every so often, it'd be her job to go feed them. And they had them things

> trained to take a hunting horn like hunters'd use – she'd carry a sack full of corn on her shoulder and go off up a mountain to wherever those hogs – thought they'd be and scatter out the corn, pretty good area there. She'd climb up a little sapling or some sort where the hogs couldn't get her – they's wild, they'd get you – and she'd blow that hunting horn, and them hogs, when they heard the hunting horn, they knew it meant food and they'd come just as hard as they could go. And once the hogs found the corn and started eating, then she'd slip down the tree and go on home and they wouldn't bother her. . . . But it must have been one of them years probably . . . wasn't no food or enough stuff to eat. But she happened to look back and saw something, just a slip of something, you know. And she didn't know what it was. And she turned around, started out back toward home and then looked back again and looked back and thought, she called a panther, which is a cougar. Probably just wasn't nothing to eat, I guess, but a large human being. And she looked, and every time she'd turn her back, that thing would creep behind her and get pretty close; when she'd turn to look at it, it wouldn't stay so close. She started walking backwards, and she walked backwards for several – probably a mile or more. . . . And she got close enough to home and she got to hollering and be – probably my great-grandpa, I guess. He was out in the field working, and he heard her hollering (and then everybody had good hunting dogs). And he went to the house and got his shot gun and everything all in a hurry, and the dogs, you know, they seen him get that gun and they was all in a big hurry to go hunting too. They took off, hauled up there to where that girl was hollering. Dogs got after it and put it up a tree and he killed it – it was a cougar!

Charles Watson also described how dangerous hunting was for the hunters:

> I had three brothers that got killed; one got killed right up there on Pinnacle Mountain, deer hunting. Down here it was raining, drizzle with rain, but they left to go squirrel hunting and when they got up yonder in the higher elevation, got up high, it turned to snow. And one of the men got to seeing some deer sign, fresh tracks in the snow and it's still snowing. And it'd just been a few minutes, feller happened to have some buck shot in his pocket. He said, told my two brothers, said: "Wait a while here, and I'm gonna see if I can track this up and get close enough to get a shot." So they sit down and waited there, sat up there on Long Ridge – old rock, it's still there where they were sitting. My two brothers sit there just, probably as far apart as me and you

> are. . . . After a while, they looked and saw him coming. He got almost back up to them, walking there in that snow and all, and stepped and his foot slid out from under him. And had an old side-hammer shot gun, . . . and he put it down. . . . And when he did, it sort of . . . cocked that hammer. And when he started to pick it up, the hammer fell and one buck shot, the main load went into the rock but they's one ricocheted off and took him [his brother] right between the eyes.

George Tanner related another hunting tragedy from "back in the early days there, some feller'd shot hisself. They gathered him up there, gonna take him to Pickens Hospital. Had to stop over there at the gap of the mountain . . . just to get some gas. So, meanwhile while they were out pumping gas, and he got out and started on down the road and told them, said, 'I'll be walking on!' He got to hurting bad."

Despite the popularity of the sport or the necessity of the activity, not everyone participated. Jason Taylor explained:

> I never hunted. I don't know. When I was growing up, everyone I knew hunted just about. My dad never had any guns. . . . But I guess he never saw the interest in – never bought any guns – and my best friends growing up, they never really had guns and they never hunted. So I was like – it wasn't big for us. Once I got into middle school, everyone I knew was hunting. They were like "Oh, yeah, we're deer hunting this weekend or turkey hunting, coon hunting." . . . [Middle school was] . . . when people started, 'cause I think that's when their dads would start letting them shoot guns. And then they would go hunting with them. But my cousin – he hunts a lot. He's already shot – or during deer season – I think he shot three or four deer. He's fifteen now? He started hunting when he was probably twelve. He got a BB gun when he was like eight. . . . I don't know why my parents never – or my dad never – took us hunting. I guess he never really saw the fun in it.

As noted earlier, Ryan Trask hunts, but at the same time he understands the relationship between hunting and food procurement:

> I think it's very important for my son and my daughter to have hunted and to hunt and to understand because if you decide to eat a piece of meat, I think that's a serious decision. I think they understand it much better than someone that doesn't hunt. . . . Most hunters that I know have a deeper and a more genuine understanding and appreciation for life in

> general. They understand the seriousness of it. . . . [My son] and I, you know, if we go squirrel hunting, I say to him, "Do you really want to eat squirrel tonight?" 'Cause if you don't, you know, we're just going to watch it. 'Cause we don't – we're not going to take a life if we're not going to use it for a reason. I think that connectedness is important. And it's something that you understand and you have to make decisions about in this environment that you don't perhaps in a subdivision. You just go buy a pack of meat. Or better yet, something that's already prepared; then you don't even have to see it raw! . . . Make a decision as you're watching it walk through there, whether or not you're going to take its life, and then think about it for the three hours that you're skinning it and cleaning it. . . . You don't throw away leftovers, for sure.

Food Traditions

As inhabitants have noted, a primary purpose of hunting is to put food on the table. More prominent in the past, but still important for many families today, are home gardens, adding to a variety of foods. The discussion of food traditions was not done with everyone, but I did acquire some information about typical foods and their styles of preparation.[11] While food preparation and cooking are not exclusive to women, they are characteristic activities, according to my informants. Many women learned to cook from their mothers, but Elizabeth Nelson faced a minor problem:

> I'm left-handed and it drove my mother crazy to see me try to do things left-handed. It just – she couldn't deal with it. So she never really taught me how to cook well – much of anything. . . . But she was a great cook. She used to cook *huge* amounts of food for lunch and then we would have the leftovers for dinner; only we called it "dinner" and "supper." . . . And she always made her from-scratch homemade biscuits every morning. My youngest brother . . . learned to make them and he still makes them! . . . And [my brother] would bring his little chair up and stand up in it and watch her make biscuits, buttermilk biscuits. That was his fascination. And she fried most everything that she cooked. There was not a lot of baking or steaming or anything like that. It was fried in a frying pan. . . . And there was always cornbread. . . . Biscuits at breakfast, cornbread at lunch. And, you know, times were hard. There were three mouths to feed. My dad was the only one working. And a lot of times we didn't have meat except on Sundays. . . . And we would have chicken a good bit; chicken

11 See also Coggeshall, *Carolina Piedmont Country*, 159–80.

> and rice and peas! Over and over and over. But that's okay. It was always good. And then, of course, in the summertime we had all those wonderful homegrown vegetables and the fruit pies. That was good eating!

Denise Craig spent time between her (Pickens) "city" grandmother's house and that of her "country" grandmother up in the mountains. "I remember, I might have been a teenager then," Mrs. Craig recalled, "but we were up here and they had squirrel stew and she [mountain grandmother] was saying, hovering around going when we were dipping it out, she was saying, 'Don't get the head. Save the head for me!' . . . And we were, like, 'Grandma, we're not going to eat the head!'"

Gregory Clayton declared that he and his family

> eat a lot of groundhog – them mountain groundhogs, they good. It's the cleanest meat you can eat. Mountain groundhog, they vegetarians – they don't eat just everything. But down in here [northern Pickens County] they cull kudzu off the sides of the road and they get fat as a butterball. Mountain groundhogs they didn't have all that much meat on them, but they's a lot better; didn't have all that fat. . . . Them groundhogs, they good if they cooked right. You got to know how to cook them. Way I like them is boiled, parboiled for awhile. Get them tender, and then put whatever herbs you want on them, and some spices. Put them in the stove and bake them. Bake them good and brown. Just salt and pepper them, take care of seasoning them. . . . Put vegetables around them. It's a good meal.

Because of her culinary skills, Anne Flowers often cooked whatever kinds of meat she was brought in order to feed her family and friends:

> My brother . . . [and a neighbor] would catch a groundhog or a coon and they wanted *me* to cook it. And so I'd always cook it for them. Then I'd call them, you know, and tell them to come on. I have a nephew – . . . Oh, he loved them groundhogs and them there coons. And he'd come up and eat with us. I've seed him setting there and eat, sweat just a-rolling off of him. He was a pretty heavy man. . . . I had a neighbor, lives right down yonder, that catched a little young coon . . . and they called me and wanted to know if we wanted it. The dogs had chewed it up pretty bad and they just saved its legs and just part of it. . . . And so, I went and fixed it. . . . [At a holiday meal with extended family], "Do you'uns remember back when you'uns was growing up?" I said, "We thought Christmas wasn't Christmas 'less we had coon and sweet potatoes."

"Every time we get together for Christmas," Forrest Sanders explained, "there's a bunch of us. She'll [grandmother] make just a *huge* spread, with corn from the field, field peas [types of beans], corn bread, macaroni and cheese, some sort of meat. She does about three or four different kinds. Then she'll make a bunch of desserts."

Bruce Anderson described a very common practice typically done around Thanksgiving, especially after the weather had cooled a bit:

> Always at Thanksgiving it was hog-killing time and Grandpa always had a big old hog out there. And we'd start early in the morning. Before daylight, Grandpa would be up and he would have big kettles out there with water boiling in them to scald the hair off the pigs. . . . It usually lasted all day. And the end of the day . . . the biggest treat of it was getting to eat lunch with the fresh tenderloin and things that was cut out of the pig right then; it was really good. And some of the things that my grandmother cooked out of the pig I wasn't real excited about, but it was good. It didn't look really good, but it was good. . . . Well, they'd take the brains and scrambled egg some brain. And actually it tastes like sausage. . . . And they took the liver and made mush out of it. They called it mush. And patted it out, and it was rounded; you could slice it off and eat it that way. I wasn't real keen on that, but they liked it. Cracklin's – I did like cracklin's. You know, take the skin and the fat off the inside of the skin and boil it down and fry it – actually fry it in a pot. And cracklin' bread, I always enjoyed eating cracklin' bread. And we, obviously they didn't have any [indoor running] water way back then. They had a well; they didn't have any refrigeration. So we used a smokehouse. And every day when they killed the hog they would take the parts of the hog, the shoulders and the hams and stuff like that and they'd go in there. And they had a big work bench in the smokehouse and it was the only thing it was used for. And they'd put the ham in there and they'd rub it down with salt and sugar and hang it up to drain. The blood and everything would drip out of the . . . meat and it would be cured, and then it would stay in there till next year when they'd cut it as they needed it. And you know, that was always real good. And of course my grandmother had a wood stove, and you had to cook with wood. And I spent a lot of days down there cutting up stove wood, splitting it up and racking it under the big walnut trees for them so that they would have wood. And it was always a good time to go down to Grandpa's [and] Grandma's. . . . We could walk through the woods; it was only about a half a mile.

After the hogs had been slaughtered and the meat had cured, John Summers remembered, one could go out to the smokehouse and "cut you a slab of ham like that, make that red eye gravy; boy, you talk about good."

Hunting, fishing, and eating those (and other) foods generate many memories for inhabitants. The smell of Grandma's mac and cheese, the taste of red-eye gravy and fresh country ham, and the touch of crispy fried chitlin's in one's hands engender fond recollections of an extended family gathered around a large dining table celebrating a major holiday. Some foods, such as possum or coon, also serve as regional or class markers, further solidifying an identity for the region. The action of patiently waiting for a prize catfish to nibble on one's bait, or quietly stalking a deer through a thick forest, might make the meat from those animals taste even more special. The social act of sharing those experiences with one's children and grandchildren creates memories that in turn generate stories that enliven the next family gathering. As inhabitants have mentioned, eating foods that a person has acquired through their own actions links human predator with animal prey, further tying people to their landscape. Above all, stories about these events link family members to each other.

Chapter Five

"The Old People . . . Don't Have to Worry About Doctors": Traditional Cures and Curing

As with every human society, inhabitants in the South Carolina Blue Ridge area become injured or ill and are also healed. While today the vast majority utilize modern medicines and standard scientific care, this has not always been the case, and even now, partly due to physical distances from hospitals or professional medical care, sometimes inhabitants need (or choose) to resort to traditional cures and curing practices.[1] Drawing upon traditions from Native American, African American, and European cultures, local healers effect cures for many reasons. It is possible that herbal or folk concoctions actually may be efficacious, or it is possible that by drawing upon the intervention of a Christian deity, cures actually work; it is also possible that psychosomatic healing may occur. For whatever reasons, inhabitants have utilized traditional practices in many situations, and a few continue to do so. Since I always have been interested in traditional culture, including traditional cures, I frequently asked for stories about these activities, and inhabitants had many examples.

A few people remembered rather difficult or painful medical treatments from their childhoods. For example, Cynthia Niles related a story she had heard from Elizabeth Nelson's father about tooth extraction about a century ago:

> Up there in Eastatoee [Valley] . . . they had a dogwood tree up there that had a fork in it. Had it hewed out for your neck to fit in

1 See John M. Coggeshall, *Carolina Piedmont Country* (Jackson: University Press of Mississippi, 1996), 97–103.

> there and had one [piece of wood] to pull down over your neck. You had a toothache, a man'd get you and hold you in there and pull that down around your neck and then pull that tooth. . . . He put them in that fork of that tree, put that other one around his neck and take a pair of pliers and pull that tooth out.

Some inhabitants used their interpretation of health care to explain and justify their advanced age. For example, Gregory Clayton attributed his senior status to his healthy eating habits:

> Well, one thing is drinking a lot of mountain water, and eating . . . a home-cooked meal. . . . I think that's the most important thing about mountain people, you know, staying healthy. . . . They ain't too many people between here [upper Pickens County] and Pickens don't have to go to the doctor every week. They probably like that all over the United States now. The old people that stays in the mountains and eats right, drinks what he's supposed to – they don't have to worry about doctors as much. Like me, . . . I've had my arm broke, and I didn't go to the doctor for that; I just tried to fix it myself best I can and keep going. Cuts? I can sew wounds up. I sewed all my kids at one time or another. They'd get cut; rather than up and go get stitches, I'd just put ice, lot of ice around where the wound was, and you'd numb it. After awhile I'd put a stitch or two in it, hold it; they didn't have to go to the doctor. It's that old stuff the Indians used. It's old green stuff that runs over rocks in a branch [small creek]. Get that and rub it on a wound, like a cut, or anything; it'll heal that wound. The Indians, they used it all the time, when they'd get shot or cut.

In a separate interview, Rachel Edwards agreed with Clayton's statement:

> We're such a generation now that we run to the doctor for every little thing. Well, back then you couldn't run to anywhere; you didn't have anywhere to go. They treated a lot of things with sulfur and lard and kerosene. They'd wrap your leg and ankle in kerosene. And I know one lady was talking about her brother got a pitchfork stuck in his leg, and about bled to death, and I said, "Well, did you go to the doctor?" She said, "Oh no! We just got a gallon of kerosene, let him soak his leg in it." Said next day he wasn't complaining at all with it, said it wasn't sore or swollen or nothing. So there must have been something healing in that.

Despite healthy eating habits, sometimes viruses would attack. To prevent this, inhabitants utilized folk cures for cold remedies. For example, Gregory Clayton used some of his family's moonshine to help with curing:

> Now you can just have your corn whiskey and you can add the honey, peppermint, and honey. That breaks up a chest cold and if you got a fever, . . . you make a hot ginger tea . . . and put moonshine in it and it'll break a fever. You got to wrap up real good and that ginger'll – moonshine, it'll sweat that fever out of you in just a little while, but you got to stay inside and stay wrapped up good.

In a general discussion with members of her family, Shirley Patterson offered a different concoction for curing colds:

> And remember, if your chest got real tight with a cold, remember Momma used to make those poultices. . . . She'd cook up corn meal and I don't know what else all be in there. Smell like onions and garlic, and they'd put that thing to your chest. But I tell you, the next morning, you wake up, you wouldn't even – you'd sweat through the night, it'd be gone. Your whole chest'd be just loosened up.

Cynthia Niles remembered another cold cure, as well as cures for related ailments. "One of the women told me you could dry the root [of pokeweed: *Phytolacca decandra*] and burn it. Get it smoking. And it would cure a cold. . . . A friend of mine said whenever they were little that they got the itch, that their mother would boil poke salad root and put that on them and it would cure them. . . . And they say it cures mange on a dog."

In his interview, Gregory Clayton elaborated on other cures that he had learned from his grandfather, who "had to go to prison so many times" due to bootlegging moonshine that he acquired a high school education and learned "all that old Indian herb doctoring":

> Yeah, they're just a lot of different herbs like that you can use for different things. Like that rat's vein [perhaps *Chimaphila umbellate*], that's good for your kidneys, prostrate [sic]– that grows in the woods. They's yellow root [*Xanthorhiza simplicissima*], all kind of ginseng [*Panax quinquefolius*], all kinds of roots you can use. Make a good tea and dig them roots from the sassafras [*Sassafras albidum*], boil them up and put a small amount of moonshine in, it makes a good drink. It's to relax you, and rest you or something. . . . They's several herbs I spot, just by seeing them in the woods.

Raised in upper Pickens County near the North Carolina line, Robert Davidson had other home remedies from his family:

> Now my grandmother and her sister used to make a worm medicine for kids. And they'd get out and dig these old herbs up and stuff and boil that stuff and thicken it down with sugar

> or stuff, and you talk about getting worms out of a young'un, it'd get every worm that was in them. . . . But that old black stuff, I remember it a-sitting on the table. . . . And you could take them white walnut roots, dig the roots up off a white walnut tree [*Juglans cinerea*] and boil it and then take something, take flour or meal or something or other and thicken that stuff down and then make a pill out of it. . . . And it would . . . clean everybody out, them white walnut pills.

"We got a weed," Anne Flowers stated in her interview, and continued:

> they call it the snakeweed [*Euphorbia hirta*?], and I gathered me some every summer. And if you get snakebit, just make you a glass of tea out of that. I know my brother . . . he got snakebit one night. . . . He walked out on the porch. And Momma had a little old couch-like thing sitting out there. And when he walked by that, there was a snake under there, and it bit him on the heel. . . . He went to hollering, you know, said he was snakebit, and they thought he was just joking. She [my mother] got her a string or something or other and quartered his leg, up here. So they throwed him in the car and started to town with him, to the doctor, and they got down here, and there used to be an old man, [name omitted]. He was a herb doctor. . . . So they decided they'd take him out there. . . . And he made him three cups of that snakeweed. . . . And he told him to drink three of them cups. Well, he did, and after he drunk that last one, he told Momma, says, "You can take that string off his leg now." So she took it off and it never did, never did bother him.

Alice Flowers, Anne's daughter, also remembered her mother using snakeweed:

> It grows on the bank up at, across from Momma's house. . . . And she would go get it and bring it to the house, and she'd make like a quart jar full of snakeweed tea. And she swore by it, that if some of the kids, grandkids, whoever, got bit that all we had to do was to feed them some of that, pour it into the holes and they would be fine. And we, thank God, we never had to test that. We did have a dog that got bit right across the nose with some kind of poisonous snake 'cause by the time it got back to the house its whole face was just swollen. And so Momma made us catch it, and [a sibling] held it, I think, and she poured that stuff in the holes that you could see in its nose, and then they opened its mouth and poured it down its throat and made it drink some and she turned it loose. She said that's all . . . we could do for it, and the next morning it showed up on the front porch and it was fine.

Jeffrey Donnelly's mother's sister "was into herbs a lot. . . . In fact, they had her . . . over at Clemson [University] talking to some doctors about herbs and stuff and she said (she's just an old plain-talking person), she says, 'I hadn't been there thirty minutes and I knew they didn't know what they were talking about.'" Donnelly's aunt's medical strategy was that "she would mix up herbs and give it to her dog and if it didn't kill it – but she was very well read on herbs. . . . She liked bloodroot [*Sanguinaria canadensis*] . . . . Said it was very good. And of course there was yellow root and ginseng." Beth Lepre knew of a local woman who "did herbs, like yellow root and ginseng. . . . She would make teas. She believed that she controlled her diabetes with that. . . . Other people would drink those concoctions. We didn't like them. It's bitter. I mean, you know, sometimes she would give them to us and we would drink them but we didn't, you know, use them as a regular [cure] but a lot of people would go to her."

"Now, in the spring of the year," Anne Flowers recalled,

> my momma and my Aunt [Cate], she'd come and stay with us a few days, and her and Momma would go out in the woods and dig herbs. . . . And they'd bring them back, and they'd put them in the wash pot and boil them. And they'd boil them down, you know, till they wouldn't be too much water. And then they'd take syrup, I believe it was, and mix in with that, and put it in a bottle, and every morning, before we ett [ate] breakfast, we all had to take a teaspoon full of that!

Alice Flowers supported her mother's recollections in an interview eight years later: "They would take Momma with them and go into the woods, especially in the spring and they would gather their roots, what they needed for the season, for – give to the kids and whoever got sick. . . . And I don't know why Mom lived as long as she did."

Pamela Charles discussed traditional cures with her first cousin, Shirley Patterson. "But that yellow root," Ms. Charles stated, my mother "always kept some that . . . she had boiled and made the liquid, put the roots in it in a jar in the refrigerator and then she would always have some that she would put in a bottle and pour corn liquor on it. Oh, that stuff taste horrible. But she said it's springtime, it's a tonic. And . . . we looked at her and say, 'Why does she do that to us?'" Mrs. Patterson interrupted: "It would be so bitter. . . ." "My baby brother, younger than me," Ms. Charles continued, "goes to the flea market. He looks for it and he buys it. . . . He brings me some."[2] "I don't think you can get kids to drink that today," Mrs. Patterson reflected, and Ms. Charles agreed: "You'd have to tie them down and force it down!"

2 As of this writing, yellow root may still be obtained at the Pickens County Flea Market, outside of Pickens.

We all chuckled at the comment, but then Ms. Charles added that she still used some of those old remedies even today. "I've chewed yellow root all my life and I ain't ever been sick," Patrick O'Connell asserted. "Good for your stomach. I ain't never been sick on my stomach." His friend Cynthia Niles added that yellow root "also protects against mouth sores. It's just good for you." For her own research project on lifeways in upper Pickens County, Deborah Mitchell had interviewed a nonagenarian, who (she said) attributed his long life to drinking "'a quart of yellow root every week.' And he had it in the refrigerator."

Anne Flowers knew of another traditional healing remedy used by her grandmother. "If some of us got hurt, got cut or something," Mrs. Flowers stated,

> why, my grandma, she'd go and get her sheep tallow and pine resin. And she'd put her some in her hand and she'd take her knife, you know, and she'd work that up real good until it'd be real good and smooth. And put it on there and it would be healed up in no time. I . . . doctored a lot of my kids, you know, when they'd get cut or anything, with goat tallow and pine resin. It'll heal it up! . . . My brother . . . was just a little fellow. And we was up there at my grandmother's; he went after her, picked up their axe – they kept that axe sharp as a razor. He picked that axe up and it just fell right between his toes and just cut it bad. Well, Grandma she run and got her sheep tallow and her pine resin. And she put that on there and it wa'n't but a few days till it was healed up.

In a later interview, Alice Flowers explained what her mother had meant: "Goat tallow was the fat out of when they killed a goat. . . . They had a big black pot beneath the yard and they would render it and then it would make it kind of hard somehow, and put it like in a jar or whatever. Mom would put it with her herbs and things."

On the other hand, not every traditional cure was efficacious. Anne Flowers's grandfather had injured his leg in a farming accident, and locals recommended: "'Heat him some tobacco leaves and wrap his leg in it.' . . . Well, we done everything people told us and it was still getting worse so we finally called old Dr. Bailey. . . . He come in and he started unwrapping his leg and he seen it. He looked at [the healer] and he says, 'Brother Jimmy,' he says, 'you're a-wasting a lot of good tobacco!'" We all laughed.

A very well-documented traditional healing practice is blood stopping.[3] For this cure, the healer lays hands on the bleeding victim and mumbles a

3 See for example, Coggeshall, *Carolina Piedmont Country*, 100–1.

secret prayer, and the bleeding (eventually) stops, according to those who have had the ritual conducted and according to those who have the power themselves.[4] In the southern Appalachians (as commonly elsewhere in the United States), the power is said to come from God in the Christian worldview. Many inhabitants told stories about this practice.

For example, earlier in her life Elizabeth Nelson had been living in a mobile home near her parents, and

> one Sunday morning I decided to go out and sunbathe in the backyard. . . . And when I started back out, the doorstep had rotted and I didn't know it. . . . And so I fell through the top doorstep. When I went down my arms went up and my arm came down on to the metal door latch and it cut through my right wrist area, all the way to the bone! And I was standing there on the ground looking at my bone and I was bleeding and scared to death. . . . Somehow I managed to get back into the house, in spite of that broken step – . . . and I called and my mom answered the phone. And I was just about screaming. I said, "Tell Daddy to come get me and bring me to the emergency room. I've cut myself." . . . And he came on out in a few minutes. And I was holding a folded towel over my wrist and putting a lot of pressure on it so it wouldn't bleed so much. . . . And so I . . . got in the truck with him. And he was puttering on down the road at his usual speed of forty to forty-five miles an hour. . . . And my dad has a gift – or *had* a gift – where he could stop blood, as they call it; or stop bleeding. And he never passed that on to me. . . . And so he was just chatting on, and, you know, being very calm. And I was still holding the towel as hard as I could against my wrist, cut to the bone. And I got to the emergency room. . . . And so one of the surgeons came and he . . . did an inner layer of stitches and an outer layer of stitches and got me all sewed up. . . . And then I looked at that towel that I had been holding on there and there's probably no more than two tablespoons of blood on it. So I knew my dad had stopped the bleeding. It's amazing. But, yeah he had that gift and people would call him or come by and see him. . . . And he could even do it when they just called on the phone. And he'd say, "Okay, where did you cut yourself? I want you to sit there and be very quiet." And of course, being quiet helps calm you down and your blood's not gushing as hard in your body, either. But it would always stop.

4 See Items 881 and 882 in Wayland Hand, ed., *Popular Beliefs and Superstitions from North Carolina*, vol. 6 of *The Frank C. Brown Collection of North Carolina Folklore*, ed. Newman White (Durham, NC: Duke University Press, 1961), 126. Hand reports that the Bible verse is Ezekiel 16:6.

> And he even did it for somebody's mule that got cut one time and it worked on the mule, too!

Beth Lepre, Ms. Nelson's mountain valley neighbor, verified Mr. Nelson's ability, explaining that her own mother had "got cut one time. She was washing dishes and she cut her wrist bad. And . . . he [Elizabeth Nelson's father] actually did it over the phone."

Several inhabitants mentioned that the gift was so strong in certain people that they had to avoid situations of animal butchering. For example, Garvin Bradshaw knew a neighbor who, "if somebody killed a hog, you know – you stick a hog to let the blood out, he said he had to walk off. The hog wouldn't bleed a drop if he was standing around. That's how powerful he was with blood; he said he had to walk off to get the hog to bleed." Gregory Clayton's father "could do it. He done that with Bible verses." In fact, Clayton continued, his father "wouldn't even stick a hog; . . . if he seen blood, he'd think of that verse, you know, he believed in it so strong, and it'd work."

"I remember one time," Gregory Clayton admitted,

> when we was at school, I was just a little – probably seven or eight years old. One boy run into the old pump handle . . . and bloodied his nose. Teacher hollered for somebody to run to their desk and get their Bible. When they got the Bible, she couldn't find the verse, and his nose quit, while she was trying to find it. You know, you just – a lot of times you just, all them kids, they was around and thinking about it. A lot of times you just think if you got a gift, you think about that verse, it'll work.

As I interviewed Joshua and Anne Flowers about their knowledge of traditional healing practices, I was very surprised to hear Mrs. Flowers quietly admit that "I stop blood, I cure poison oak, and take fire out" (see below). Mrs. Flowers mentioned that her aunt had taught her, and then provided examples of her skill:

> I had a woman to call me yesterday morning and said her husband, he's a-having nosebleeds. . . . And they carried him to the emergency room one day, and they cauterized his nose up in there, but it'd still take spells bleeding. And his wife called me yesterday morning and said his nose was bleeding, and wanted to know if I'd doctor it, and I told her I sure would. . . . When [Norman Cleveland] got run over [in a job-related accident], . . . well, they couldn't get his blood stopped, the doctors couldn't. . . . Well, my sister-in-law is down below Pickens. She called me and told me about it. . . . I doctored him and they said about eleven o'clock that night, it'd stopped. Now whe'r I'd done – I didn't do it, the Lord done it – whe'r it was me or whe'r the doctors done it, I don't know. . . . My children, some of them's

> want me to teach them. . . . I'll just sit down and write it down and give it to them.

In another interview, I had been talking to Benjamin and Denise Craig, and Mrs. Craig knew a lot about traditional healers. In fact, she is related to Anne Flowers, and thus to the aunt mentioned earlier. "And she passed it to my daddy," Mrs. Craig continued, "and then he passed it to me." Mrs. Craig described a time when the aunt cured her of warts by praying and touching them. "I had my little doubts," Mrs. Craig admitted, "but then a few weeks later I looked down at my hands and . . . they were all gone and I don't know when they went away. It's amazing. Even the big seed wart on my finger. When did it go away? I don't know. But it went away." I asked Mrs. Craig if the healer recited a specific prayer or just generally prayed, and she replied, "It's a special prayer. But I can't tell you!" I chuckled and assured her that I was not going to elicit forbidden knowledge, but I did ask her if she had ever used it. She replied, "Well, I've used it on me! . . . And I've used it on you [her husband] when you burned yourself and you said it went away. . . . And I know it works. . . . But I guess you just have to believe that . . . it means something even if I don't understand it. And part of it's plain. You know what you're talking about. But there's a section of it that's like, 'Okay. I'm saying this?'" When I asked her if she recalled a specific instance of her helping to heal someone, she cautioned that she has not advertised the fact that she is a traditional healer. "But I think you're not supposed to advertise it," Mrs. Craig explained; "I think your people are just supposed to come to you. So then I couldn't, you know, set up a little stand!" Or "hang a shingle," her husband joked.

In fact, Denise Craig admitted, her son-in-law seemed very skeptical when he heard about her gift, "so I really haven't told many people. In fact," she continued,

> I didn't memorize it for a long time. . . . It's written down. Daddy wrote – gave it to me. But we didn't discuss it. It had the instructions. And then there's in the old Bible, there's the copy that Aunt [Cate] gave to Daddy. . . . And he just gave me the envelope. He didn't even discuss it with me. So, there was no talking about it! No insider's advice, you know. . . . But now this little boy at the church . . . he just finished second grade. And he has a wart on his knee and he wanted me to pray it off. . . . So now I prayed on it last Saturday. . . . So we'll just have to see. I told him that it will take a few weeks and it will just be gone.

As the conversation continued, Benjamin Craig confirmed that his wife could cure warts, stop bleeding, and talk out fire. When I asked if the prayer was the same for all three conditions, she said yes, but the healer must specify the different problems. Then the healer rubs the affected area while praying.

Mrs. Craig admitted that her father was a bit of a "character," and so at the end of the ritual he would puff his breath, gesture with his hand, and say, "Poof!" "But that was my daddy," Mrs. Craig continued; "he wasn't like a loud person or something but he was really funny." When I asked Mrs. Craig if she was going to pass the prayer on, she hesitated and replied, "Yes. I don't know to whom yet. . . . I don't know. I don't know. You know our children are town people!" I then asked if the prayer had to be transmitted from female to male to female, and Mrs. Craig agreed, but added, "You don't have to be related, though. I still don't know why Aunt [Cate], out of – you know, it was a gigantic family – why she would give it to Daddy. Especially since we didn't even live up here. But she asked him."

This same woman mentioned by Mrs. Craig was Robert Davidson's paternal grandmother, and he also recalled her healing talents, including her ability to stop blood:

> And they said she could really stop it, too. There was a bunch of fighting up there one time and they cut each other all to pieces, and some of them went and told Grandma that they'd been in a fight over there and they'd cut up each other pretty bad and wanted her to stop the blood and she wanted to know their names and all. And they told her the names and everything. And [one victim], he always swore that he, he tells, "I believe I know whenever they got to her"; says, "I felt that blood stop running on me." He told me that hisself. He says, "I believe that I know," says, "I believe I'd've bled to death if they hadn't a-got to her."

Garvin Bradshaw acknowledged that "there's been a lot of people can stop blood." In fact, Mr. Bradshaw recalled a time he had had a facial operation and then later, standing in a store,

> blood just come, started just running, dripping, pouring out of my face here. Someone said, "You better go back to the doctor." [A friend] got me in the car, and we might've went from here to that house up there; [the friend] says, "You ain't bleeding now, are you?" I said, "Nope." "Well," he said, "I stopped the blood." I didn't know he could stop blood, but he told me he did. [Another neighbor] . . . told me, she could tell one man, or a man could tell a woman, said there's three verses from the Bible, and she told me she'd tell me 'fore she died, but she moved to Greenville, [and] she never did tell me. But [another neighbor] said if you'd take a double-bladed axe, then go to a branch and just set it down like that and let the water run against it – it would stop blood.[5]

---

5 Although this sounds like a folk belief, I was unable to find it in the *Frank C. Brown Collection*.

As previously mentioned, those with the healing ability to stop blood likely also have other powers. Anne Flowers, for example, has many. In fact, she related, "somebody called me the other day and wanted to know if I could stop – cure thrash[6] on a baby. . . . I says, 'I'll try it.' So I tried it and I ain't heard nothing. I don't know whe'r it cured him or they had to take him to the doctor." Garvin Bradshaw described another neighbor lady who lived

> down yonder. If you had the thrash or something you'd go down there and tell her what was wrong. . . . And she would cure the thrash, and pour out blood, draw out fire. If you got burnt, you'd go down there and she'd draw that fire out. If you got cut, she'd stop the blood. And me and [Brian Alexander, my brother-in-law] . . . was a-working down here at Keowee Keys [lakeside community]. A man had a big oak tree down there he wanted us to cut, and it was in the summer time. . . . Well, tree was about that big around, you had poison oak all over that thing. Well, I pulled my shirt off (it was hot that day), and I used the chain saw. And that stuff broke out all over me. It broke out on my face! Well, they said [the lady] lived over here at Pickens; they told me she could cure poison oak. . . . I went to [her]! Three days' time, my poison oak was gone.

In contrast, Bradshaw continued, his brother-in-law Brian Alexander "went to the doctor," and Alexander's wife interjected, "Got shots, and it didn't help!" "Didn't help him a bit!" Mr. Bradshaw agreed, and added, "then he got the thrash on top of that, and I took him down to [the healer], and she cured the thrash and his poison oak both!"

In a conversation several days earlier, Brian Alexander related that he

> knowed a man down here. . . . You'd just call and tell him your name and your poison oak'd dry up. Sumac – that old sumac? It'll dry up. And you had warts on you. I had a wart on my arm, and I called him and had that wart went off. . . . And my wife, she had them shingles, and she just kept going to the doctor; it kept getting worse. I called him [the healer], and he said he never had done nothing with no shingles, and he'd read and see what he could find about that. But it wasn't less than a week and her shingles started drying up.

As inhabitants have already noted, closely related to the tradition of stopping bleeding from wounds and removing the pain of skin irritations is the traditional ability to "talk out fire." In this practice, the healer lays hands on a victim, recites some secret prayers, and (in most US locations) channels the power of a Christian God to remove the pain from the burned area –

6 This ailment is more commonly known as thrush, or an oral yeast infection.

sometimes almost immediately, sometimes delayed.[7]

In our conversation, Anne Flowers admitted that she had this ability. When I asked her how she removed the pain from burns, she replied, "Just like I doctor poison oak. . . . And I'd, you know, kind of rub it, and talk it out." As she explained what she could reveal about the ritual, she joked that her husband wanted her to teach him because "there'd be young girls who'd lay out in the sun and get blisters. And they'd come here and want me to doctor them, and I think he wanted to doctor. Get to rub back there and rub her!" Joshua Flowers, her husband, admitted that "I'd burn myself" on the stove sometimes as he helped his wife cook, and then he would "just stick my hand" out and say, "'Take fire out of my hand' and hand it to her and work right on. She'd take the fire out and I never did know what had burned. It quit hurting and then there was nothing no more to it." Anne Flowers retorted, "I told him, I said, 'I think you done that on purpose just to get me to hold your hand!'"

Several inhabitants related stories of having the ritual performed on them by local well-known traditional healers. For example, as a child on an upper Pickens County farm, Philip Valentine helped his father make charcoal for sale by burying smoldering trees. Valentine's job was to tamp down the burning pile. He continued:

> One particular morning I went over to pack it down, and I went down inside [the pile]. And I got – my whole leg was burnt, all the way up to my midsection. And I can tell you, I was hot! And I ran down to the little creek and got in there to cool myself off. And my mother . . . wrapped me up with a tow sack, put Vaseline and stuff, you know, so I could get some comfort, 'cause it was really hurting. After that she went up to [a neighbor] up on the hill over there. . . . So what he did, he went into the house, he stayed for a while, and he came out with his Bible. And he went to some verse in the Bible, he read it out of the Bible, and he had me to hold his hand while he read to me in the Bible. And telling me that he talked the fire out of me during, through the Scripture, reading of the Bible. I don't know what section of the Bible it was.

Brendra Kendrick, raised in another Upstate county, described a situation shortly after she had married. Her husband was outside on a riding mower,

> and somebody called the phone or whatever and I had walked out through the yard to get his attention and he stopped the tractor. And I stumbled just before I got to it and I grabbed that [exhaust] pipe. I mean, my whole – the inside of my hand was just one huge blister. And he called this guy that we worked with or used to work with and he said, "Do you need to see it?" And

---

7 See for example Coggeshall, *Carolina Piedmont Country*, 100–1.

> he said, "No." And he said, "She should be okay in about ten or fifteen minutes." About fifteen minutes later it wasn't hurting. . . . And I don't have a scar or anything.

"Well, I'll tell you an experience I had about taking out fire," another man related to a group of us as we sat together in an outdoor gazebo. "And this is true," he added somberly, and described an incident one summer as he worked at a local textile mill. During a minor repair, a spark caused a flame, and then

> that whole thing just blazed up, right on my face and my arm. Well, they got the fire put out there and everything, and I was hurting so bad and they got me and carried me to Travelers Rest. The doctor saw me, give me shots, and put Vaseline and all kind of stuff on me. And I was hurting so bad. [A friend], he was working up there and he brought me home. And 'fore we got home he said, "My mother can take fire out." Said, "Do you want to go by and let her take that out?" And I mean, I was really hurting, you know, I was burning, my whole face and burned my hair off and everything. And I said, "Sure." So she went by there and looked at it and did what she did. In about thirty minutes, it quit hurting, never did have a scab on it, never did do anything. And then that was that, that quick. And I don't know, I mean it was just gone.

As several inhabitants related stories of traditional healers to me, they regretted not learning the traditions themselves. For example, one of Brenda Kendrick's relatives "could tell you what you could take for the tummy ache or the headache or what you need to go get out in the woods, like the yellow root and all this stuff. He knew what it was for and what it was used for and what you need to get and how you need to make it." But no one in the younger generation learned the information. Alice Flowers reflected on the traditional medicinal knowledge of her mother and grandmother and also regretted not having learned more. "Every year in the spring she wanted to go to the creek," Ms. Flowers explained, "and we loved it, you know, and so we'd go and she would show us things. I guess she was trying to teach us, and you know I could pick out a few things [today] but nothing that I would be brave enough to give somebody!" "You don't really hear people talk about that anymore," Mrs. Kendrick reflected; "but it used to be a fairly common thing, I guess. . . . You used to hear about it quite a bit, but I haven't even thought about that in quite a while."

On the other hand, Gregory Clayton joked, anyone could proclaim themselves to be a doctor. "One time there was a doctor," Mr. Clayton explained to me, and then implied that the professional was being rather dismissive of Clayton's herbal expertise, and so he replied:

> "I'm a doctor." And he said, "What kind of doctor are you?" And I said, "I don't know; I'm an herb doctor." And he said, "Does it work?" and I said, "Yeah, it works." I said, "I'm a – I delivered a chicken one time." And he said, "How in the world did you deliver a chicken?" And I said, "I cracked the eggshell and let it out." He looked at me. That's delivering a chicken, ain't it?

Although today largely replaced by more modern medical practices and improvements in transportation to medical facilities, traditional cures and healing practices remain in mountain culture, but generally hidden discreetly from external view. Traditional healers still exist, maintaining traditional knowledge, despite having fewer and fewer relatives to whom to pass that knowledge. Many residents, when asked, recall their own experiences with traditional cures and healers, helping in another way to preserve the traditions by acting as verification of the efficacy of such practices. I have seen botanical materials such as yellow root available for purchase in regional farmers markets. Like many other folk traditions deemed by standard American culture to be "old fashioned," curing traditions remain, but in the more private realms of local knowledge.

Chapter Six

"Everybody Was Closer Together": Stories of Social Life and Activities

This chapter includes stories about specific places (e.g., country stores or rural churches) as well as traditional activities associated with them (e.g., church functions). Descriptions of these places and activities help to paint a general background for some of the stories about them, and together create a more complete picture of life in the mountain counties. Of course, churches and stores were also places where people gathered to tell stories, and understanding the context of those stories is also important. Many of these social activities commonly occur throughout the South and have been well documented for the region.[1] The following stories generally were solicited as I asked inhabitants to reflect on their lives or to describe favorite memories. This time, readers are invited to drop some salted peanuts into a co-cola, sit on the worn wooden step of a country store, and give me a listen.

Rural Life – Houses

In his engaging speaking style, Robert Davidson described how his grandparents recycled an old home:

> My granddaddy and [a neighbor] tore a house down in the Rocky Bottom. And . . . hauled it to the Cane Break in a one horse-wagon and a club-footed mule. The old mule was club footed. And he hauled that over there and built that house up there where he lived at all the time. . . . And Grandma'd sit and drawed nails out

1 John M. Coggeshall, *Carolina Piedmont Country* (Jackson: University Press of Mississippi, 1996).

Figure 6: Typical country home in Pickens County.
People and Places - Pickens Area, Digital Collections file, Pickens County Library System.

> of them boards, and the nails, she'd set out there and straighten nails for him to nail back, to put back. I remember sitting there straightening them nails as well as it had been yesterday.

Denise Craig described an old log home that had been inhabited by elderly relatives: "And my grandfather had put siding on it, and they were so upset because they wanted holes in there between the logs because they said it would make you sick to close up your house.[2] . . . They would keep their door wide open even when it snowed. . . . They were tough people."

A young Joseph Yeats faced hard weather conditions when as a child he was allowed to spend the night with his cousin, "and the weather got real cold and I didn't notice the doors when I went in. There was no door knobs, just the latch. I woke up the next morning; it was awful cold and I looked. 'Uncle Bud,' I said, 'it's so cold last night, the door knobs froze off!' He never did let me forget that as long as he lived."

Charles Watson described the general characteristics of his grandparents' home:

> Yeah, I remember going over there. The thermometer – the bottom just felt out of it one evening, one day. And Momma was worried about Grandma and Grandpa 'cause they's getting up in years then, and she wanted to go check on them, and we went

2 Although this sounds like a folk belief, I was unable to locate it in the *Frank C. Brown Collection of North Carolina Folklore*. However, it certainly would prevent carbon monoxide poisoning.

> over there. It'd already dark got there [*sic*], they had done gone to bed, and they were real fire conscious. But Grandpa had done roked [raked] all the ashes up in the fireplace in a little mound and watered them out and patted it down with his hand. They didn't want no fire in that fireplace with them in bed asleep. They had plenty of quilts on the bed, sleep through it. Wake up next morning, be maybe where your breath'll be blowing; there'd be ice, you know, on the wall. Or the floor, big ol' cracks that you could see chickens underneath! And Grandma wouldn't allow a sprig of grass in the yard; she'd dig it up or something – dig it up and throw it out at the edge of the woods. And they'd go right there to the sand pit and had a sand bank out there, you go out there and get a special type of sand for some reason and bring it in the house and scatter it out in the house on the floor. That was to keep down body lice and stuff like that, or so I hear. 'Course them body lice was before my time, I reckon; people got a whole lot cleaner.

As with Watson's grandparents' home, many inhabitants recalled older homes with gaps between floor boards where roosting chickens could be seen and cold air could come up. But sometimes these gaps had a positive function, as Denise Craig explained:

> My great-great-grandpa was wanting to fix the floors [in their cabin] and everything. Well, she [his wife] wouldn't let him. I mean, she was really upset, because there was a hole in her little kitchen area – in the floor. And that's where she had – it was wonderful, because all she had to do was reach down in there and get the hen eggs because they had nests under the floor. And so, she had such convenience because all she had to do was reach down and get the eggs out.

Many inhabitants described local homes as very simple. For example, Rachel Edwards visited many mountain homes in her childhood because her family performed as a traveling gospel group:

> Some of the homes were very sad. There would be a – there wouldn't be a partition or a wall; there would be a curtain. They would have hooks, and they'd have the rooms partitioned with like a bed sheet, I guess, and they would curtain it off. And some of the homes wouldn't have running water or plumbing at all. And my mother was curious and she went into the kitchen of one of the homes, and just talking to the lady while she prepared our supper. And she was cooking in Jewel Lard[3] buckets; that was her pots that she was cooking in.

3 Jewel Lard was a brand name, popular in the early to mid-twentieth century.

Claudia Alexander was raised in a home her father built by himself back in the mountains of northern Oconee County:

> We had a living room and we had a wood stove. And in the living room in the corner was a[n] iron bed. Momma and Daddy always slept – everybody back then had a bed in the front room. I think they did that because they had to keep the fire going. We had a kitchen, and then it had a[n] upper room (we called) – it was a bedroom. We had two iron beds: one at the foot of the room, one at the head of the room. The back room had one iron bed. The boys all three slept in one iron bed, and then us girls had that bed. And Lord I slept with my momma and daddy till I think I was eight years old. I did. I got ashamed – everybody was making fun of me; my brothers'd make fun of me.

Many country homes were heated by wood, including that of Charles Watson's family. According to Watson, cooking in this manner once caused a horrible tragedy with a family pet:

> Well, they had an old fireplace to heat the house and they had just what we call a cook stove to cook on. Cook stoves put out a lot of heat 'cause Momma could bake a pone[4] of cornbread and got through, you know, just take and open that oven door and let it stay down and it'd heat the house up. I think the old feller that lived over here, he did that. He couldn't hear; he was like me, couldn't hear good. . . . He baked him a pone of cornbread, you know. . . . He let the lid down, and it was cold weather, and as the stove cooled down, one of the old house cats jumped up on that door, good and warm to that cat, so it went back in the oven and laid down in there, still nice and cozy and warm. And Dale couldn't hear a thing. After awhile he passed by and just shut that oven door, and that cat in there. Well, he went on the next day, . . . he fired the old stove up again, he couldn't hear the cat yelling and meowing and screaming, but he noticed when he put his pan in there, he felt it hit something and he looked down and there his cat was, he done been cooking it about two or three days! . . . I couldn't eat out of there no more.

Without electricity, the Bradshaws' childhood home used oil lamps, but before that, Claudia Alexander explained, "well, they didn't even have that. You know what my dad and momma used? They took a[n] iron frying pan and put pine splinters in it and set it on fire and the iron pan was sort of like what you'd say, a candle holder for all their little pine splinters." "Kitchen'd be cold – freezing," Claudia continued. Mother "would get up early in the

---

4 Cornbread made without milk or eggs (closer to Native American traditions).

mornings and go in there and make biscuits. And it cold as it was in that kitchen, she'd try to crank up that old wood stove in the kitchen and run to the living room to get warm by that wood heater, get warm and run back to the kitchen and see if that wood stove's got it warm in there yet." "Now you used to have to tote stove wood up and down this ridge here," her brother Garvin Bradshaw recalled; "take a[n] axe up there and cut me down a pole of wood about that big around, come down here and cut it up. . . . Went to work in a cotton mill . . . and I bought an electric stove for my momma and that stopped the wood getting right there."

Peter Abney "was twelve year[s] old when we got power up in here [upper Pickens County]. I really, really thought it was something to have one light bulb in each room! . . . Then you could see to study. Before that it was oil lamps and the glow of the fire that you read your books and studied by." Alice Flowers could "faintly remember when we got electric lights. And we did not have [an] indoor bathroom. I got married in 1967 and I took a bath in a wash pan. . . . But in 1967 they [her parents, Joshua and Anne Flowers] still did not have an indoor bathroom."

"Would you believe it," Cynthia Niles asked me, "I was in a twenty-four by twenty-four" square foot home when I first got married. She chuckled, and continued:

> And this [her current home] is the first house I've had hot water in. And I don't feel sorry for kids today, girls today, that have babies. I had three children in two and a half years. . . . I had them in the hospital, but I had to carry water, and we didn't have no bathroom in the house. And today they have diapers, hot water, and all this. I don't feel sorry for them today because I know what I went through yesterday! But it wasn't that bad because where my parents live, where we was raised at we . . . had a well. But [at my first home after marriage] I got water out of the creek. . . . You grow up fast. You get educated fast.

Just a generation ago, indoor plumbing was still considered a luxury. "Tin tubs was fun to take baths in," Claudia Alexander remembered. To do so, she explained, one had to "carry in water, heat it up and put it in a[n] old tin tub and get in that thing. That was fun. . . . We'd take bird baths and then we'd take big dunking baths too. . . . I'd jump in and take my bath and wash my hair every night. Even though we were poor, we knew to stay clean." Peter Abney, a contractor, was building a house for a client and a special-order sink had not been delivered to the job site on time. Both the manager and assistant manager of the supply store tried to apologize about the delay, but good-natured Abney simply replied, "'Think nothing about it; the boy [the customer] was twenty-one before he ever knowed you could put water in the house anyway.'"

Community Social Activities

In addition to social activities associated with school (see Chapter Seven) or church (see below), communities frequently held various social activities for the entire community.[5] Anne Flowers, born early in the twentieth century, recalled several types of communal work activities. She explained:

> In the fall of the year we'd have cotton pickings. Everybody'd come in. You know, the last of the cotton, they'd just go through the field and pick off the bolls where they was about half-open. . . . And then after we got the cotton picked out, we'd have a square dance. So – that was our entertainment. And they'd have corn shuckings and wood choppings. And after they'd get through, they'd have supper. Everybody'd eat supper and then after supper they'd start up that string music and everybody'd hit the floor!

Jeffrey Donnelly also recalled wood choppings: "Everybody'd get together and go to someone's house, and their grandmother would cook a big meal for them and maybe ten or fifteen men or so would get out and cut wood, and that family would have enough wood for the winter and all the women would get together and cook a big meal for them and there was no charges, it was all free."

During her interview, Anne Flowers recalled a regional holiday from her childhood, one that would not have been celebrated in the North – Jefferson Davis's birthday: "Well, [when] . . . I was a-growing up, the third of June, they had what they called Old Soldier's Day in Pickens [Jefferson Davis's birthday]. And I mean the people would come." A friend interjected: "Everybody would come," and Mrs. Flowers continued: "*Every*-body would come. They'd have sack races and, oh, everything. . . . And then . . . people would go up there and they'd sell lemonade, you know. Oh, just have a great big washtub full of lemonade. Old Jim Chapman – . . . he sold it. And he would holler, it was 'lemonade made in the sun; if you ain't got the money you don't get none!'"

Family Social Activities

Given relative social isolation and frequently high birth rates, large families created multiple opportunities for social activities. When Harry Edison was a child, his family owned a country store in Eastatoee Valley. Edison reflected on this time: "I just couldn't ask for a better life than what I had growing up," he stated. "All of the kids in this valley they loved my dad," Edison recalled, because of the adventures his father would organize. For

5 See also Coggeshall, *Carolina Piedmont Country*, 105–24.

example, Edison continued, when it would snow, his father would

> get his old car and put the chains on it. . . . And we had homemade sleds and Daddy'd hook them behind the car. . . . It's wonderful nobody got hurt [unclear sentence]. But he'd pull us all the way back through those mountains on one of them sleds. You talk about having a ball – we had it. And all them kids they loved my dad for that, you know.

Brenda Kendrick reminisced about her girlhood, growing up in Oconee County. "I remember, I couldn't wait" to go barefoot in the summer, Kendrick recalled:

> Momma always told us you can't go barefoot until the first of May[6] and we couldn't wait to get those shoes off, running through the pasture and fields and the grass . . . and go play in the creek and this kind of stuff. Everybody went barefooted. . . . I was the youngest, and I had two older sisters and then my brother, and then my sister and me, so it was – a boy was right in the middle of four girls. I was the tomboy of the family. Wherever he [my brother] went, I went with him. I could climb any tree that he could climb and do it better. I went hunting with him. Anything he did, I could do, you know, I was that into it. . . . We played outside, we played with the neighbors' children, we'd all gather together. I can remember just as a kid that we had a large pasture area, down below our house, along the river. A bunch of young guys and boys would come over on Sunday afternoon and my dad would go down there and my brother and they would play softball down in the pasture. And of course, my sister and I, we'd go down and watch. And they'd be just dozens of kids down there, you know, but we were always busy. There was always either something to do around the house, working in the garden; we played cards a lot. In the wintertime, you know, I can remember Mom making taffy. You'd have to butter your hands and pull the taffy, you know, and cut it; I can remember that when I was a child. She loved to make chocolate fudge in the wintertime, and she was a wonderful cook. My dad was a lot of fun. He would, when we were kids, I mean, he'd work all day and just at dusky dark[7] he'd want us to get us out and we'd all play hide and seek.

Neighborhoods full of large families had plenty of children for playmates.

---

6 One should not go barefoot before the first of May, item 479 in Wayland Hand, ed., *Popular Beliefs and Superstitions from North Carolina*, vol. 6 of *The Frank C. Brown Collection of North Carolina Folklore*, ed. Newman White (Durham, NC: Duke University Press, 1961), 75.

7 "Dusky dark" is twilight. See also Joseph S. Hall, *Smoky Mountain Folks and Their Lore* (Asheville, NC: Cataloochee Press, 1960), 66.

Figure 7: A gathering of families, Big Cane Break.
Stanley Aultman Collection, Digital Collections file, Pickens County Library System.

For example, Marsha Baird "had ten siblings," and most of her father's brothers also had big families,

> and so the cousins were pretty close. . . . And one of my biggest memories is of going to the river, to the Keowee River, on a picnic. And it would always be in the hot summer. And we'd take watermelons and put the watermelons in the river. And I can remember just as well going down a long sandy road by the river with the corn being so high you couldn't see over it. And it was like the corn and then the river, and the trees that grew along the river. And there was obviously an area that was sort of like a pull-out section of the road, where people had used it on more than one occasion. And there was a big tree hanging over the river and a rope on the tree. And my brothers would swing out over that rope and drop in the water – cold water! But that's the kind of vacations we had.

Raised in the Carolina mountains, Gregory Clayton and his brothers swam frequently in human-made ponds. But

> Mother, she tried to keep us out of them, 'cause back in the '40s, polio was going around a whole lot. . . . They didn't know; they thought maybe water was what's causing it. She'd tell us to stay out of them ponds. She kept telling us, said, you know, there's crawfish in water. . . . They got them old pinchers on there, they'll pinch you. Well, she'd tell us them things'd get

> ahold of our toes and wouldn't turn us loose till it'd thunder.[8] Scared us; we was scared anyhow. And one day, my brother, he wanted to go get in the water so bad, he got him a piece of tin and a big club. And he done that, he said, "Now I'm gonna get in that water." And he said, "If you hear me yell," said, "you get that piece of tin!" What he'd do is bang it so it'd make a sound like it's thundering.

Brian Alexander and his wife, Claudia, recalled even simpler pastimes from their childhoods. Mrs. Alexander began: "But it was just a happier day back then for me, because to me going down to the creek and playing was fun, putting a string on a June bug – you know. . . . We would tie a string on a June bug and it'd fly –" And then her husband interrupted with "It would fly around and around and around." And then Mrs. Alexander continued with other entomological entertainment: "Yes, and catching lightning bugs and putting them in a jar. And we would play with our imagination. I would take a stick and draw on the dirt, and that was my living room; this other little square is my den. But you know, you just used your imagination."

Raised in upper Oconee County, Claudia Alexander as a child did not have many material possessions. One time, she recalled, her uncle

> went to the dump. Some well-to-do person left some old toys there: a doll stroller, a little tin-looking kitchen outfit. We [she and her female cousins] thought we were rich up there in that yard playing with all that stuff that's been thrown away. And he brought it home from the dump and we got all those new toys!

As a child, Gregory Clayton had different sorts of toys. After his parents had gone to bed, Clayton and his siblings would sneak out of the house and

> hang a lantern up on a limb, get old lantern, and old bats, they'd come to the light. Get the bugs. We'd get out there, we'd make us a – have a board and hew it down and make a handle on it. Throw things up, now and the bats come down to, trying to get it. We'd bat them things and bust them all to pieces. Anyway, that's the way we had our fun. But you can get the old bats flying around; you throw something up and they'd fall, they'll come down with it. If you got a good bat, you can knock the soup out of them.

Allen Hill confessed to a different episode of harming animals. As a boy, Hill spent the weekend with a friend of his out in the country, and one Saturday his friend's parents had gone to Greenville. Hill continued:

---

8 Crawfish (family Cambaridae) hanging on until hearing thunder may be found as item 7016 in Hand, *Popular Beliefs*, 7:359.

> We wanted to go hunting. Well, we decided not to go hunting. And shoot the chickens with the BB gun. And we thought he [the patriarch] wouldn't notice it when he got back. Well, you know how kids are! . . . We shot his laying hens. We didn't kill them, we just crippled them. They was a-hopping around the yard. And he came in the house, . . . says, "Come here, boys!" . . . He said, "I should give you a whupping about crippling my chickens." And we looking at each other, "Who told him we shot them chickens?" He said, "But I want you to go catch every one of them crippled chickens." And we knowed how to catch them, you know. At night, they'd roost. But he didn't want them on the ground, because they couldn't fly up to roost; they was crippled. So we had to catch them, and he would put them in that cage where the foxes and stuff couldn't get them. But it took us an awful long time to catch them.

In recent decades, families are smaller and travel is easier. Donna Trask grew up in Eastatoee Valley but had no nearby children or relatives to play with; her cousins lived in Pickens, and it was a treat to spend the weekend with them. On the other hand, at the time of our interview, Mrs. Trask and her family lived near her sister and her family, and so the cousins are raised together, as many families did in the past. "When their [her children's] cousins come from Georgia and Mississippi," Mrs. Trask explained, "you know, it is a *huge deal* to get to come over here and play, go fishing, and go four-wheeling, and just do all the things that they do. Yeah, a lot of times they'll camp outside; . . . they set up a tent up right here, and just camp out here."

As a Pickens city girl, Stephanie Jamison loved to spend the weekend at her grandparents' place in Eastatoee Valley, where they ran cattle. One night, while camping out in the yard, she and her compatriots

> left one night [and] we went out cow tipping, up at Granny and Grandpa's farm and we snuck out and we went up there, and the cows were just grazing or sleeping and we would just go tip them over. Well, Grandpa forgot to tell us that he put a bull on that pasture that weekend. . . . Somebody hit the bull and that thing come charging and oh, mercy! . . . Lawd, I didn't think we was going [to] ever get out of that field. I think, was it [my cousin] climbed the tree and the bull was pawing at the tree and we're like, trying to get the bull over here. . . . At last she crawled and got out but we never told Granny and Papa, but Papa knew. The next morning, he said, "Y'all went out there and messed with my bull last night, didn't you?" I said, "Why?"

> and he said, he said, "He's got dirt rut in his horns." I guess he was trying to get it out of us. . . . I mean, you know, we did stuff like that when we was up there. When I'd come home I had cartoons and I had TV and stuff but if you – I would literally rather spend my weekends there doing that than I'd be at home watching TV.

In another interview Beth Lepre echoed those same sentiments: "I liked to be inside and cook and, but then, I'd go outside and play if there was somebody to play with. . . . In the summer, we weren't in the house watching TV. That wasn't what we did. Because, first of all, there was no TV. Like, we got one station . . . . We had an antenna and you'd turn it and it'd just be all this 'snow,' and just was not really worth it. . . . I didn't have anything different until Dish[9] (whatever) came out."

Before contemporary mass media (such as television), Brenda Kendrick explained, entertainment

> was more community based; you went visiting on Sunday afternoons . . . after church, and family get-togethers on the weekends. That seems to have kind of gone by the wayside a lot. It was – I can remember even after I was grown, and my sisters were married, the ones that lived in the area we'd all usually meet at Mom's, Mom and Dad's on Sunday, you know for Sunday dinner, and we'd all stay till like late afternoon. The children would get together and, you know, play outside; we were never inside.

Ryan Trask reflected on the differences in social interaction between his childhood and that of his own children:

> Everybody went to every family reunion when I was a child. That was nonnegotiable. And you wouldn't think of missing it. But I also know that at that point in time, everybody was closer together. They were more connected. They kept up with each other. It wasn't as awkward. But you know I think it seems like families drift apart or fall apart in a shorter period of time than they did in the past. I may be wrong but I think I see people, you know within one generation sometimes it's over. You just had that tie for that one immediate group. Whereas I grew up remembering you know probably four generations of people in the same room and the same setting that knew each other at these family reunions. . . . But it seems that you don't have that intergenerational connectedness that I think

---

9 Satellite or cable TV. "Snow" on television refers to a grainy white random pattern of tiny dots.

Figure 8: Campbell's Grocery Store.
People and Places - Liberty, Digital Collections files, Pickens County Library System.

> was probably a part of human culture for a long, long time. . . . I think we're worse off because of it.

Rural Life – Country Stores

A century or so ago, while many rural households produced much of their food, certain items such as coffee or shoes or some hardware had to be purchased commercially. But few homes had vehicles, the rural roads were mostly unpaved and muddy, and horses and mules were needed for farm labor. Thus, country stores arose at crossroads and in small communities, within walking distance (several miles) of most rural homes. Because of the time and effort needed to arrive, many customers lingered at the stores, catching up on community or regional news, which made crossroads country stores important gathering places in most rural communities.

For example, Rachel Edwards remembered, "back then we had so many little stores. Every, you'd go one mile or so and there'd be a little store. It'd have every kind of thing that you could possibly want. . . . They sold gas and then kerosene and just small commodities. Didn't have a whole lot, but –" and her husband James added: "Dopes[10] and candy." Mrs. Edwards then continued: "I remember what fascinated me about some of those old stores was the smell,

10 Coca-Cola soft drinks were nicknamed "dopes" because of small amounts of cocaine in the original formula.

Figure 9: Rocky Bottom Store.
Stanley Aultman Collection, Digital Collections file, Pickens County Library System.

because they would always have apples and bananas and tobaccos and all these things and the smell was so fascinating to me. . . . But that was a . . . congregating place. Everybody would go there and swap tales and probably swap their flour and meal."

Harry Edison's father had been a moonshiner, but after a conversion during a revival,

> my dad came home and poured out the only living he had and friends and family went in and built the store right over there next to where my mother lives, which is between where I live and where my mother's house was over there. . . . So that store's built in 1954. . . . People would come here every Friday, Saturday night . . . and we'd sit around the store, you know, and talk, and it was just a great time back . . . to live in those times and have all those good neighbors and everything. But 'course the supermarkets and all just about did away with them. The grocery store did real well in the '50s and, you know, up in the early '60s. . . . We had bananas and canned goods mostly. . . . But then they moved it [the highway] in '69 over to where it is now, so. . . . We finally closed it down about '73 or '74. And finally I tore the store down in 1976; that's when it was torn down.

I then asked Mr. Edison to describe a typical Friday or Saturday night at the store, and he elaborated: "Well, there would be people sitting around.

Sometimes the people would come in to play music and it was just an enjoyable time." "But especially at that store," Edison continued,

> people come up there to the store and sit around and talk. . . . And I guess that is [the] . . . reason I'm not a bashful person because I grew up with them. I got to know a lot of unique people over there at that store. People would come here from all over, from everywhere you know. . . . And I would just meet them and talk to them. And I would take nothing for growing up like that.

A similar store existed in the little community of Rocky Bottom, and Ryan Trask recalled that a married couple ran the store, and "the husband was a pretty famous bootlegger. . . . On the weekends they'd have dances and music." Since Robert Davidson grew up in that community, I asked him in another interview to describe that same store in more detail:

> Well, it was just an old long building and had a kind of a side room off to one side of it, went along with it, that they kept the feed in there. You could go there and buy about any kind of feed you wanted to, but they kept most of the stuff there in the store. People'd go there and buy soup beans, but I've seed [seen] a man go in there and buy as much as fifty pounds of soup beans at one time. And coffee, they'd go there and buy twenty-five, thirty pounds of coffee, and all that kind of stuff, and take it back to the mountains with them.

Daniel Hall, who spent the summers in the community as a youngster, added that the store "sold gasoline. . . . And you bought kerosene. . . . They . . . mostly had canned goods, and . . . coffee, sugar, or flour, that sort of thing. Not produce unless somebody brought it in there to sell it, you know."

Another man elaborated on the informal economic traditions that store operators had to have:

> And [this man] run this little store that's over here on the highway. Well, he was really nice and he would bring up a pair, some shoes if we'd tell him, if my daddy'd go tell him what kind we wanted. And we always got a new pair of tennis shoes in the spring laced up, you know, ankle-high tennis shoes to work in the field in. And he would bring us up a pair for me and my sister every spring and get what size we wanted. So, and he had cloth; he had material in his store and sewing needles and things like that which you had to have. He was very nice. And the thing of it was, he didn't require cash. You know, you could pick up a chicken off the yard and take it and he'd take that in on it or eggs or whatever we had that we had to spare. So it was right convenient.

Patrick O'Connell remembered the informal bartering in his neighborhood store but also cautioned about the potential for relatively slow merchandise restocking: "We'd take eggs up there and swap them for coffee and stuff like that. If you bought any candy you had to look at it real good and make sure it didn't have no holes in it. . . . It done been there so long, the worms'd get in it. If it had a hole in it, it had a worm in it."

In his neighborhood in Oconee County, John Summers remembered their local store and the owner's economic flexibility, necessary for a cash-poor society:

> That building right there, that was Gladys's old store. . . . And everybody had credit there. Everybody bought their groceries there. And when they got, most of them got their check once a month, what little check they got, they went and paid Gladys with it. . . . She helped the community out. I'm gonna tell you, if it hadn't been for her, they'd been a lot of people starved to death. They'd went real hungry. But if you made any effort at all to pay her, you'd get anything in that store you wanted. As long as you made a[n] effort down the road to pay her.

A quite memorable country store nested in the upper Jocassee Valley, now submerged under the lake with that name. As a teenager, Alice Flowers was a frequent customer. "If you turned [into the valley] and went on up a dirt road and you crossed over a creek at one point, and went all the way up, well, about three-fourths of the way up [a man] had a store." In a separate interview, the owner's daughter described her father's place:[11]

> A few years before he died he just had a[n] old store up there; he sold picnic supplies. Anybody could come up there and want to buy them – and Cokes, and stuff like that. And he had some picnic tables there under the, one of the old big trees. . . . They'd come and have picnics and want to buy supplies from him. . . . It'd just give him something to do. Like a hobby I guess is more or less what you'd call that. He didn't make no living at it; it's just a hobby. It probably cost him as much to go out and back [from Pickens] as he made.

But the store had a tremendous impact on Alice Flowers and her friends. "On the side of the store," Ms. Flowers recalled,

> there was plywood and he would push it up and put a stick in under it, and that's where you went and ordered your Coke and pack of crackers. And he had a jukebox. Man, if I danced to that jukebox! And our favorite was "In the jungle, the quiet jungle, the lion sleeps tonight."[12] We would borrow money to

11 For a photo of the store, see Claudia Whitmire Hembree, *Jocassee Valley* (Pickens, SC: Hiott Printing Company, 2003), 95.

12 First line of "The Lion Sleeps Tonight" by the Tokens, from 1961, but originally written by Solomon Linda (from South Africa) and recorded as "Mbube"

> play that and then we would – we'd dance. We'd all get out there and dance, and that was our hangout in the summer time. . . . My sister Doris and her boyfriend (whom she married) . . . had like a '39 or a '40 Chevrolet or something, you know, and when we turned into the Girls' Camp [in Jocassee Valley] he stopped. We all piled out and piled *on* the car, you know. No fun to drive up there in his car. So he would *fly*, and we would be holding on to the back windows! Or you know, or standing on the running boards, or up on the – if you were really lucky and got there first you could sit on the rounded fenders up front.[13] But we'd do it. Like somebody would drive one time and we'd float down on inner tubes and then we'd go back and we'd do it again! . . . And then we'd stop and get our pack of crackers and Coke and dance. And it was just wonderful. It was *wonderful*! It was heaven. . . . No roughnecks, no fighting; you didn't have to worry about anything. You just went up there and enjoyed the day.

As a teenager, Donna Trask helped her father manage another very popular country store in northern Pickens County. She remembered:

> when I was a teenager, I spent a lot of time working in it. . . . We pretty much did everything. . . . Sometimes I'd cook. . . . We had like a snack bar. Short order, I guess. . . . On the weekends and holidays there would be people coming to the lake [Jocassee or Keowee], going to Table Rock, or going up to the Wilds.[14] . . . We had lots of people that would come in, go over there and sit down by the fireplace and they'd stay – that was their habit. Or sit outside. . . . So it was kind of neat for us because then we got to know people in the community. You know, I had known people in the community my age, but this was – this kind of broadened that for me. And I remember it better than any of my other siblings, I guess, 'cause I was the oldest. But you know, even all the way up to Rocky Bottom, we had customers that . . . never left their house I don't guess and would call in an order, and we'd pack it up and somebody'd come by and pick it up and take it up there.

Nancy Abney Daniels frequents that store occasionally and agreed that it "is another way that people get to know each other." But then her young adult son interjected: "Especially guys," to which Mrs. Daniels admitted: "That's a guy thing, yes. . . . I hardly ever go. Yes, I may go in and get, you know, a loaf of bread every once in awhile, but now [my son and] . . . my husband, oh, yes, they

---

by his group, the Singing Birds.

13 A 1939 Chevrolet coupe had wide flat front fenders and running boards.

14 This could be a reference to "The Wilds," a Christian camp in Brevard, North Carolina.

probably – [my husband] goes to the store every morning probably before he goes to work. My dad [Peter Abney] visited the store every day. When he died, they sent over biscuits. I mean the store is like a huge part of the community." And if a person lives in this area, Mrs. Daniels added, everybody simply calls the place "the store." If someone says they are going to the store, she explained, everyone knows the person is not going to a chain grocery store in a larger community, but to this crossroads community gathering place.

Nancy Daniels's son Edward offered more details:

> There's a little café part, and they just sit there [Nancy Daniels laughs] and drink a drink. They just sit there and talk or even hang out on the porch. And that's about it. And talk about, like if it's like bear season – that's a *huge* week. And the store is just packed out all the time that week and they're just sitting there. I don't know if they're lying or what about what they ran or killed or whatever. But that's about all you do is you sit there and talk. But a lot of people like it.

Mrs. Daniels added that her brother, like a lot of community men, will visit the store and "eat breakfast and stuff like that. My dad would, even though [his wife] tried to put him on diets, he would sneak over there and eat! . . . That's just part of being like a man in this community. They're just going to go to the store." Ryan Trask, also an occasional customer, concurred, observing that "you can go any morning and just eat breakfast and sit there long enough. And a lot of the same people are still there. The old timers are gone but it's still – it's still a vibrant general store, country store, for people in the local community."

As with other stores, the owners of this store also needed to be generous with credit toward their customers. Ryan Trask reminded his wife that her family "had to provide a lot of credit, I mean, you – you had the books of ledgers, keeping up what people owed you." Donna Trask agreed: "Yeah, we inherited like, I guess, the guy that had owned that store for probably, I don't know, twenty, thirty years maybe when we bought it from him. He had a certain amount of people that he gave credit to. So when we, you know, we just kind of inherited that and that was fine. It wasn't a big deal. We kept it on index cards and a[n] index box."

Rural Life – Country Churches

Another community place that served both as a locus of stories and as a source of them was the church. While multiple denominations (and sometimes multiple churches in the same denomination) served the larger cities, fewer buildings and fewer denominations could be found in the rural communities. Churches not only serviced the souls of attendees, but they also acted as social centers. Many community activities swirled around the buildings and their congregations, as the following stories attest.

Kayla Radcliffe, a college student at the time of her interview, described how important the church was for rural communities in the area:

> It's like the culture to go to church. If you don't go to church you're like, oh man, that's weird. You know, you don't go to church. Like, who are you? So, you get all these people in there and they're not always there because they're religious. They're there because they grew up there. . . . I think that it's almost like a social thing. Because the people I knew in high school – that was their social life – going. . . . Well, in ours, the main social thing like before and after, you go and people'd get there thirty minutes before it starts and just stand in the foyer and talk. There are men who stand out there the entire thirty minutes and just talk to people as they come in – it's not their job, they just do it. And then afterwards, another thirty minutes afterwards, people are just talking and talking. And the families within the church are usually related. . . . And in youth group we would go separate from the congregation during service and have activities and that sort of thing, so there was a lot of bonding going on there.

Kayla Radcliffe's friend Jason Taylor, attending a different denomination in an adjacent county, described his activities after church:

> We used to always play football after church. Or after we would eat we'd play football. And then I had two of my friends I grew up in church with – they're best friends – that I'd always, we'd always try to talk our parents into going to each other's houses after church. Now we just go home after church. You don't try to run off too soon. You might stick around for a little bit and talk to each other, 'cause I mean, with the youths, it's like you grew up together in church and then it's like, you probably don't hang out too much but you still have stuff to talk about after church. So it's like, the old people that sit there like my mom and other people would talk until like one o'clock after church. And now we're trying, we're starting to do that 'cause we don't see each other as much, so we have more to talk about and get caught up on.

One very common annual church activity was a revival, often extending over several days with multiple preachers, some singing groups, and an expectation of salvation.[15] Many inhabitants remembered revivals, typically held in late summer. Brenda Kendrick described those from her childhood:

15 See Coggeshall, *Carolina Piedmont Country*, 145–58.

> And it was – I don't know why, but it was always in August at the, you know, heat of the summer, in that little white church that we used to have up at Salem [Oconee County]. . . . Well, you'd get a preacher come in, you know from outside, and it was more of a, I guess you'd call it "down home gospel preaching." I can remember, you know, it was, well, like the "hellfire and brimstone" kind of thing, back when I was a child. I don't know if they were trying to get you to walk the aisle and give yourself to the Lord or scare you to death! It was a little different than it is now. . . . And some of those pastors probably, I know a lot of them, especially mountain pastors back then, they had no formal training as a pastor; they just read the Bible and they preached strictly from the Bible. This is what it says, and this is how it is, and that's it. You know, which I have seen grown men go down that aisle crying. You know, you can feel the Presence there, all the time.

As a child, Rachel Edwards sang in a traveling gospel group with her family, and they received a request to sing at what became a very well-known revival in Eastatoee Valley, in upper Pickens County (the same revival where Harry Edison's father gave up moonshining):

> And my dad got a call about the revival if we would come and sing. My dad was very hesitant. . . . He said, "that's some mean people up there"; said, "they're bootleggers and chicken fighters, and I've had to go up there [as a deputy sheriff] several times for murderers." . . . Well, my mother said (she's got the strong faith), she said, "If you're doing God's work, He's going to take care of you. I don't have nothing to worry about." . . . So the revival started, and it lasted six weeks. And the bootleggers, a lot of them got religion, and the chicken fighters, and they changed their ways. And they had a big baptizing at . . . a fishing lake at that time. Five thousand people turned out for this baptizing [JMC: Wow!], and we also had three gentlemen that were known for their liquor. . . . They were huge men, over 350 pounds some of them, and it took three or four preachers to get them under, immerse them under the water, they were just so huge. I don't know if the turnout of people was to see this happen, or what, but it was amazing, this revival.[16]

Brenda Kendrick described what it felt like to be immersed in bodies of water outdoors rather than a baptismal pool inside a building:

> I've always been afraid of the water. I don't swim, I can't swim; I've always been afraid of water. Of course that river [Little River], it might not be deep, but the river's really dark and you

16 For a description of the Eastatoee Revival, see Hembree, *Jocassee Valley*, 175.

> can't see too well. And I think there were about five or six of us maybe that day and we had to walk down to the bank, and then there was a rock there. You kind of stepped on the rock; . . . my foot missed that rock. I thought I was gonna get baptized before I actually went under, and that terrified me. And the pastor (he was such a sweet gentleman), and he caught me and he said, "Now, steady girl, you're not quite ready yet!" . . . You don't usually hear of a lot of baptisms on rivers or lakes or anything like that; it's usually baptismal pools in the church, but it's just the – to me, it's just kind of a special time if you are baptized out like that. To me it makes it more spiritual, more, I don't know, it's just something different about it. Maybe that's how I was raised and that's what I saw growing up, but it's just a special time if you go to a river bank, stand there and maybe sing "Shall We Gather at the River" while somebody's being baptized.[17]

Another major annual church activity was a homecoming,[18] significant for a number of reasons. Homecomings emphasized and synthesized the Southern cultural importance of several dominant symbols: home, faith, family, and food. Kayla Radcliffe described homecomings from her church:

> Those were like– those were big mostly 'cause of the food, because people could cook really good. But I guess they may've been more of an element for the people who were older, because when I was going to them, I was like a preteen and stuff like that. So I was just there for the food. And I guess the significance of it? Yeah, I think I missed a lot of that. . . . Well, we always had ours in the – we called it the Fellowship Building. And it was actually the old church. It was built in like 1940 or something, so it was a tiny, tiny building. . . . And they tried to fit like 200, 250 people in there, so what it ended up being is that they just hoped that they picked a good Sunday for it so everyone could sit outside after they got their food. And there'd be a service where it was Homecoming, older people would come back who had gone to be at other churches and stuff like that. And usually, I mean, it was a pretty big thing, because the people at the church, they were really proud of how far the church had come from being in a small building, and from being unrefined, I guess. . . . But the afterward part is the part I look forward to, 'cause of the food. And like each

17 In a separate interview, when discussing traditional riverine baptizing, an African American congregation spontaneously began singing "Take Me to the River," because the discussion brought back favorite memories. See John M. Coggeshall, *Liberia, South Carolina: An African American Appalachian Community* (Chapel Hill: University of North Carolina Press, 2018), 146.

18 Coggeshall, *Carolina Piedmont Country*, 154–57.

Figure 10: Picnic.
Rogers Collection, Digital Collections file, Pickens County Library System.

> family had this dish that they were specialized in. Like, I still remember this lady; . . . she has the best beef roast *ever*. Wow! Like, you'd always look forward to Homecoming when she would bring her crock pot roast. It was amazing. And you just hoped you got in the front of the line so you could get some of it before it was all gone. And like my mom always made macaroni and cheese, and certain people would always make certain things, and you'd know what to look forward to. And then mostly the older people got to sit inside, like at the tables and stuff, and then the kids and some of the younger adults would be outside, and we'd eat, and just play around. And then like, most of the women help with the cleaning up. . . . And honestly? I think the men like maybe took out the trash or something, but for the most part, they [the women] were like, you know, get out of here!

Although shortened for families with weekly wage earners, homecomings and revivals continue in the region today, still generating the fervor of old-time gatherings. Homes now might be brick bungalows, air-conditioned and focused on the TV room, but extended families still gather at grandparents' homes for Sunday dinners and tell stories about family. Small, family-owned country stores have been replaced almost completely by standardized quick-market gas stations or supermarkets in towns, but if the gas stations still provide a place for eating and sitting, people still gather and tell stories. In other words, the stages for performances may have changed over time, but the scripts continue to be written, produced, and performed by the next generations of actors.

Chapter Seven

"We Learned the Old Way": Stories About Schools

Another significant social institution experienced by everyone with whom I spoke was school. Although inhabitants varied from having an incomplete grade school education to having advanced university degrees, they had all experienced some form of state-sponsored education. Depending upon their age, some inhabitants had attended one-room schools in outlying rural areas prior to consolidation in the 1950s. African Americans were forced to attend segregated (and inferior) schools until South Carolina's desegregation in the late 1960s. Recreational activities after school and on weekends differed by decade and depended upon transportation and income, among other variables. Despite the vast distinctions between a clapboard one-room school in the South Carolina mountains and an air-conditioned and professionally taught school at the county seat, those who attended remembered stories from their school days, often including the names of favorite or feared teachers and administrators. Since I often asked interviewees about their school experiences, I collected some informative and entertaining stories.

Grade Schools

Prior to consolidation in the 1950s and located generally within a child's walking distance (perhaps several miles, though) were numerous grade schools, typically consisting of one or two rooms and serving the local community of closely related families. These schools contained six grades and could be taught by one or two teachers. Josephine Chavis taught in such a

Figure 11: Oolenoy School.
People and Places - Pickens Area, Digital Collections file, Pickens County Library System.

school in upper Oconee County, where "I had all the grades for two years" in one room. In order to teach and to maintain discipline, Mrs. Chavis explained, "you can put one group to work and go to another group and get another group going."[1]

Bruce Anderson described his childhood school, also in upper Oconee County:

> We had six grades. And three of them was in each room! The first year I was out, there was two in each room, and then it shrunk a little bit and they were able to put three grades per room. . . . The rooms were probably forty by sixty [feet]. . . . We'd have ten, fifteen people in each class; we'd have forty-five people in the classroom, something like that. Edith Phillips was my teacher in the first and second grade. And then Bessy Matheson . . . she taught me in the third and fourth grade, and Miss Irene Willbanks, . . . she taught me in the fifth and sixth grades. . . . It was just a little country school. Everybody knew everybody. Every class had a certain time for certain subjects

1 See also John M. Coggeshall, *Liberia, South Carolina: An African American Appalachian Community* (Chapel Hill: University of North Carolina Press, 2018), 147–52, for a similar African American experience.

> that they taught, and not only did you get to listen to your stuff but you got to listen to the stuff that was being taught for the next grade, and the next grade on up, and you kind of learned a little things ahead of time.

During her interview, Julie Jackson recalled her favorite teacher:

> I can still hear her voice. I can hear her teaching us. I can hear her reading to us. . . . She's been dead for years. But I can still hear her. . . . She had a strong voice, you know. And she . . . read books to us that we – she would read, if we'd be good, you know, and do what she said. . . . But she read three or four chapters of *Black Beauty*, or three or four chapters of *Huckleberry Finn*, *Tom Sawyer*, which we probably never would have read on our own, unless she made us. . . . But she did that every day when we came back in from recess. That was a cooling down period I suspect now that I can look back on it. But we'd play and run, and you know she'd bring us back in and read to us for about thirty minutes or maybe a little bit longer.

In many rural communities, a local church doubled as the schoolhouse.[2] As Garvin Bradshaw explained, "they'd have church . . . Sunday morning in it. And they'd have school through the week in it. And they'd teach six classes in that room there." In some church/school buildings, such as McKinney Chapel in Oconee County, the backs of the pews were slats. Jesse Alexander told a humorous story about "a big old long-legged boy" who "got his leg all twisted" in one of the pews during school. "Said they had to help him get untangled," Mr. Alexander added.

Even if the schools were in a separate building, the two local institutions frequently intertwined, as Deborah Mitchell explained:

> And we started each day with Bible reading and a prayer. And in August they had a revival meeting at the church across the road. And we would go to the revival meeting in the mornings. They had a morning service and an afternoon service, and we would go over for that. That was part of our instruction, you know. And that was very informative for all of us. We look back now – I've talked to some of the kids that were in school, and how important that was for us, in establishing our Christian principles, and establishing our Christian faith, and that kind of thing.

These rural schoolhouses frequently had no indoor plumbing and rather poor heating. Garvin Bradshaw described his Oconee County school: "It had a wood heater in it. We toted our water up from the spring about a three

2 See Coggeshall, *Liberia*, 101–2, for another example.

hundred yards down below it. It had a[n] outhouse – girls' outhouse on one side and the boys' outhouse on the other side." Joseph Yeats worked for his rural school. "I made a little money. I built fires, two heaters [the school] had for the winter, and . . . two teachers would give me a dime apiece; I was making twenty cents a week. Go to school an hour early, I'd build fires in two heaters. . . . And another thing – that little old school . . . didn't have a well. There were days where I had to walk down to the local store and get water and the entire school drank out of two dippers and two buckets."

Before roads were paved and before families had multiple vehicles, school children walked – another reason for the small, scattered, community rural schools. "But there wasn't no traffic or anything on the road," James York explained, "so it wasn't no problem." Garvin Bradshaw recalled some of his challenges in upper Oconee County. One year it had snowed, presenting Mr. Bradshaw's sister with an attendance problem, but the schoolteacher's husband "toted her in that day, snow on the ground. He toted her in on his shoulders." In upper Pickens County in the late 1920s, Robert Davidson "had a long ways to walk – most of the people had a long ways to walk to go in there. We was walking about four mile. And there was other people coming the other way a-walking as far as we was."

In the narrow Jocassee Valley (upper Oconee County), "school was about three or four miles down the river," Joan Randall recalled; "lots of times the road was under water and then we couldn't cross the river" to attend school. Her former neighbor, Douglas Edison, explained:

> But the road was almost as low as the river bed, so it didn't take a lot of water till the river would get out in the road. And Miss Mary Wiggington was the teacher. She lived at the head of the valley. And when it got – you know, had a lot of floods and what not, we didn't have school, for she couldn't make it to school. Then they was some that lived across the river, on down on Keowee, that come to school by boat. . . . And when . . . the river would get up, they'd be afraid to paddle that little old boat on that swift water. One of the girls, I remember, would spend the night with my sister a lot, you know – they was in the same grade, and she'd just spend the night with us.

Teachers, too, struggled to attend school, especially in the upper mountains. Elizabeth Nelson explained that her father taught school in the 1930s so far into the Jocassee Gorges area that "he would walk across the mountains for ten miles to the schoolhouse and board Monday through Friday and then on the weekends walk back home." In a separate interview, Harry Edison added that Nelson's father "would walk through these mountains with a flashlight, I guess 'fore daylight, and go back in there and stay till Friday night, and he'd walk back by flashlight on Friday night. Back out of there to where he lived with his mom and dad before he married." "Take enough groceries with him to last him a week," Norman Cleveland added. "Three hundred fifty dollar a year was all he made teaching school." Another teacher, Bradshaw recalled, drove "an old gray mule and a buggy" to school, while Brian Alexander's grandfather slung old military saddlebags over a mule and rode eight miles up to teach school at McKinney Chapel (upper Pickens County) in the 1920s.

In these smaller schools, discipline might be swift and physical. For example, Bruce Anderson attended a two-room school, also in upper Oconee County:

> And my aunt, my mother's sister, was my teacher, and she showed me no mercy! If I did something wrong, I still got a spanking. But those were days in school that, you know, if you did something wrong, you were disciplined. Not beat, but disciplined. . . . I think that's real important to young people growing up, is to know what discipline is. . . . And they say education is better but, you know, we learned the old way.

"I remember my teacher was Pearl Chastain," Charles Watson recalled, and continued: "she'd teach one class and she'd give you a bunch of homework, study material, and then she'd go to the next class and be teaching them, and you'd better be doing your study material. She called up her big fat hand – boy, she could lay blisters with it!" David Nelson, a pupil in a one-room school in upper Pickens County, described a situation where one unfortunate student, probably in a household with illiterate parents, struggled to read and write. To motivate him, Mr. Nelson reported, the teacher "would whip him, in the room, among the children. Just whip him and [the child] would just beg him to stop. He'd a-beat him like everything and kept us all scared to death of him."

At that time, David Nelson noted, "it was not unusual for grown people to not be able to read. It was not unusual at all." For example, Claudia Alexander admitted that her father "couldn't read a lick. My mother had to stand there and read every letter and every bill 'cause they didn't have any education. My mom or my dad they like went to school, maybe just a couple of years. The mail come, you know he would say, 'Read this, old woman.' . . . And she would read him the mail, or something like that." Mrs. Alexander's father eventually learned to read in his seventies, as he finally "got saved" and baptized. "He had such a hunger to read God's Word," Mrs. Alexander explained, "that he would sit and read, and he really (with God's help) learned how to read. Before he died at the age of eighty-three . . . he had learned how to read just about anything he wanted to in the Bible. . . . To learn how to *read* at seventy years old by hisself just sitting and pronouncing syllables, you know, that was amazing." Garvin Bradshaw, Mrs. Alexander's older brother, also struggled to get a grade school education, as he admitted: "I never did get no schooling. Third grade's all I ever got. . . . I had to stay home and help my daddy. All the schooling I got I learned in the woods staying lost. I never did get no schooling like these girls out here did," gesturing toward his younger sister and his daughter. Robert Davidson attended school until his father was killed during the Depression, "and I never did get to go to school no more. After that, well, then I had to go to work."

Because students might have to drop out for a year or two to help their struggling families, or because the quality of instruction might have been poor, students of varied ages might be in the same grade. For example, at Holly Springs School (Pickens County), Charles Watson admitted, "I went to school with some of them that got to go vote. I think then (if I ain't mistaken) the voting age was twenty-one," and the voters "were still in grammar school. You can imagine how big they looked to a little fella like me!" Higher up in the Pickens County mountains, Harry Edison had heard from his father that his great-grandfather "was dating the schoolteacher. She was probably about sixteen or seventeen years old; he was about fourteen!"

Cafeteria times were also fondly recalled. For example, in his Oconee County school, John Summers remembered lunch time: "We paid a nickel to eat lunch," he recalled, and women came to the school to prepare the food while classes were in session. "And boy, you talk about eating. We was just kids; we could smell that food cooking, you know. And boy, we sure done some eating." In Deborah Mitchell's Oconee County school,

> I remember the neatest thing that happened was that somewhere, . . . maybe when I was in the fourth or fifth grade, that somehow they got a lunchroom program. And they had a lady that came in and cooked our lunch for us. And we thought that was the greatest thing in the world, you know, was to have this lunch program. . . . I remember that they'd have little boxes of raisins, and they'd give us extra things and we'd take them home; we just thought that was wonderful. I never see a box of raisins today that every now and then I don't think about that.

And then there was recess! "And if it was a-raining or anything, and we couldn't get outside to play," Anne Flowers recalled, "why, we'd always play games in the school." She and her husband tried to recall a game where a boy and a girl would step out of the room, think of a name for themselves, and then other children would try to guess what they were. "And ever-who guessed what it was, why then they would be 'it,'" Mrs. Flowers continued. "And we'd . . . go out in the woods and play," Margaret York remembered. "That's all we had to do, make our playhouses, the little girls did," she continued; "we'd have little broke pieces of glass or something and that was our tea set, you know!"

Figure 12: Oolenoy School Children.
Sims Collection, Digital Collections file, Pickens County Library System.

"And us boys would go out and cut us a crooked stick with a limb on it and that'd be our car and we'd run around [with that]," her husband, James, added. "That was the days when nobody would've ever thought it'd come down to guns in school and killing people, you know; it was good old times," Mrs. York concluded.

The Yorks elaborated on other childhood or recess games. Mrs. York mentioned "'Tag,' 'Ring Around the Rosie,'[3] and 'Hopscotch' and what we called 'Annie Over' – that'd be throw the ball. One group get on this side of the building and the other group on the other side of the building and we throwed the ball to each other." Mr. York continued: "'Annie Over' – that was like a baseball game now. Throw that ball over the building." "And you didn't know when if you was on the side, when it was gonna come at," Mrs. York explained; "if you caught it then you done good, we thought." Children at Deborah Mitchell's school played the game as well, "but boy, if you were on the lower side of that building toward the road, you had a lot of running to do. I guarantee you, we probably weren't any problem at school because we wore ourselves out at recess playing!"

Deborah Mitchell described several other children's games, such as "Drop the Handkerchief":

> Well, . . . all the children are in a circle, and one person has a handkerchief. And one child is running around with that handkerchief in their hand, and let's say they drop it behind

3 W. W. Newell, *Games and Songs of American Children* (New York: Dover, 1963, orig. pub. 1903), 127–28.

> you. Okay, then what you've got to do, is you've got to run – and you may not even know it's dropped – you've got to run and tag that person around that circle. . . . And then when you tag them, then you'd run around, and you'd have to drop it for someone else and then you run as fast as you can. And then we played "Dodgeball." . . . Ooh, that's a hard – you've got some big boys, that's a – I bet you know about "Dodgeball," don't you? And then we'd play a game called "Red Rover": "Red Rover, Red Rover, send [Deborah] over" and you'd try to break through those hands. Wow! That was a dangerous one with the big boys!

The oldest couple that I interviewed, Joshua and Anne Flowers, described box suppers and "cake walks," traditional activities from their school years early in the twentieth century. When I mentioned that most people might not know what those activities were, Anne Flowers agreed, and elaborated:

> Well, they'd have box suppers. The girls – now over there at [her one-room school], back then, they taught 'bout to the tenth grade over there. And they was strong girls, you know, going to school over there. Well, they would fix boxes and fix lunch, you know. They'd have fried chicken and everything. And then the boys would bid them off. . . . And ever who [*sic*] got the box, then, them and the girl that had made it would go off and sit down and eat it. . . . That's the way they'd raise money, you know, for the school. . . . Then they'd have a cake walk. And we would – they'd start up the music and we'd walk around the house – around the school building. And whenever the music stopped, ever who [*sic*] was standing on the line got the cake. . . . They'd just draw a line, you know. And who would stand on the line would get the cake. . . . Oh, they would be a good crowd, bunch of them, you know. Boys and girls who didn't go to school would be there. . . . But they weren't supposed to know, you know, whose boxes they was, but some of them'd slip around, you know, and find out.

Many inhabitants reflected fondly on their years in one-room schools. "And you know as it turns out, we were just, our education was just as good," Julie Jackson said; "we had just as much coming out of [her school] as they did coming out of a mill hill school and the other schools, when we had tests and when we got evaluated. So you know, we didn't lose anything by going to a two-room school. I don't think." "Probably, as a matter of fact, we did better," her neighbor, Shirley Patterson, added, and elaborated: "I think it helped us to strive to get to where we are with our accomplishments that we have done now."

Despite the potential benefits of these tiny rural schools, the state of

South Carolina began rural consolidation in the 1950s, by busing children to larger multiroom schools. "Jocassee [Valley] School had gotten way down in attendance, and that's, of course, the reason it was consolidated," Deborah Mitchell observed. But, she continued, the community had already lost the post office, and now the school, and she wondered if the reason many people refused to sign the petition to close the school was because "they felt like . . . they were really truly losing their identity and community, you know?" Reflecting on more recent potential consolidations, Brenda Kendrick added: "I don't know if that would be a good thing. The school, I think, is about a part of a community, but I think you have to think about the education for the child. When you think about keeping the school or getting rid of it, would it be better for the child to go to a larger school?"

In Oconee County, several schools condensed into one in the small community of Salem. Brenda Kendrick described the school:

> When I went to school there, . . . the high school and the grammar school was in one building. The grammar school was on one end, the high school was on the other. I remember in seventh grade, I think there was maybe thirty-something people in the seventh grade, . . . and we graduated eleven. Some of them did miss grades and graduate later, some of them dropped out, some of them went to service, you know. But there was eleven or twelve that graduated with me that year, and those of us that are still living, we try to get together once about every two to three months and have lunch. . . . We were *all* close friends. We still are, even boys and girls.

"I've had some wonderful teachers" at that school, Mrs. Kendrick recalled:

> I can remember in the third grade at school, Miss Estelle Nickelson was my teacher. . . . What impressed me most about her was she waited at the door when you went into school, in the room every morning. She always hugged your neck and told you that she loved you. . . . Every morning we had Scripture lesson before we started school. . . . She made us memorize Scripture verses, and one time she wanted us to memorize a psalm. And I remember I memorized the first psalm and had to stand up before class, and at that time I was a really shy child. I didn't like to say much, but you had to stand up in class and recite this; I never will forget that. . . . I had some really wonderful teachers at church and at school, at Salem.

The benefit of living in town was the availability of after-school activities, as Mrs. Kendrick explained: "A friend of mine that I was friends with all through school, her dad had this little store downtown and of course the school was right there close, and we'd go down there. They'd let us walk downtown, you know, sometimes if we had some reason to go. You could take a nickel and buy a huge bar of candy at that time."

By the early 1950s, several Pickens County rural schools had consolidated into Holly Springs Elementary School, attended by Nancy Daniels:

> Then you just had one grade for each class because I guess there were maybe two hundred students there. There could be as many as thirty in a class. There was no kindergarten. There was just first through sixth grade at that time. I can still name every teacher. I was a very quiet, shy little girl! But I made friends then that I'm still friends with; some who still live right here in the community. . . . But at Holly Springs it was [a] very strict little school at that time. . . . We had a very strict principal back in my growing up years. . . . And, of course, teachers could paddle. I had one teacher that, my first-grade teacher, who I dearly loved. But she would take a little string and tie you to your seat if you'd been up too much, and if you broke your string you got a paddling. But, for some reason I was never afraid of her. She was – I *loved* her. And I never broke my string! I was one of those good little girls that always, you know, set [sit], and did what I was supposed to do.

Elizabeth Nelson attended the same school several years later:

> The kids were from . . . rural communities around in northern Pickens County. There were no wealthy families that had kids in the schools. . . . Some of their parents did work in the cotton mills, so we were all about on the same economic level. And we all grew up in the country with bare feet, playing outdoors. . . . Those were very good years. Had good teachers; they were mostly older people. I don't remember having any young teachers like we do now. . . . We had no male teachers; no male teachers. And our principal was Miss Katie Hendricks, an old maid. . . . And she was this *tiny* little lady with salt-and-pepper hair. She used to wear these little cotton shirtwaist dresses that almost came down to her ankles. And she was hyperactive. She was always moving at a hundred miles an hour and she would spank you in a heartbeat! Everybody was afraid of Miss Katie! Oh! But she ruled with a strict hand and everybody minded, most of the time. We had very few incidents of misbehavior – significant misbehavior.

Attending Holly Springs School several decades later, Beth Lepre had very similar memories:

> We had a principal named Miss Katie Hendricks, and she was like really tiny. Like probably four feet, eighty-something pounds, and she was really tough. I mean, she . . . did the paddling. And

> I mean, she would think nothing about taking us, and some of the sixth grade boys were big and probably older, because back then a lot of the boys did still miss some days of school to help on a farm . . . so some of them were probably older in the sixth grade. But it didn't faze her to take them to the office and paddle them. So she was tough.

While generally avoiding punishment, Elizabeth Nelson confessed to one memorable transgression, running afoul of the same first-grade teacher as Mrs. Daniels:

> I remember in the first grade I had a couple of – learning experiences. They had us sitting in little rows beside each other and [a neighbor girl] was sitting to my right and she said, "Here, pinch me as hard as you can. It won't hurt." On her arm; and I said, "No. I don't wanna do that." And she said, "Come on. Do it. Pinch me as hard as you can. I promise it won't hurt." And I said, "No. I don't wanna do that." Well, she kept on and kept on. And finally I did it. Well, Miss Ida May Simmons, our teacher, saw me. It didn't bother [my friend]. She didn't cry or scream or anything, but both of us got to spend one day inside for recess instead of getting to go out to recess. And what she did to us – this was very unique – she tied our hands to the back of our little chairs with sewing thread and if we broke it, then we got a paddling. And so we knew we better not break that sewing thread! And we didn't!

Elizabeth Nelson also remembered a type of writing paper familiar to many of us from that generation:

> We had writing pads. The paper wasn't really white. It had blue lines. Some of them – every other line was a solid line and in between that was a dotted line. And that's how we learned to write our ABCs. The capital letters went from solid to solid line and, of course, the lowercase went from the solid line on the bottom to the dotted lines. And we used these large pencils that did not have erasers. . . . If you made a mistake and you wanted to get rid of it, you wet the tip of your finger with your tongue and then you wiped it off that way. That was our eraser!

Artistic creations seemed to be Elizabeth Nelson's forte:

> I remember the very first day in first grade. . . . And they'd let us sit in the room and color with crayons, which I dearly loved. I had a picture of a duck. Not a real duck, but like a rubber duck. I colored it bright aqua blue and it had an orange bill, because I thought that was pretty. . . . That was my first experience in school. . . . And in the third grade, Miss Alma Grant was my

> teacher. She was my favorite teacher in that whole school. I liked them all, but she was my favorite. And I was kind of a teacher's pet. And she would buy these borders, picture borders, to go all the way around the wall, two walls, in the room. And she always let me take them home and color them. That was a treat. I loved to do that! And for some reason – . . . I would get I think aggravated. Probably some boy was sitting next to me irritating me or something. But I'd get aggravated and I would ask if I would could go into the big walk-in coat closet and do my work during class. And they would let me do it. They probably thought I was crazy.

"And the food!" Elizabeth Nelson continued; "we didn't have junk food when I was in elementary school." Instead, she continued:

> We had the ladies – the cafeteria ladies that prepared our food every day. And they were local people's mothers! We knew them and it was all good food. Except – well, in elementary school we had – you can count on the same thing on the same day of the week each week. But it was all good. Wednesday was one of my favorite days. We would have homemade vegetable soup and the sandwiches would have peanut butter and honey and raisins mixed together – very nice. And then we'd have an apple.

Elizabeth Nelson also remembered recess:

> We didn't have all the amenities they have now. We had the big tall swings, which we loved. And we had seesaws and I think that's the only equipment we had. We played softball a lot. They would not let us sit down at all. You had to be active. You had to be up and moving. And then they didn't have a fence around it [the recreation field] then. So on the northern side up this way there was lots of bushes and honeysuckle and stuff. And a bunch of them got out in there and cleared out a bunch of that to play in; and got in trouble of course, at the same time. I never did go out in that. But usually we were on the swings. That was my favorite. I liked playing softball, too. . . . And we all played and we were all active. Nobody sat down.

Several decades later, Kayla Radcliffe attended the same grade school and played on the same playground, with slightly different cultural changes:

> We had a really big playground. . . . It's like three acres, it's *huge*. . . . And the creek was always a constant source of amazement, because we couldn't touch it because we weren't supposed to get wet. . . . And a lot of it was just little games. I mean a lot of the girls, they would congregate together. There were the "girlie" girls, the ones who liked to braid each other's hair and that sort

> of thing, and they'd stick together. And then the guys, they would try – there was a lot of soccer. We loved soccer as little kids and then we grew up and we're like "football!" I mean, soccer was really cool because, I think it was because we could play it easier. All you had to do was kick the ball, whereas football you have to know how to throw it, you have to know how to catch it. . . . And tackling wasn't allowed, so that wasn't as exciting as kicking someone who had the ball!

As with inhabitants from earlier generations, Kayla Radcliffe reflected on the quality of her primary education at Holly Springs School:

> In fifth grade, we had really good teachers. . . . And I remember I had Miss Smith and Miss Duncan. And Miss Smith was all for applying for like national competitions. . . . And the year before my class, they had tried this new thing where they were applying for this national book competition where the class writes and illustrates the book and they see if they can get it published and they did. They won this national competition. So my class did it and we won it, too. I actually did the illustration for the book and then we all wrote it together and it was really cool and we're like, "We're awesome!" Then they won it again.[4] So that was something to look forward to, I think, was getting in the fifth grade and having the cool teachers and getting to do things like that. So I think they made us feel really – they made us feel important even though we weren't in the most important places, that we could do things that were noticed by other people.

"Holly Springs was a really good school," Beth Lepre summarized; "we were well prepared when we got to junior high."

Despite being academically well prepared, however, children from smaller rural schools often had significant social adjustments when paired with students from other rural areas or even small cities. "Now when we went to middle school" or junior high, Beth Lepre observed, "it was quite frightening because, you know, we'd never been around that many kids and changing classes, so it was kind of traumatic for some of us." According to Mrs. Lepre, one significant change was the increase in field trips, and she remembered one unforgettable trip to Clemson University, the state's land-grant university, "to see the cow that I think, if I remember this, and I hope I'm not imagining this, that they had the cow that you – it had its stomach open and you could see its digestion. Seriously, I remember that."

4 One of these publications, "We're on Our Way to See King Bear," is still available: https://www.amazon.com/Were-Our-Way-King-Bear/dp/0439150124, accessed July 9, 2024.

Harry Edison also remembered a significant learning event from his middle school years:

> When I was in eighth grade, . . . we'd always have gym and . . . when we got through taking a shower every day we had to put our towels in this hamper. We went in one morning and the coach says, "Okay, somebody left a towel on the floor – who was it?" And nobody said anything. . . . So every class he had that day he made us bend over in our underwear against our lockers and he used this razor strap, belt, and he hit every one of us. And I had that imprint of that on my rear for about three days and . . . families went in and complained about that. But I remember I was proud of my first cousin. He was a couple of years older than me. . . . He was in my class. He looked, he says, "I did not leave that on the floor and you're not going to use that on me." And he [the coach] says, "Get on out here." So he ran him out, but my cousin just stood up against him. He wouldn't take the punishment. You just couldn't imagine somebody, a teacher doing that this day and time, could you?

Unfortunately for that same coach, Harry Edison lamented the fact that his junior high football team had not taken advantage of the strength and skills of his rural friends:

> Back when I started school in the eighth grade we had a really good football team, but like my tenth, eleventh, twelfth grade we only won about three ball games the whole time. And I think about some of these guys that I grew up with – we played cow pasture football. Now, boy, I tell you, you talk about rough. Now we played over here at my uncle's house, and broke arm, broke collar bone, stuff like that. We played some rough football, you know. It's all cow pastures then, but some of these guys, they would've been great football players at Pickens but they just didn't go out. I know this one guy, . . . boy, he was so good. He got a year behind me 'cause he failed like the seventh or eighth grade but every time he's over there at the junior high and he went out for football. And they said in practice he would just run all over everyone. And the coach just jumped all over him; the coach said, "You got to follow your blocking." He says, "You want me to follow blocking or you want me to score a touchdown?" And he said, "I want you to follow blocking," and he said, "I'm through!" so he quit.

High Schools and High School Activities

Inhabitants' stories about their high school experiences varied by almost a century in time, and so their stories described a range of institutions and activities, from small rural schools before public transportation, to modern countywide places where many students had their own vehicles. As schools increased in size and their territorial draws expanded, young adults with varied backgrounds came together, often recognizing social differences. After-school activities also changed, from having to do farm chores to participating in social clubs or athletics. High school sports rivalries grew in community importance. With an improvement in roads, an increase in personal transportation, a growth in family income, and an expansion in leisure time came a concomitant modification to teenage social activities. While I did not ask everyone about their high school experiences, some inhabitants elaborated. For a few people, their experiences were so entertaining to me that I asked them to expand even further.

Before families had multiple automobiles, and before public school buses deployed, some inhabitants boarded with relatives or friends in town because of the distance from their rural homes to towns. For example, David Nelson's family rented a room for him and his sister in Pickens:

> They gave us a little hot plate – one-eye burner hot plate. And then they give us vegetables. Wasn't much to carry back with us. We did our own cooking in a room down there the first year in high school. . . . I stayed in Pickens two years and then the third year I went to Brevard [College, North Carolina]. . . . Well, my sister had, she finished Pickens. I would have been down there by myself. . . . They'd give us food to take, vegetables and stuff to take back with us, and canned goods to take back with us. . . . They knew if they'd gave us money we'd buy candy with it. So, we used to carry food with us.

In high school during World War II, Joseph Yeats had to walk four miles to the nearest high school, but sometimes his farm chores interfered with his attendance. "In crop years I'd have to cut school at twelve and walk the four miles home, then plow a mule till dark," he explained; "many a time I walked that four mile and plowed the rest of the day." Joshua and Anne Flowers proudly proclaimed that they sent all their children through high school, except one son. "And he hated school, and he'd beg and plead . . . for us to let him, you know, quit," Mrs. Flowers explained, and elaborated: "He told us to come in one day and said, 'Daddy,' he says, 'I'll plow!' . . . He says, 'I'll plow that old mule from sun up to sun down,' says, 'if you'll let me quit school.' He just kept on till we just finally told him, so we let him drop out."

Prior to World War II, Carrie Jackson noted differences between the students from town and those (like her) from more rural areas. "It was hard for us because we always considered ourselves underdogs," she explained. "Those city students, they kind of looked down on us little country students. . . . See we had no, anything out in the world to teach us, I mean like the . . . telephone or the radio or anything like that. And they did. And they knew things that we didn't know." Mrs. Jackson continued, "And they all went to the movies, you know, and they'd sit there in English class and talk to Ms. Chastain the whole period long, three or four of them that had been to . . . seen the movie. And we wouldn't. 'Course we didn't know what they's talking about. . . . It was not only the students that did that [ignored us]; the teachers did too. . . . They didn't seem to understand that we were from the sticks up here."

After World War II, when Carrie Jackson moved her family from "the sticks" to Pickens, her daughter Julie Jackson felt "scared to death" when she started school, a sentiment echoed by her neighbor, Shirley Valentine. "They made fun of us," Julie Jackson continued, and "called us little country bumpkins. And mountain hoosiers – they called us that, too." "And see you didn't wear the same kind of clothes like the city girls," Shirley Valentine interjected, and then Carrie Jackson remembered one girl in her class decades earlier whose father owned a business in downtown Pickens,

> and of course she had everything, you know, that she wanted. Well, she had her friends, you know, that were just like her that had plenty, I reckon. And they dressed different from what we could dress. Yeah. They didn't know what cotton stockings were. And we didn't know what socks were. . . . I was not dressed like they were. . . . Some mornings we'd go in there, with the bus stuck down in the mud and be late getting in. And when we had to get in and out of the bus, there'd be mud knee deep and things like that, you know. . . . We were just not up to their standard.

On the other hand, Denise Voight's father owned a store in Salem, and consequently "everybody thought we had a lot . . . but as a matter of fact we didn't." However, after school the bus would stop in town and Ms. Voight and her friends would "get out and get drinks . . . and moon pies" from her father's store for free.

Initially, Cynthia Niles and her family "lived out in the country probably about two, three miles," but then moved about a mile from Salem (Oconee County) while she was still in grade school. This allowed Ms. Niles, a self-described "tomboy," to play basketball, and she proudly proclaimed, "I started playing basketball when I was in the seventh grade, . . . and I got my first block letter in the seventh grade." Basketball, she continued, was the only sport available to girls at that time, and the teams sometimes played on Friday nights. Even though Ms. Niles had been raised Seventh Day Adventist, her mother let her play on Friday nights (the beginning of the Sabbath for that denomination). One memorable game, Ms. Niles proudly recalled, she stood at the center line and, "right before the buzzer sounded, the ball left my hand at center line. It went straight into the basket!" To her knowledge, that remained the longest female basket in the school's history. "I was a good player," she stated confidently.

Denise Voight played for the same team at about the same time and described basketball as "my life" at that time. "Didn't you all even beat Walhalla [the team from the Oconee County seat]?" her friend Helen Urban asked as I interviewed them over lunch at a local restaurant. "We almost won the championship," Ms. Voight replied; "we went to the last game and White Plains beat us. I remember crying . . . when that happened!" At that time, girls played by different rules: "We jump-balled [after every basket] and the guards stayed on one end and the forwards on the other end," Ms. Voight explained; "I was a forward so I got to stay on the one end. We didn't even run the full court." She continued, "But we would go long distance, you know, to play and get home in the wee hours of the morning and then have to get up and go to school." Then I asked her if it was unusual for girls to play sports at that time, and whether it helped or hindered meeting boys. "Oh yes, it helped meeting the boys. 'Cause I, you always had a boyfriend," Ms. Voight explained; "you tried to beat the others to the bus so you could get on the back seat!"

At that same school in Oconee County, Deborah Mitchell remembered one unforgettable teacher and a life lesson. The teacher, "Miss Dorothea Thode," was from Walhalla, originally settled by German immigrants, and she taught chemistry. At one point, Miss Thode and her mother went on vacation to the Caribbean, which amazed the Walhalla students. But, during the teacher's absence, Mrs. Mitchell continued, "someone got ahold of the test. Well, guess what we all did? You know, kids are kids. And, I promise you, when she did the makeup test, I think everybody – I mean we probably made ten or fifteen on it. Someone taught us a lesson."

A memorable class for Carrie Jackson was home economics, popular with girls at that time. She elaborated:

> I took home ec, and we had a fashion show. We had to make a dress. . . . And we had to do it all by ourself. . . . I made a two-piece dress, and it was a skirt and a top that come down over it. And it buttoned on the shoulders; had three buttons on the shoulders. And it had bound button holes. . . . And I thought I never would – it had to be right! . . . Ms. Hendricks wouldn't accept them. . . . And I thought I never would get them little button holes made, but I finally got them done. I learned a lot in home ec. . . . I learned how to can, and I learned how to cook. Just staple foods, I mean you know, I didn't learn no fancy foods like they do now.

"And the boys, they took agriculture," Mrs. Jackson remembered, but "they had a lot of field trips, you know, to go on in the agriculture class. And the boys that lived up here [upper Pickens County] couldn't . . . because they . . . wouldn't have any way home after school was out and the bus came on."

At that time, older students often drove the school buses. In northern Pickens County, "all this was dirt roads back then," Joseph Yeats proclaimed, and "I drove a school bus my last two years in high school. . . . Kept a pole in there, a long pole under the middle seats; I'd get stuck I'd put that pole between the dual wheels on the back, ride the mud hole out! I can't imagine though now a kid sixteen years old driving a bus on dirt roads full of kids!" Denise Voight proudly stated that she "was one of the first girls . . . in Oconee County to drive school buses." Even though she admitted to hitting a mailbox one time, Ms. Voight concluded that she "did all right." Typically, though, the girl drivers were assigned the less mountainous routes, and "the boys had to drive the ones to go up to Jocassee [Valley] and all that." "And we were so envious" of our female friends as bus drivers, Helen Urban related, "because, see, they were employed and they could buy all these pretty dresses. They probably got thirty dollars a month!" Decades later, Donna Trask proudly stated that she "was the best school bus driver of the year; I got the award!" At first surprised by the announcement, Mrs. Trask discovered that "they told me I was the only one that hadn't wrecked! And that's how I got the school bus award."

Claudia Alexander and her family lived on an unpaved road into the mountains of Oconee County, and

> it was nothing but just a narrow dirt road full of ruts. . . . It was real steep back then but it had a lot of ruts, and when the weather was bad and it would snow or sleet and get real messy, then it would freeze. The bus sometimes couldn't get up that big hill back then. . . . And I would pray it would snow where I wouldn't have to go to school! . . . So I can remember when the weather was bad in the winter sometimes I'd be out of school a week at a time.

Even decades later, Forrest Sanders explained, "Sunset [a tiny Pickens County mountain community near the North Carolina line] would always save us when it snowed. 'Cause if they couldn't come, no one could come. It was great."

Charles Watson started high school in the early 1960s, and described the difficulties still faced by students whose parents lived out in the country along bus routes. "Well, back then, as far as playing sports or anything, a country kid didn't have much of a chance, 'cause wasn't no way out and back," Mr. Watson explained. "Most of the time it'd be town boys would be on the team. Country kid didn't have much of a chance." He added that he "always worried about not being able to find the bus when school'd get out in the evenings," because "the bus driver wouldn't be parked in the same place. It'd be scattered around different places in the parking lot. Always worried about finding that bus 'cause I thought if I had to spend the night in that big city of Pickens, it'd be the end of the world!"

In "the big city of Pickens," one of Margaret York's favorite activities about this time was that she and her friends

> went to the [roller] skating rink. They'd have an old tent that'd come and set up in town, and they would have a skating rink there. And that was the funnest thing I ever done. You talk about bruises from my ankles to the top of my head learning how to skate, but we used to have a lot of fun doing that. . . . I mean, these poor old gawky farming boys go down there and put on a pair of skates. And they was like myself – their feet'd go out from under them, and we'd all be on the floor. I don't know how I could skate from not having broken bones, but, oh, that was a lot of fun. But mainly the movies were the biggest thing that you could go to.

"When I was growing up, teenager," Beth Yeats recalled, "there was a bus came from Brevard [North Carolina] to Greenville. You could catch the bus and a lot of us girls would go to a movie and it wasn't the danger it is today, and we'd window shop up and down the street and get a hot dog or something and ride back home."

"Then as I got in high school" in Pickens, Margaret York explained, "I used to go to football games every Friday night." While her husband admitted that "I never did care for the [foot]ball games; . . . I'd make me a good sling shot and go bird hunting or something," Mrs. York loved the games. "Easley's always been our biggest rival," she stated; "they was a bigger town than Pickens, and they thought they were better than we were!" Mrs. York believed that the rivalry may have been based on class, because "they was the rich people, and we was old country people up here. And if our old country boys could whup them Easley boys, that was a thing!" In order to attend, Mrs. York related, "my mother would take me and let me out and I'd meet whoever I was gonna see there. After the game she'd come out and pick me up, 'cause she didn't go."

By the early 1960s, the cross-county rivalry between the Pickens "Blue Flame" and the Easley "Green Wave" had escalated. Charles Watson explained:

> In fact it got so bad they cut it out just before I got in high school, and they went for years and years and they didn't play. Then when I was a senior in high school they played again for the first time. Lord, that was the awfullest mob you ever have seen in your life. That was the first ball game I ever got to go to. Momma and them was – they was so religious they wouldn't *hear* of you going to a ball game. She'd say, if I'd go to a ball game, "What if the Lord come back, you down at that hellhole," that's what she

> called it, a hellhole. Well, my oldest brother . . . was gonna take me to that ball game since I was a senior in high school. And at the house Momma was squalling about us going to a hellhole, and said, "What if the Lord's coming back and you down there, where you gonna go?" Well, I went on anyway, and Pickens won at that time. And in later years, my older brother and all, they had kids of their own and them grandkids growed up and they all got playing sports (you know, times got better – had a ways out and back), and Momma got interested in football. . . . She wouldn't miss a ball game!

While students like Charles Watson had to be bused to school from outlying rural districts, African American students like Shirley Patterson Valentine faced an even greater challenge. Because of segregation, and after her mother demanded it from the local white-dominated government, Patterson and her siblings obtained a small county school bus to drive them from the Liberia area in upper Pickens County, past the white Pickens County school building, to the center of town, to await the arrival of another bus to take them another eight miles to the nearest black school, Clear View, in Easley.[5] Because of segregation, African American students spent about three hours a day on the bus, coming to and from school.

Several inhabitants remembered desegregation at Pickens schools. Raised in upper Pickens County, Harry Edison believed that "we weren't prejudiced; we just didn't know the blacks; all I saw of them was on TV." At Pickens Junior High, Nancy Daniels encountered her first black classmates "because there was no black children up in this community; that was a little bit of adjustment for me. Because I mean I was raised that you loved everybody. But just all of a sudden being in class with little black children was an adjustment for this little country girl." But eventually she became friends with her black female classmates.

"Now, I can tell you this," Harry Edison stated: "My senior year in high school was when integration came to Pickens High School [1969], . . . and there was like six or seven black kids came from Clear View High School out of Easley." Mr. Edison continued:

> I remember one, name was [Allen Hill].[6] He was a big, tough black guy. And because my name was [Edison] I had study hall with him. We sat next to each other and I became friends with that guy. I thought a lot of him. I didn't know any of the others, but I got to know him quite well. . . . And I had other people that

5 See Coggeshall, *Liberia*, 149–51.

6 By coincidence, I interviewed Allen Hill in February 2009, and then in May interviewed Harry Edison about his high school experiences, and only then realized Edison was describing someone I had already interviewed. Of course, their actual names would be close in alphabetical order.

> I thought were supposed to be my friends; they would tell me to stay away from him. But I didn't, because I was raised – my parents raised me to do unto others as you'd have them do unto you – to treat people the way you want to be treated. And that's the way my parents were and that's the way I grew up.

Despite the fact that some of Edison's white "friends" threatened him for befriending Hill, "I'll tell you one thing they didn't do – they didn't bother him," Mr. Edison explained, because Allen Hill played football, and was quite strong. In another interview, I discovered that Hill spent many weekends with his friend Don (Shirley Valentine's nephew), in rural Liberia.[7] Today, Edison works with a man who attends Hill's church and reported that "he still remembers me when I was his friend, and that makes me feel good to know that."

By the early 1970s, despite the increase in the availability of transportation, many mountain inhabitants still faced the problem of physical distance transforming into social distance. For example, Elizabeth Nelson lived in far northern Pickens County,

> and I didn't get to do a lot outside of school because I didn't have a means of transportation, living this far out in the country. I didn't – I couldn't participate in sports after school, which killed me! Or any of the other little clubs that met after school. I couldn't go places and do things with my friends very much. Now I did get my driver's license when I was seventeen years old. But we only had one vehicle, which Daddy drove to work every day. So there was not a question of me having a vehicle to drive. . . . Now, I didn't like that, because that made me feel isolated, because I knew a lot of kids were doing things after school together and I couldn't. I guess that was the main thing I resented about living way out here when I was in high school.

Ms. Nelson specifically remembered one night, "I think it was our senior year," when she got to spend the night with a female friend, "and we stayed up practically all night writing our term papers for a class together. And the electricity went out, but we had manual typewriters so it didn't matter. A candle, manual typewriter's all you needed. We did our term papers together."

Most of the time after school, country kids like Beth Lepre "got off the bus and usually did some work, like in the garden or the yard, or whatever we had to do. We did our homework and went to bed by about eight o'clock." Nancy Daniels, also from rural Pickens County, had a very similar routine:

> But when I'd get home my time was pretty much spent with homework. I was one of those studious girls. And I'd . . . have a

7 See Coggeshall, *Liberia*, for some of Hill's adventures.

> snack, get my homework done first. And then supper and then we would watch some TV in the evenings. But we were in bed by nine each night. So, as far as having a lot of fun after school, again, it was just right there with my mom, my dad, and my brother. . . . 'Cause at that time we pretty much had – always had a cow, two hogs so we spent our time right there.

But Beth Lepre did remember a special treat. Occasionally, she fondly remembered her father walking from his factory several blocks from downtown to the high school, where father and daughter would "walk uptown . . . and go to the drugstore and get, like, a fountain drink and just kind of shop around in the little stores up there; . . . that was kind of a big thing for us. And then when I would go stay with my friends that lived downtown," Lepre continued, "like usually their moms would take us to the movie or maybe some, you know, fast food restaurant. . . . And then when they would come up here they would want to swim in the creek and walk around and look at the cows, and see Daddy and Momma milk the cows in the morning, and just things like that."

On weekends without football games, Beth Lepre and her friends participated in a very familiar teen pastime from the mid-twentieth century:

> On the weekends, we would – and this is silly too, but we would ride around in Pickens, and it was like a traffic jam on the weekends at night. . . . Kids would just get in their cars and just ride around and around the city, and I mean over and over for like, from dark until like, as late as you could stay out. So we would do that and see all our friends up there. Just things like that. Nobody really had a whole lot of money, it didn't seem like, to do any big things.

"And in high school the big thing was cruising down Main Street," Nancy Daniels remembered, and she and her female friends "did that some. . . . We'd just go out and have a good time as far as watching the boys on the street and things." In Oconee County, Brenda Kendrick admitted that Salem

> was just a small town, [and so] . . . if you went to a movie, you had to go [to] Walhalla or Seneca on Friday or Saturday night. And of course, we'd go to Walhalla and just cruise up downtown with friends. . . . There really wasn't much to do in that area back then, but we had fun. . . . I can remember hanging out in, at the church parking lot, or in front of my friend's house, or downtown, or you know, you just meet up somewhere and a group of us like would ride to Walhalla or sometimes maybe get together and go to the river. If somebody responsible and their parents would let us go, even to Jocassee.

"After I got big enough to have my own car," Harry Edison explained, he and his friends would

> go to Greenville. We'd go to the Palmetto Drive-In, the Little Rebel Drive-In – well, that Palmetto Drive-In over in Greenville . . . boy, that place stayed packed out.[8] And these black curb hops they had to be real smart 'cause they would go from one car and they didn't even have a pad in their hand. And they would get orders from car to car and they'd come back and they'd bring you exactly what you ordered. I don't know how in the world they would do that.

"Usually it was like on Saturday and Sunday night, Friday, Saturday, Sunday night," Edison recalled, "unless there's a football game, you know, on Friday night." Edison and his friends would "cruise" from one fast-food stand to the next and then circle around again. Then Edison turned to his wife and asked her, "Did you ever get to go over there? Other than with me?" and with a slight smile she replied quietly, "Mm-hm," and we all laughed.

"Friday night was always high school football," Nancy Daniels stated; "we *loved* to go to the Pickens games. My mom and dad did too. My brother played. And we didn't miss away games or anything." Prior to the early 1970s, Mrs. Daniels continued, Pickens did not have a great team. "But beginning in the early '70s, Pickens did this dramatic change and became – they didn't lose anything. So it was very exciting. And the stands were always full. And just a lot of crowd enthusiasm. And you lived for those Friday night football games. So it was great fun." Accompanied by her best friend, Mrs. Daniels typically sat with her parents at these Friday night games.

Perhaps as a way to leave their mark on the land, daredevil Pickens High students drove up to the top of a monadnock about a mile outside of town, walked to the edge of a curving granitic surface, and painted their high school graduation dates as large as they dared on the bare rock.[9] While Beth Lepre knew of the practice, "I was a chicken. I mean, I was good," she admitted. Ms. Lepre also thought that the primary culprits at that time were boys and acknowledged that "we had some pretty devilish little boys. They were daredevils and they would do anything."

By the 1970s, students at the larger county high schools recognized divisions between country and city students, but they still "mixed and mingled," according to Beth Lepre. "No, they didn't really look down on us," she continued,

> but, I mean, they were like, "Oh, you live up there where you have to pump in sunshine!" And, I mean, people made fun but

---

8 Opened in 1959, the restaurant remains at the same location: https://palmettofinefoods.com/, accessed January 30, 2025.

9 See John M. Coggeshall, *Something in These Hills: The Culture of Family Land in Southern Appalachia* (Chapel Hill: University of North Carolina Press, 2022), 81 and Figure 2.

> it was in good spirits and they . . . didn't like say, "You bunch of bumpkins." At least not to our face! We were so goofy we didn't know it, I don't know. We were pretty naïve. . . . My best friends from middle school through high school were from the city. They were city girls and they would come up here and spend the night with me and I would go spend the night with them.

Many high school students like Ryan Trask "loved to hunt and fish and pick bluegrass music," whereas "some of the wealthy people whose parents were doctors in Greenville . . . didn't have those experiences." But, Trask continued, "there were dividing lines in what you did, perhaps, but not in valuing somebody's worth and friendships." "But, no, I mean, it wasn't that clique-ish in Pickens," Andrea Bowers described, because "it was never big enough to be a city to have a city versus country; it was just like, it was country and then there was the sticks!" In fact, Mrs. Bowers added, rural activities drew her school friends to her parents' home in northeastern Pickens County on weekends. "They loved it here," she exclaimed; "I mean they wanted to stay there all the time" because "Mother would feed them and they'd get to hunt and swim and do whatever." On the other hand, Mrs. Bowers marveled at the suburban neighborhoods of her friends and thought it would be wonderful "to have just neighbor after neighbor after neighbor."

Living in far northern Oconee County, from a modest financial situation and without a personal car, Claudia Alexander felt that she missed out on a lot of high school activities but also that her high school guidance counselor "should have told me that there was financial aid for poor people; that could have helped me. I felt like I was one who fell through the cracks, really." Mrs. Alexander believed that her grades were sufficient,

> and I felt like I could've been, I could've went on – I really feel like with my personality and my drive that I could've went further if I had somebody who would have encouraged me in school as far as, "you can go to college"; "this is here for you." But being in the mountains I felt like I was one of the kids who got dropped through the cracks, I really do.

During my research, I interviewed three then-current Clemson University students who had been friends at Pickens County High School, and they described in great detail the lives of high schoolers in the early twenty-first century. Because they were also outgoing and insightful and humorous, I enjoyed talking with them and thus obtained a great deal of information. As readers will discover, despite significant changes to American culture over the past several decades, the social lives and observations of high school students have not changed significantly.

For example, Jason Taylor compared his middle school experiences, where "you've been around the same . . . hundred people in your grade for the past like eight or nine years and you're just kinda getting tired of it," to when he entered Pickens High School:

> I remember freshman year, that was one of the most fun years 'cause I met so many people. I just met, you know, I met a hundred more people. They were all really fun, fun people to hang out with. They had little . . . parties. And it was like, we'd play "Capture the Flag" and stuff like that. And like get together and play basketball all the time, play football. There was always something going on. Going to football games on Friday nights, that was like a big thing to do. And then – everyone had really good personalities, you know. Everyone's like always having fun, just having I guess regular old high schoolers having fun, not really paying attention in class.

Taylor's friend Kayla Radcliffe also enjoyed her high school years, especially engaging in the age-old high school ritual of cutting class:

> I remember back in high school, we would – especially my senior year – we would leave early and go fishing a lot. We did that a lot. We . . . knew how the system worked, and if you stayed forty-five minutes in a class, you were counted there. So after that forty-five minutes, . . . especially on Fridays, we'd get out about – we were supposed to get out at one, and we'd get out about twelve fifteen and go on and start fishing. . . . We'd go either to, up to the Eastatoee, and go fishing at the creek there, or we'd go just to one of the ponds around Pickens.

Kayla Radcliffe described the cliques at her school in much the same way that Ryan Trask had done for that same school decades earlier:

> See, there were a lot of cliques but there weren't people who were just like, "Oh, no, I can't talk to them or everyone will think I'm unpopular." It's like everyone was on speaking terms but everyone didn't like each other, so it wasn't completely separated. There were a lot of good ol' boy cliques, you know. "I wear Justin boots[10] and tight jeans and I like wearing cowboy hats so I'm a good ol' boy." And part of that image was the dip, like, chewing tobacco. And the funny thing was you get caught with cigarettes and you're like [snaps fingers] boom, you're gonna get writ up. But if you get caught with dip, most of the administrators were like, "Man, I wish I could dip at school anyway" and they're just like, "Ahh, don't do that anymore." . . . And then there are cliques like, well, a lot of the Honors kids stuck together, really because it was such a small school that we all had the same classes

10 Justin Boots is a Texas-based boot company.

> together. . . . There were some people who were like trying to be impersonization of skaters. There – that was that going on, but they were usually the ones that everyone liked. So it wasn't like we're gonna shun you because you're not like us. They were just the comedians, mostly, of the school. Other than that, there wasn't a lot of really big divisions.

When I asked Ms. Radcliffe if there were "good ol' girls," she replied: "Not quite as much. Most of the girls tried to follow the general pop culture view, wearing the latest styles, a lot like the sororities here [at Clemson University]. They look like them. They act like them. . . . The girls who were kind of country were the ones that were poorer, so I think they weren't able to – I guess try to be a part of that group, you know." "Pickens was mostly country," Forrest Sanders admitted; "you had the country kids, and then you had the preppy-type kids. . . . You have the real country people, and then you have the people that get to high school and decide to dress country." When I asked him what that meant, Sanders replied: "Well, the Carhartt pants.[11] I mean, granted I own Carhartt pants and wear them all the time, but you had the Carhartt pants, and the Dixie Outfitter[12] shirt on, with a camo[uflage] hat. That was the general, everyday wear." Jason Taylor noticed that some of his friends altered their dress as they moved from Dacusville to Pickens: "They dressed like they were, you know, all countrified, and like cowboys."

According to Kayla Radcliffe, the surrounding rural middle schools provided most of the "country" students. Radcliffe mentioned places like Dacusville, "because Dacusville is even smaller than Pickens. It's like hardly a town! . . . And the Pickens kids . . . – the good ol' boys were the ones like I went to elementary school with, so the ones from back in the mountains. I mean, they'd have a horse in the backyard and they're like 'I'm a cowboy!'" According to Jason Taylor, when they had classes, the Dacusville boys would "usually sit together, just 'cause we knew each other pretty good."

Jason Taylor offered a heteronormative male perspective on the high school student divisions:

> By senior year, it was more of a, everyone kinda knew each other and didn't really care what the other person did. But freshman, sophomore year I think was worse with girls just because, I don't know, I guess, they made fun of each other more; I don't know. Guys are just like, I don't really care what the other guy thinks; I'm just going to sit here and talk with this group of friends. But we had different tables at lunch and you always sat with the same people for – the few who you knew. And there'd always be

11 Carhartt is a Michigan-based maker of work pants.

12 Dixie Outfitters is a Tennessee-based clothing company that manufactures, among other items, Confederate-themed T-shirts.

> the popular table and then like the people at the band table or – just all – just different kinds of people.

As others have observed, Taylor felt that "city versus country I guess wasn't really a big deal, 'cause everyone – everyone knew what the country was like. And I think . . . with girls it was Dacusville versus Pickens. . . . And all the guys [from Dacusville] thought that Pickens girls were hot and all the guys from Pickens thought the Dacusville girls were hot."

While "city versus country" may not have been a significant social division, family names and reputations still carried weight in these small Southern towns. Jason Taylor believed that Pickens is "really controlled by names, I would say. . . . Like, there's certain names in the community everybody knows, and like those names seem to be able to get what they want." For example, he argued that Dacusville kids had to excel at athletics just to surmount the name recognition that Pickens kids already had. "My sister, she was a cheerleader, and the first two years she didn't make it. She was a great cheerleader, but they didn't know her name; they didn't know who she was." But by junior year, with a new (outsider) coach, Taylor's sister was selected just on her talent and not by name. "And then I know another girl that didn't make the squad," Taylor continued, because she had an older sister with a bad reputation and was not selected for fear the tainted family name might damage the squad's standing.

I then asked Jason Taylor if he thought cheerleading was a popular activity, and he replied: "I think it was. I mean, I think the cheerleaders thought it was. . . . Like I think you always consider the cheerleaders are popular. . . . You might not like them, but everyone does know who they are." Taylor's sister eventually made the squad, and "she really enjoyed it." However, he admitted, she recognized that she had been a self-described "really nice girl," but after making the cheerleading squad, "she said she wasn't a nice person after that. It's like, I don't know, something about the cheerleaders, a lot of times I think they thought they were above other people, so they could do whatever they wanted. By senior year, everyone had caught on and we were past all that . . . and we were like, 'No, we don't care what you do. No, you're just stupid.'"

One of Pickens County's rivals today is Daniel High School, closer to Clemson University and thus enrolling the children of many Clemson faculty and staff. Donna Trask, the wife of a Clemson administrator, attended high school in Pickens but early in her career taught at Daniel, and "they *do* have a big difference in where you're from over there. But yeah, the kids – even now they'll call themselves 'rednecks,' which is a term I don't like, but those are the ones that . . . hunt, the ones that fish, the ones that are into outdoor activities, four-wheeling, that sort of thing." "There was two different types of Daniel kids," Forrest Sanders stated; "you had the Six Mile [a small town outside of

Clemson] kids and then you had the Central and Clemson area kids. I think a lot of it was more the professors' kids, but then you also had the Six Mile kids that were just country people."

As many inhabitants have stated already, for at least the past half century, high school football enlivened Friday nights in regional communities. "Football was *huge*," Kayla Radcliffe recalled:

> I mean there were people who didn't like football who went to football games just because that was a social event. No one – very few people'd actually watch the game; they'd just go to talk to people and . . . just hang out with others. Like, I didn't like football and I went to the football games just because there was nothing better to do, really. And then there are people who are die-hard about it, like my brother. He thinks I'm insane for not liking football. It's – sports are *huge*. I don't know why, but they are.

As in decades past, for the Pickens High School Blue Flame, the rivalry with the Easley Green Wave generated the greatest excitement. "Everyone goes," Jason Taylor exclaimed:

> everyone from past years that's already graduated goes. I've went to the past two we've had, and I don't even go to school there anymore. It's a pretty big deal. . . . You'd have a lot of former students and their families come, and then community people . . . that, you know, grew up in Pickens, and then they just stayed around Pickens. . . . If you went to Friday night football games when you were in high school, you're probably just going to keep going to them when you have kids or if you just want to go. Because people keep up with it and talk about the roster, especially the older men of the community.

Momentum begins building the day before the game, Jason Taylor recalled: "Around Thursdays, people start getting pretty excited about it, and you actually buy your ticket at the school, . . . so you don't have to wait in line. . . . And then of course you'd figure out with who all you're going with, because that's always a big deal." The day of the game, Kayla Radcliffe recalled, students wore T-shirts with slogans like "The Green Wave will never extinguish the Blue Flame," or everyone wore blue T-shirts to school that day. Football players wore their jerseys as shirts, because "that was their pride thing to get psyched up for the game," Radcliffe explained. "And sometimes there'd be a pep rally," Radcliffe continued, "like the cheerleaders would come out and do their routines, and the seniors would all sit together and the juniors and freshmen and it was kind of like the hierarchy. And the seniors got preferential treatment."

Not all the students appreciated the pep rallies, however. For Kayla

Radcliffe and her student friends, the rallies were "kind of annoying" because they disrupted their art classes, "and talking about something we really didn't care about." Radcliffe believed that poorer students, like a girl she knew, also did not care about the pep rallies because they belonged to a different class; these students, Radcliffe admitted, actually called the events "'prep rallies' . . . because the girls who were the most popular were the ones who were the cheerleaders. And the football players – the most popular – were the ones who were getting the attention. And it was sort of a jealousy thing, I think. And then they'd go to the football games anyway because it was the best thing to do on a Friday night."

Before the game, some fans would tailgate, as if they were at a collegiate or professional game. Between school dismissal at three p.m. and the start of the game, Jason Taylor and his friends would

> get there, you know, six o'clock to get a good seat, or just to hang out with people. And then cars, cars would line up the streets. The students usually parked in the student parking lot, . . . and then all the school parking lot would be packed. The Lightsey Square [in downtown Pickens], which is a community parking lot, that'd be packed. All the church parking lots around it would be packed, so if you didn't get there early, you'd be parking way off. . . . And then a lot of times, starting our senior year, we started tailgating before the football games. . . . And it's like someone would have like a grill and we'd just chill out, grill, have some hamburgers, and then go to the football game. And then we'd – it was always fun to do the tailgate at other people's schools, just to say, "Hey, yeah, we're that school spirited."

"So – and the games?" Kayla Radcliffe elaborated:

> I think they would always start at seven and some people would get there early and just socialize. You'd find there was the home side and the visitor's side and then in the middle was the concession stand. And the place to hang out was the hill between the concession stand and the home side, because the adults didn't sit over there. You could go back behind the concession stand and all kinds of things would go on. People would get in fights. That was the cool place to be, and that's also where the police officers tend to hang out and break up fights. . . . And then when the game started you'd watch it for about five minutes, and then you'd start to go and get food and go talk to someone else and then maybe you'll watch a little bit again. And then halftime starts and the band people go play. Oh, the band people, they were their own little group. . . . And honestly, they would say the only reason that the football games existed (that was their joke) was so that they could go play on the field! So

> they were very proud of that. And then the big thing was if they won the game the football players were allowed to wear their jerseys again on Monday, and if they weren't they couldn't. It was like their shame that they couldn't wear their jerseys.

Jason Taylor, who was a much more engaged fan, elaborated on his former classmate's description:

> And like you walk in [to the stadium], and it's just packed, like you can't move at all. You probably aren't going to be able to find a seat. If you do, you're going to be squished. And getting there, there's just like tons of people. You probably have to wait in line for ten minutes to get a ticket if you didn't get one beforehand. . . . And then at our home field in Pickens, you walk in the main entrance to go down the side of the stadium.[13] . . . There's like the band section, . . . and then you go down a little bit further and you'd have like, there's gonna be like families and stuff, and then you get to the student section. The student section was like pretty much at the fifty yard line, and like all around the student section are season tickets, because you can actually buy season tickets to the games, and you get like a special parking spot and everything like that. . . . So you get there early and you get a good seat in the student section, and a lot of times it's the juniors and seniors that sit there. . . . My freshman and sophomore year we sat at the very end, like, of the stadium, but it was still packed out down there. . . . And then finally like you would migrate closer and closer, and then like senior year you'd sit in the middle of the student section and all the fun. . . . It was just amazing 'cause it was like, made that transition, you thought you were something else then! . . . A lot of times there'd be younger girls sitting there. Not too many times were there younger guys. I guess maybe the guys controlled it. We were like, "We don't want a younger guy sitting here; bring those girls over. We don't mind if they come!" That was like the highlight, when you'd get to sit there.

By the time he was a senior and had "made it," Jason Taylor explained, the game had become "just like a complete social event. . . . You just . . . pretty much just cut up [joke around] for the whole two and a half, three hours or however long it lasts. . . . I don't know if anyone ever watches the third quarter unless something fun happens. The fourth quarter, everyone usually watches it." Girls, according to Taylor, mostly went to socialize: "They'd just go, you know, and cut up. Half the time I don't even know if they know what's going on with the games." But, Taylor continued, "you wanted to go to the football

---

13 Taylor described the "old" Pickens High stadium, now Pickens Middle School. A new high school and new stadium, opened in 2011, sit farther out in the country.

game 'cause there were a whole bunch of girls there. So you wanted to meet and socialize with them."

I asked Taylor how students knew where to sit, and he explained that "you would just go in and there would be everyone sitting there already. And I mean like, as a freshman or a sophomore, unless you were like really popular, you'd probably be scared to sit there. Like 'cause it was really intimidating. I was like intimidated when I was a freshman and sophomore, so we'd go down to the end and there'd be like – there was a big group of us that all sat down there, and we'd love to watch the football games."

During Kayla Radcliffe's interview I asked her what happened after the game, and she replied, "Well, by that point it was like eleven thirty and a lot of people had to be home for curfews. But there was a lot of hanging out behind the high school because that's where everyone parked their cars for the game. And many people hang out at McDonald's [less than a block away]. I mean even after school that's a big hangout place. . . . Sometimes people would decide to go see a midnight showing of a movie. But after that I don't think any parties went on or anything."

On the other hand, Jason Taylor (perhaps due to a different family religious background or different gender) had a much more active social life after football games. He elaborated:

> Well, freshman and sophomore year the biggest thing to do after you left the football game – *home* football games – was go to "Fifth Quarter," which was like, they had it at East Pickens Baptist Church. And like everyone was invited and you could go down there; they had free pizza and drinks and then they had music and you just . . . hang out with friends pretty much for a couple hours. And we'd wait till the news came on and watched *Friday Night Hits* or *Friday Night Blitz* [local sports shows] to see what happened on our football game once again. . . . And then near the end of Fifth Quarter, right before the football would come on, they would have like a preacher or something talk to us for ten, fifteen minutes. . . . And then like someone's parents would pick you all up and y'all'd go to one person's house and just hang out. I don't know, watch movies and go to sleep.

For young high school students, though, there was an added benefit of attending Fifth Quarter at the Baptist church, as Jason Taylor explained after a brief pause:

> The walk to Fifth Quarter was really fun too, 'cause . . . to get to the church you had to walk through like this older mill neighborhood kind of, and some like dark roads. So you'd always have like a group of people walking together and then you'd have the couples, like couples walking together, and then

> they'd go off onto one of the – there was like a different road you could take, and they'd go down like a dark road and then everyone else'd go down another road and get there and like wait for awhile to get there.

For area high school students, Friday night football served as a critical entertainment and social event. But when I asked Kayla Radcliffe if other sports were as popular as football, she thought that the volleyball and basketball teams were fairly popular because they were inside a gym and people could sit and watch, whereas baseball and soccer were less popular because they were outside. In fact, Radcliffe recalled, "I actually remember a movement from the soccer team to try to get more people to come to their – like they started the 'Soccer Fanatics' club and like five people joined. So no one cared about their sport!" Football also was outside, "but it was such an established thing," she explained, that everyone attended. "Like so established that my dad was *extremely* disappointed that my brother didn't play football because in high school that was my dad's life."

I asked Jason Taylor, at the time of his interview a sophomore in college, if he felt odd attending high school football games as a college student, and he replied that perhaps he would feel strange at a less-critical game, but "going to the Easley game? I think you can always go to the Easley game and no one's going to look at you funny. You're not going to feel weird about it 'cause *everyone's* there." When Taylor meets his former high school friends there, "I think we watch the game more now instead of just" socializing, because they know fewer people today. "You've got your group of friends you kind of always went with; . . . it's just like you kind of pick up where you left off. It's like you've been going to school all week together and it's a Friday night again; you just talk about what you're gonna do after the game. . . . So I mean, it's really no different."

Unlike a lot of teens in previous generations, those born in the twenty-first century typically had more accessible transportation. "Seems like when you're a freshman or sophomore," Jason Taylor stated, "you go home, and if you want to do something, you gotta tell your parents to do it. But when you're a junior or senior, you know you can just go do whatever you want, whenever you want." Greater access to transportation also provided greater work opportunities after school. Taylor explained: "My junior year of high school – we would get out of school and a lot of people would have to go to work at four, either at Pizza Inn or I think some people worked at the Ingles [grocery store] in Pickens." Taylor especially remembered the numbers of students working at local pizza places:

> *So* many people worked at Pizza Inn or pizza places in general. That was like the place to work. . . . There's a pizza place in

> Dacusville called Dacusville Pizza Stop. . . . I think junior and senior year of high school, two of my good friends worked there, my age. . . . All the girls that worked there were always from Easley for some reason. . . . And then at Pizza Inn in Pickens – that was a big pizza place in Pickens – and I think just about *every* guy worked there. . . . Like you could go in at any time of the day and you'd probably see someone you know working; that's how it was. But it was fun because you'd just go in, hang out with people.

As students acquired after-school jobs, social life after school also evolved, as Jason Taylor explained:

> It'd be funny 'cause like freshman and sophomore year you just wanted to get out of school and go home, and then it was like junior year, here we would be like standing outside of school for like an hour, talking in the parking lot. . . . Some days we'd be out there close to five, just hanging out and talking. And it would be funny, the schoolteachers would just try to run us off, and I'm like, . . . "You're gonna run us off so we can go do something bad?" 'Cause that's what happens when you leave school; you just wanna cause mischief.

Jason Taylor provided numerous stories of mischief, and I delighted in asking him for examples of episodes from his high school years.[14] Some of these escapades involved sports, especially football, Taylor confessed:

> Not every year, but every few years, there's something that happens – one school does something to the other school. I think, maybe my junior or sophomore year, the Easley kids came and painted – it was so stupid. The football players, I think they came and painted like their football numbers on our parking lot and they left spray paint cans there, and I think they, you know, put "Easley rules" or "Pickens sucks" or something. But they ended up getting caught, 'cause they painted their numbers on the parking lot, which was stupid. . . . Usually if you do anything school spirit, or any sort of vandalism to the other school, you can't go to the game on Friday night and you'll probably gonna get suspended for a couple days if you're a football player or not, it depends. . . . If you're a football player and you get caught doing something, they may let you go a little bit sooner so you can play in the game the next Friday!

I had noticed that Jason Taylor referred to this activity as "school spirit," and he explained: "The kids like to call them school-spirited type of things. I mean, I guess the principals see it as vandalism." Another time, Taylor

14 See a description of another episode of Taylor's in Coggeshall, *Something in These Hills*, 81.

offered, students from Pickens "may have did something" to Easley's football practice field, and so "then the Easley people came over and did something to our practice field. And it's the kind of thing that if it happens to one school, definitely . . . the other school is gonna fight back and do something else."

Because the senior class president was a "pretty cool guy," Jason Taylor said that he came up with "crazy ideas" for seniors:

> We always had "Spirit Week," where you had "Hat Day," and "Hillbilly Day," and all the different days – . . . where you could break the school rules, or dress code, a good bit. But then, near the end of our senior year, we were having like, just random things we'd do. Like one day we just, all the seniors wore togas to school. Or, not all of us, but as many people as we could convince to wear togas to school. Another day we were supposed to all wear like, dress up as pirates, another day like ninjas, or Ninja Turtles. It was hard to do some of them, but . . . for "Toga Day" a lot of us had togas on and that was pretty fun, 'cause it wasn't any sort of special day; it was just a random like thirty people walking around in togas.

"Senior Skip Day" was often difficult to negotiate, Jason Taylor explained, because all the seniors had to agree on a date and no tests or major projects could be missed. "And every now and then," Taylor continued, "our teachers would trick us" by scheduling a test that day. Eventually, a common day would be agreed upon. However, for his Senior Skip Day, Taylor elected to attend because of a project deadline, and he and his close friends found themselves as some of the few seniors there – in fact, many juniors skipped as well, and most of the attendees that day were only freshmen and sophomores.

As a senior in high school, Jason Taylor and his friends felt like they owned the school. At that time, the high school had cordoned off one hallway for exclusively freshman classes, but Taylor's Advanced Placement Calculus class met in that same hallway: "So we'd get out and it'd be class changes and all the freshmen would be changing. . . . And a lot of times we'd walk down like standing right beside each other, so the freshmen had to walk, perfectly walk around us."

"And then, the meanest thing we came up with," Jason Taylor admitted, was "Kick a Freshman Friday." The goal was "you were supposed to just randomly kick random freshmen on Friday." They singled out only freshmen they knew, and Taylor wondered if other freshmen wondered why only certain ones were selected. "But we tried to okay it with our principal that we could actually have a 'Kick a Freshman Friday,'" Taylor continued, and explained their strategy: "It'd be like a spirit event and we'd have T-shirts and we weren't actually going to kick them; we were just going to give them a 'kick-start' in school. But he didn't think it was a good idea! . . . But we thought it'd be cool to have 'Kick a Freshman Friday' shirts."

About a week or so before graduation, Jason Taylor remembered, there was also "Class Day":

> And all the seniors wore white and different classes'd wear different colors. Freshmen wore green, sophomores, I think wore red, I don't know. Juniors wore pastels. And then we'd have a senior slide show and you'd give out senior superlatives. . . . Superlatives were like the cutest couple, most spirited – . . . all that stuff. . . . And then at the end we would sing a song to everyone, to all the other classes. I don't even remember; it was a weird song. It was about what the freshmen did, sophomores did, and the juniors did. And then the juniors sang it to us and we left. And usually on "Class Day" you peaced out, did whatever you wanted to, skipped school.

Jason Taylor described his high school graduation day with a touch of sentimentality. For many area high schools, the ceremony is held annually at Littlejohn Coliseum, Clemson University's basketball arena. Taylor did not remember much about his particular ceremony, but afterward

> we walked out of the tunnel, like all of our teachers were in this tunnel like clapping for us as we went out into the world, and that was like one of the coolest things. And then we got outside and everyone, it was just kind of like significant – showed what after school is gonna be, 'cause everyone just like went their separate ways, like went to where their parents were and then like took pictures with their friends, and that was it, you know? The people . . . you took pictures with on graduation day are the people you're probably going to hang out with after graduation day. Everyone else you're probably not going to see maybe once or twice at high school reunions.

Then I asked Jason Taylor what he missed most about his high school years, and he replied:

> I think I miss like – high school, like you went into class and like you had a ton of different people in there, you know, and you *knew* all of them. . . . And you had a couple good friends in each class you went to and you'd cut up like all the time. [Unlike college], . . . it was like you were all together there for like a whole six and a half, seven hours and you might've ate lunch together and you were always doing certain things. . . . I like that it enclosed things so you're just walking down the hallway and you like see random people you know. As a freshman that's kind of intimidating 'cause it's like, there's so many people! And then

> it's like, as a senior you're just like . . . walking around the hallway like you own it. And then after school you . . . might hang out in the parking lot; go to a basketball game that night, or a football game. Then you go home and that's where it's probably a little bit more boring 'cause you don't really do much; might do your homework and that's about it. . . . The cool thing about college is that everyone has goals in mind and they actually care about school. Our high school, that wasn't the big thing. Not many people really cared about school.

Because I was curious about the social lives of high school students and how these activities had changed through time, I asked my three college-aged informants about their extracurricular social activities. Kayla Radcliffe replied:

> It depended a lot on where you lived. . . . A lot of times people would just go out driving. For a while there was this legend that there was some monster living in Fox Squirrel Ridge [a rural Pickens County road] because these people from Dacusville took their girlfriends out driving and played a trick on them. And like a year later I'm sitting in this freshman class and they're talking about going out to look for the monster. When I knew the guy who made up the story. . . . He was one of those people that was like, he'd make up a story just because people would want to hear him talk. . . . So people would just do, go drive and pick up something to eat and then, you know, go home and watch TV. I mean, that's really all that there was to do, honestly, but it's what they did for fun.

Perhaps because Jason Taylor was from a less conservative religious background than his friend Kayla Radcliffe, he had a much more active social life. Taylor noted a division in social activities between his freshman/sophomore and junior/senior years. During his first years in high school, Taylor and his friends would

> just get together and we would still watch movies a good bit. There was nothing much too exciting. Every now and then someone would have a little party, not like a wild party, it would just be like a little get together. . . . We had a lot of bonfires. . . . One friend of mine had a pool table. We'd go over there and play pool. Just hang out. We'd get ten people over there and we'd just have a ball just playing pool and just joking around. We'd always have a bonfire at the same time. . . . Our friends like tore off the back part of their house and they built a new part on. They had all this wood. . . . So we built a giant fire pit, had a bonfire probably at least once a month. That was what we did ninth and tenth grade.

Social activities changed by Jason Taylor's junior and senior years. When I asked him why that transition occurred, he replied: "I think it's you get to the point where you're hanging out together and you don't have anything to do. And I guess maybe if you drink, you feel like you're doing something. But every party I've went to, if you were drinking, . . . they're not doing anything more than they would be doing if they weren't drinking. . . . They'll be having a conversation with a beer in their hand, they're having a good time. They're having a conversation without it, they're bored."

At his university, Taylor asked his college classmates from other parts of South Carolina if they "partied," and he reported that they denied doing so. Then Taylor suggested that

> in the country there's not much to do on the weekends. Your parents – a lot of people's parents – won't let you do much, and if you go out, you want to do something, so you I guess "stick it to the man" maybe. . . . It's really odd. . . . I really feel that people from the rural part of the state end up partying more. I guess that's why you get so many jokes about rednecks and their Lite beers, 'cause I mean they end up drinking in high school and they drink for the rest of their life. They might not be getting drunk for the rest of their life, but they enjoy having beer.

Then I asked Jason Taylor to describe the types of parties he attended during his junior and senior years. Taylor admitted he had attended "a few," and described some where the hosts would proclaim that their parents were out of town – "and that would be the party that would be the really wild one." On the other hand, most of Taylor's parties were held at homes with "a whole lot more liberal parents" who "didn't care if kids drank at their house." The rationale, Taylor explained, was that these parents reasoned that high school kids were going to drink, but that "if you do it here we won't be worried about you." Those parties typically were "pretty relaxed. And we'd usually have bonfires at those parties, too. . . . They had a pool and we'd swim in the summer a little bit."

I asked Jason Taylor to describe these more relaxed parties in more detail. He replied that people would be sitting around the bonfire, talking, perhaps playing a guitar, with some inside playing video games. "All you were really doing was just having conversations – with a beer in your hand," Taylor explained. Most of the party attendees were males, perhaps because fewer girls were "into it," Taylor speculated, but he did admit that when girls attended, "there was just more drama. But when they did come it was fun with them, too." Female guests included girlfriends or "girls that the guys were interested in," Taylor recalled. Typically, though, the male hosts planning a party would know that "we need to invite some more girls over, . . . and then we never would!" Taylor speculated that some "popular" girls had started attending parties while still under sixteen.

College Life Stories

While stories about college and college life were not a focus of my research, and while not many informants my age or older had attended college, some had. Mostly my questions about college life were driven more by my personal curiosity as a college professor rather than by professional interest, but I did ask how inhabitants from relatively isolated mountain regions adjusted to the much wider horizons offered by higher education. Assuming more recent informants such as Kayla Radcliffe and Jason Taylor had been raised with television, mass media, and the internet, I expected that their adjustments to university life had not been quite as dramatic as those of previous generations. As a faculty member at Radcliffe and Taylor's university, I also wanted to avoid any conversations with them that might reveal academic or student conduct violations, as well as any potential conversations about academic life or colleagues that might make them feel uncomfortable in the context of my office on campus. Thus, the stories I have selected offer some perspectives on how inhabitants have viewed higher education through the past century and not more recently.

Deborah Mitchell had been raised in Jocassee Valley (now inundated under Lake Jocassee) but had desired a wider stage for her life's adventures since girlhood. After high school in the late 1950s she wanted to continue her education and had considered enrolling at Clemson College [now University], but her father felt the institution had too many males per female.[15] Instead, Mrs. Mitchell received a scholarship to the region's all-female teachers' college for $500, which almost paid her tuition for one year. She received other scholarships to cover her remaining years in part, but she also worked part-time as a babysitter for families summering in Jocassee Valley as well as at a garment plant in Salem. In between her junior and senior years, Deborah Mitchell served as a waitress in a hotel on Clemson University's campus; as a home economics major, she believed she could handle the job. She roomed in married student housing because she also lived with and worked for a faculty spouse whose husband was away on a research project that summer. After two days she was promoted to "night hostess," and using her "wonderful Southern hospitality" skills, she charmed her guests. Because she roomed very close to the hotel, Mrs. Mitchell also worked the breakfast shift the next morning. Since the same customers saw her working both at night and again that next morning, she thought *they* thought she must be desperate for money, so, she admitted, "I got some *darn* good tips!"

While "chemistry was about the death of me," Deborah Mitchell confessed, "I did graduate in four years, which is a miracle!" When I asked

15 Clemson first admitted female students in 1955, and so the ratio of males to females still would have been significant in Mrs. Mitchell's time.

her if students from other regions had noticed in her speech or behavior any hints of her mountain origins, Mrs. Mitchell did not believe so. Since her parents had always emphasized "us speaking correctly and learning the King's English," she did not believe that she had "any mountain twang or anything like that." But she and her roommate, from the city of Pickens, felt that their friends across the hall, from Pauley's Island [South Carolina] on the Atlantic Coast, were more sophisticated – "you know, the worldly girls who knew how to shag[16] and all this stuff." As a joke, Mrs. Mitchell and her Pickens friend "made up this story about that we couldn't come back [to school next year] because our daddies – their liquor stills had been cut down!" "Oh, we shot them a line," she said, laughing.

About a decade later, when Elizabeth Nelson considered her path into higher education, women's roles in American society barely had begun to change. Ms. Nelson's parents expected her to attend college, but she really wanted to get a job and become financially independent. As a compromise, she enrolled in a two-year private religious college about thirty minutes' drive from her home, expecting to graduate with an associate's degree in "secretarial science." But after only one year, Ms. Nelson discovered that "I didn't have what it took! I couldn't do dictation at a hundred and twenty words a minute and I couldn't type at a hundred and twenty words a minute. And I squeaked through those courses with a C and I thought, 'I gotta rethink this. This just isn't going to work.'" Instead, she took a personality test, loved art but believed she could not make a living that way, and discovered that she was better suited for the social sciences. She enjoyed her sociology class but hated her psychology teacher, and so majored in the former.

As a professor myself, I was intrigued by Elizabeth Nelson's antipathy toward her psychology professor, and discovered that, in effect, he had trouble accepting the changing roles of women in American society in the late 1960s. As a preface, Ms. Nelson described herself as having been a shy person in high school and during her first year at college, but a specific incident helped her to overcome her shyness and to gain in self-esteem. At the time of her attendance, Ms. Nelson explained, the college "was going through a change on campus." The dress code for female students permitted only dresses and not slacks, but "there was a movement underway" to change the dress code to allow women to wear slacks to class. The college deans voted in favor of the change, and so one day Ms. Nelson wore slacks to her psychology class. Unfortunately, she continued, the professor "was the school's minister and he

16 The "Shag" is the official state dance of South Carolina, which had its origins in African American nightclubs on the Atlantic coast frequented by a few daring white teenagers in the late 1940s, then spread to white nightclubs. Like "rock and roll," the word originally referred to sexual intercourse, and still means that in British and Canadian slang.

was old and he was ultra conservative." And so, during class, the professor "just quit teaching, put his book down and said, . . . 'I just want you to know that sloppy dress is indicative of a sloppy attitude.' And then he went back to teaching. . . . And that's when I decided, 'I ain't taking that guff! I'm not listening! You hear me? I'm not listening!'"

Because she needed to take some credits during her second summer semester at the school, and because the institution did not have an August graduation, Elizabeth Nelson had to wait until the next May to graduate. "And we were all in there getting ready in the room" and that same conservative psychology professor came in, looked at all the graduates, and pronounced, "'I just want to commend all of you who finished on time.' And that was a slap in the face towards those of us who had not finished on time. And I thought, 'You turkey!'"[17]

During her time at the college, Elizabeth Nelson resided in dorms on campus and loved her time in the little college town. Without a car, Ms. Nelson did not come home very often, but "my girlfriends and I would walk uptown and visit. It was a great experience; perfect place to go when . . . you're shy and naïve and, you know, this is a good first step away from a rural life – a sheltered rural life." When I asked Ms. Nelson if the other students teased her about her accent, she admitted that "I was teased a number of times by kids, because I had such a pronounced Southern mountain way of talking, the drawl and everything. And I'm like, 'I'll show you!' So I purposely changed the way I spoke. . . . I did it as a means of self-preservation so people wouldn't make fun of me."

While the stories in this chapter document adventures in various levels of educational institutions over almost a century, the stories also illustrate significant changes to American culture, as reflected in the daily lives of upper South Carolina residents during that same time period. Early in the twentieth century, many rural students attended one-room schools taught by devoted (or strict) teachers often without advanced college degrees. By the middle of the last century, schools consolidated, highways improved, and education professionalized. Automobiles became more common and attendance distances increased. Desegregation altered minds and classrooms. Teenagers and their activities entered into mainstream American culture, and increasing affluence and idleness modified their extracurricular activities. In addition to acquiring an education, pupils in school at any level also might utilize that institution to acquire a spouse. Stories of couples constitute the next chapter.

---

17 "Turkey" was a term of mild ridicule popular in the 1970s but in common use decades earlier. See the *Oxford English Dictionary*.

Chapter Eight

"It Was Meant for Us to Be Together": Stories About Couples

During the course of my research, I sometimes had the opportunity to interview married couples, and I always enjoyed their interactions as they recalled events from their collective or individual pasts. In total, I interviewed seventeen couples, fourteen of whom were inhabitants and so I will focus on their stories. Of these fourteen, two were African American and the others were of European descent. Often as a way to help my informants become more comfortable with the interview process, and to assist in establishing rapport, I would ask them to describe how they met, and I delighted in hearing their varied perspectives on this occasion. Male and female informants without spouses present (or those widowed) added their own stories as well. Since this group ranged in age from their forties to their nineties, stories of dating and of married couples described life in the mountains for over a century, and document major changes in southern Appalachian and American society. I have organized the stories by general topic, and then chronologically within topics. Despite their variations, the stories still demonstrate the love and sociality that drew these people together and that have kept them together, often for decades. Perhaps there are universal truths to be discovered in these stories, but at least the stories serve as entertainment.

As readers will discover, these stories describe the gender binary and heterosexual relationships commonly found in American society. While I did not ask my informants about nonbinary individuals or homosexual relationships because that was not the direction of my research, hints of both did occur in some stories. For example, I remember one story told by one inhabitant about two men who quarreled, with one killing the other; the narrator had implied that their disagreement may have been due to a romantic breakup. Lucille ("Ludy") Godbold (one of the two sisters who managed the Jocassee Girls' Camp) to contemporary eyes fits the definition of a nonbinary individual,[1] and was even indirectly described as such through the mid-twentieth-century cultural lenses of some of my informants. Since my research, one of the inhabitants quoted in this book has come out publicly as gay and has married someone of the same sex, but this person did not present that identity during the interviews. Despite these gender alternatives, virtually all the following stories illustrate the majority of American cultural perspectives on gender, courtship, and marriage.

Stories of Initial Meetings and Dating

The personal history of married couples logically would begin with meeting and/or dating potential spouses. Before consolidated high schools and sprawling suburban neighborhoods, meeting potential spouses could be challenging. David and Marie Ellison, a married couple in their seventies, originally met because "his parents and my parents were good friends," Marie remembered, and continued: "I recall the day – [her husband interrupted] – that we went up one Sunday, you know how country people used to go and eat lunch with their friends and neighbors and spend the day." Then, she looked at her husband and asked, "We were about ten years old, Papa?" "I think," Mr. Ellison replied, and Marie continued: "And he had a playhouse. They had a branch [small creek] running down there by the side of their house, and we played in that playhouse and played in the playhouse and we just kept on being friends, I reckon, and I guess we knew each other pretty well!"

Other couples met in their church youth groups. For example, Ryan Trask explained that he met his future spouse "when I was three and she was four at Vacation Bible School. And we were always friends. I've known her obviously my whole life." In a later interview, Donna Trask agreed, explaining, "We have pictures of us in, like . . . maybe Bible School . . . where we had gone to see the fire truck and we're all standing in front of the fire truck. So we had known each other a long time. And our parents went to school together so – and our grandparents knew each other." "But we never dated until we were both students at Clemson," Mr. Trask explained in his earlier interview, but "she was the editor of the annual staff when we were in junior high school and high school. And I had to work for her. I was her photographer and layout person, so she's been telling me what to do since I was in junior high!"

1 See her description in John M. Coggeshall, *Something in These Hills: The Culture of Family Land in Southern Appalachia* (Chapel Hill: University of North Carolina Press, 2022), 43, 187n18; see also Claudia Whitmire Hembree, *Jocassee Valley* (Pickens, SC: Hiott Printing Company, 2003), 162–64.

Elaine Parker met her husband Robert because "we grew up in the same church. . . . And you know back years ago that's where you would get your boyfriend, your husband, wife – at church. 'Cause that was the only place we got to go, really, was the church. And maybe a ball game every once in awhile, a movie." Robert Parker agreed, adding that about fifty-seven years ago, "that's where I winked my eye at her!" Mrs. Parker continued their story, explaining that her future husband's family eventually moved closer to her own family, and

> I had a cousin that lived right up the road right up from us here [and] . . . he [Robert] had a girlfriend that he would bring to my cousin's house. And you know how we young people were back then. You'd get together Sunday afternoon after church. And we all would, you know, go to my cousin's house, and that's where we'd have our little fun. You know, act up and be silly and all this kind of stuff. . . . I did have a crush on him, you know! . . . So, I think that's where it started at my cousin's house. He would come to my cousin's house and [eventually] didn't bring his girlfriend. I didn't understand; I said, "Why he didn't bring his girlfriend today?" . . . And see, he and my brother, they were friends. And he would come to my house. . . and pick up my brother like on a Saturday night, and they would say they [were] going to get a haircut. . . . Okay, so we would be home Saturday night . . . getting ready for church Sunday. . . . We'd be sitting on the porch, you know, polishing our shoes and combing our hair, and rolling up our hair on this brown paper. . . . And my brother would get so upset. "I thought we was going out tonight." He [Robert] said, "No, I'm not going nowhere now, I'm gonna stay here." . . . I think this was after he done winked that eye at me. That melted me! So . . . my brother he . . . said, "I'm gonna buy me a car, 'cause [Robert] ain't gonna be riding me no more."

Other couples, such as Joshua and Anne Flowers (married for about seventy-five years), met in one-room rural schoolhouses. "I was about twelve and he was about thirteen," Mrs. Flowers explained, "and we claimed one another for sweethearts. We'd write notes and he'd always put me two plugs of Juicy Fruit chewing gum in his notes. . . . We claimed one another for sweethearts the whole time we was in school." Joshua added: "Married when I was twenty-one and she was twenty." Mrs. Flowers specifically recalled a school function called a "cake walk," where parents donated cakes to the school to be auctioned off as a fundraising event. "We walked in the cake walk over there one night," Mrs. Flowers related,

> and me and him won the cake. It was a big old coconut cake. . . . The teachers . . . wanted to know, said, "Now, do y'all want that cake? Or do you want us to" – they'd put it up and auction it off, you know. And we told her go ahead and auction it off. So they [someone else] paid about five dollars. And she divided the money between [us] . . . . We had two dollars and a half, and we thought we was rich!

At that same one-room school, James and Margaret York also met each other, but it was not until their teen years that they became more connected. When Mr. York was a young teenager, he worked at a sawmill, and Mrs. York's father ran a part-time beer joint where Mr. York and his friends would gather after work. Mr. York described his future father-in-law as "kind of a 'ill' fellow; he might shoot you, or he might go slap you or whatever, you know." At this, Mrs. York did not contradict him, but just laughed. "But I always got along good with him," Mr. York assured us.

One afternoon, several boys were teasing the owner about eventually marrying his daughter (then about ten years old), and Mr. York proudly remembered that the owner pointed to him, then about fourteen, and said, "'Boys, I'm gonna tell you something.' Says, 'Right here is the man that's gonna marry my daughter.' And I never will forget that as long as I live." Margaret York added that "I wasn't nowhere in to marrying at that time. . . . I didn't even *like* him, then. His sister was my best friend, and me and her was real good friends all through high school – grammar school and high school. But he was so mean, I didn't like him at all. I couldn't stand him!" When I asked her to explain, Mrs. York said that her future husband was "always just aggravating, just picking at you. I think he wanted your attention, but he didn't know how to get it!" She laughed and continued: "So he'd just be in his little clever way aggravating to me. I just thought it was awful!" Mr. York added sheepishly, "But you liked it, though, didn't you?" and his wife replied, "No, I didn't then. I don't know how I got tangled up with you!" and both laughed. After Margaret York graduated from high school, the couple married and remained together for over fifty years until death took them both.

Childhood friends John Summers and George Tanner grew up together in the now-flooded Jocassee Valley, and as teenage boys, they remembered trying to infiltrate the barrier of the Godbold sisters, guardians of the girls' camp in Jocassee Valley, in order to meet girls, especially those from other places in the state and region. I interviewed both men as we sat around their campfire at a state park, and Mr. Summers reminisced: "Boy, me and him used to have times on that river up there when they had the girls' camp up there," and we all laughed. Mr. Summers would carry Mr. Tanner on his bicycle about a mile from their rural neighborhood up to the camp, and Tanner added, "We'd go down every once in a while and put the girls on a show." Specifically, Mr. Summers would ride past the camp with Mr. Tanner standing on the back of the bike, holding on. "We'd get all kind of comments from them, too!" Mr. Summers said with a chuckle. On Saturday nights, with permission, the boys would attend the frequent skits performed by the girls at the camp.

As a teenage boy, Harry Edison also rode his bike over to the girls' camp. The father of a friend knew the Godbold sisters, and so Edison and his friend could attend the Saturday night skits, too. "We didn't talk to the girls, you know; we just you know smiled at them," Edison admitted shyly. "And I guess the first time I seen 'My Fair Lady,'" Edison remembered, "they put that on one night and that's the first time I'd ever seen that play. . . . And they did a good job of it, too." In a later interview, Edison said that he and his friend also would "go swimming right up above the camp and watch the girls go swimming."

In a later interview, John Summers described a particular incident of girl-watching at the girls' camp:

> But I plowed all day and I come back by the girl[s'] camp down there, and there's a bunch of girls playing tennis, you know. Didn't mean nothing to me. Old Sarah [Godbold] that run the place – she hated boys and she'd run a man off right quick. . . . I was just walking down through there and I reckon I looked up that way but one of them [girls], right sassy, said, "I hope you get your eyeful!" And see I was tired, worked all day, you know, and I said, "I don't see nothing to look at to get it full!" And I just kept on walking.

John Summers described another opportunity several years later to meet the girls at the summer camp:

> After I finished high school I was working . . . in Charleston and I come home one weekend and I rode up in the valley, come back and there's a bunch of girls and (you know where the baptizing hole is), they's all in swimming there. And I stopped and looked a second to see the 'old big hen,' you know [Sarah Godbold]. I walked down there where they's at and got to talking; it was nice. And see, I had *learned* about Charleston, you know, and I was staying down there. One of them asked me where I was from, and I knew if I told her from up there – I said, "I'm from Charleston" (I was, right at the time, you know). And she said, "What part of Charleston?" and I told her, you know. Well, she lived on that same road! She says, "Oh my," says, "you've caught me hook, line, and sinker!" Said, "That's my hometown; that's where I live!" Been a-telling her a lie!

In the same Jocassee Valley lived Deborah Mitchell's natal family, and Deborah believed that in her youth "my daddy was *very* protective of his girls and who we dated, or who stopped and talked to us. And I always wondered why; I'd get so mad at him, like, you know, 'That boy's so cute, I'd like to talk to him.' 'No, no, no.' So my daddy always had this innate ability; . . . maybe he knew things that I didn't know. But he was very protective of us."

At that time, Cynthia Niles observed, many girls in high school got married because, as she explained, "really wasn't anything in Salem to do except take a year of home ec[onomics] and get married!" Mrs. Niles recalled three of her high school classmates who "got married in the ninth grade. . . . And I was in eleventh grade whenever I quit and got married – seventeen." She always teased her husband, who was employed by the federal government, "that he was like Strom Thurmond: He had a government job and a young wife!"[2]

Born in the 1950s, Harry Edison and his wife had met in their neighborhood church, but he did not ask his future wife out on a date until high school. At that time, Mrs. Edison explained, "the first date we went [on was] to a Liberty–Pickens football game and then he really did wine and dine me because he took me to Capri's in Easley, which was one of the nicest restaurants around."[3] A fanatic high school football fan, Harry Edison teased his wife that while they were dating, she would attend all the games, "even in the rain! She'd sit under an umbrella in the rain." But after they were married, "times have changed since then," Mr. Edison said slyly, looking at his wife, and both laughed.

A teenager decades later, Jason Taylor described how boys in his larger, consolidated high school met members of the opposite sex:

> People went out at our school, [but] I don't really see it as like dating, like going out to eat for dinner by themselves; it was usually just groups. . . . I think a lot of times relationships started up at football games, because you'd like be sitting with people, and then you'd just like be cutting up with these people, or a girl, and finally just moved into the relationship stage. I think I know a few guys that did that. They just hang out with girls at football games. . . . You wanted to go to the football game 'cause there were a whole bunch of girls there. So you wanted to meet and socialize with them. But as for sitting, a lot of times it would just be like – it would be a mix. By senior year, we all knew each other pretty well, so we'd just sit with whoever we wanted at that particular game.

2 Strom Thurmond was the US senator from South Carolina (serving from 1954 to 2003) who, at age sixty-six, married a former "Miss South Carolina," then twenty-two.

3 Opened in 1944, the restaurant is still in business in Easley.

Although they had known each other earlier, Joseph and Beth Yeats met again by coincidence after high school graduation. On his way to a Sunday afternoon date, Mr. Yeats had stopped for a hamburger at a small restaurant and overheard a patrolman talking about having to go retrieve a drunk by the side of the road. Mr. Yeats had just seen a friend of his in such a position, and so Mr. Yeats immediately left and picked him up first, before the police had arrived. As they drove around to sober up, the pair passed a young lady walking by the side of the road. His friend said, "'I know that old girl. Let's stop.'" But then the friend added, "'Yeah, she's an old stuck-up schoolteacher. You wouldn't enjoy dating her.'" Instead, Mr. Yeats took a chance and made a date, to return next Sunday evening. But, in the meantime, Beth had had a wisdom tooth pulled; "her face was swollen, her eye was black; I mean she looked terrible." And Mr. Yeats thought to himself, "'Good God, she can't look that bad all the time,' you know? . . . And eight months later we were married." Beth Yeats concluded: "People said it wouldn't last, and it's what, fifty-eight years?"

At nineteen, Claudia Bradshaw Alexander also met her future husband Brian after high school. She asked her older brothers, working at a nearby textile plant, to try to get her a job with them so she could carpool and save enough money to buy a car. At the same time, Brian carpooled to another textile mill, but his friend's wife worked with Claudia. Whenever his friend stopped to pick up his wife, Brian "would watch me." Eventually he would write her notes, and then finally he worked up the courage to ask mutual friends for Claudia's phone number. However, at that time Claudia lived far into the Oconee County mountains, and her family did not have a telephone. So she gave Brian her brother's number and instructed him to call her at five p.m.; she would then walk up to her brother's house and answer the phone. Brian did, and he asked Claudia out on a date.

Claudia first consulted with her "very strict" mother, who told her, "'I don't think you are'" ready to date yet, to which Claudia replied, "'Uh-huh. I am too; I'm nineteen.'" On the other hand, Claudia's father learned of Brian's family name, one that carried a great deal of local prestige due to another Alexander, a pastor, having served with honor during World War II. Although Mrs. Bradshaw gave the couple a curfew of nine p.m., Mr. Bradshaw allowed them to date, due to the family's reputation; in fact, Claudia recalled, Brian was the only boy her father ever approved of her dating. Upon first meeting, Brian Alexander took Mr. Bradshaw's hand firmly and greeted him, because "I've always been raised: You respect your elders. And he shook my hand, had a firm grip, and I knew right then me and him were gonna get along. And as long as I ever knew him we never had to cross words." "Never!" Mrs. Alexander confirmed immediately.

"Oh gosh, it was a whirlwind romance!" Claudia Alexander recalled. Brian started: "We dated –" and Claudia interrupted, "three months and you asked me to marry you. And then we were engaged three months. Six months total." "And we were married on the – December the twenty –" Brian hesitated, and Claudia interjected: "First." Simultaneously, Brian confirmed: "Twenty-first," to which his wife warned, "You'd better remember!" "Yeah, I remember," Brian affirmed. Then Brian recalled the moment he asked his future father-in-law for his daughter's hand in marriage. When Brian began, Mr. Bradshaw interrupted and said he need not ask, but Brian asked for his permission and blessing out of respect. Brian recalled, "He just kind of grinned; and he had a tear coming down like that. I'll never forget it. And he said, 'Well, what you waiting on?'"

Unlike most inhabitant couples, Benjamin and Denise Craig met as college students at the University of South Carolina. Denise had wanted to take an English class from James Dickey, a professor who had just published *Deliverance*, but she felt intimidated: "I always wanted to take one of his classes, but my mechanics in English weren't probably in good enough shape to take a writing class with him. He'd probably take me apart!" Instead, she and her husband met in a political science class, which Mrs. Craig had avoided until the last minute. "But I guess it was meant to be," Denise Craig said with a smile; "then you were there. If I had taken it without putting it off then we would've just been like ships passing."

Ryan Trask's grandfather attended Clemson College (now University) in the 1930s. At that time, Clemson was an all-male military college, and the students drilled on Bowman Field, in front of Old Main [Tillman Hall]. As Ryan Trask explained, his grandmother had come into town with some friends to have a picnic and watch the cadets parading, as many local residents did. Out of the cadet corps, Mr. Trask's grandmother picked out his grandfather, then a junior, "and he quit school and got married."

Unlike almost everyone else I interviewed, Josephine Chavis met her husband after she had gotten a college degree during World War II and had begun her career as a teacher, then one of the few professional jobs available to most educated women. First she met her future husband's brother [Joseph, a pseudonym], but "everybody told me how good looking [John, pseudonym] was; they said he's just handsome." At one point a local school held a box supper, and even though Mrs. Chavis did not teach there, she donated a box supper anyway. Josephine believed that the local schoolteacher secretly told John which box supper she had brought, so he bought hers. "And he brought me home that night. And then I think he came back the next Sunday; I think he came and we went to ride," Mrs. Chavis recalled; "and we dated then for five years. We'd break up and then we'd get back together. I think it was meant for us to be together."

Married Life

Because of cultural prohibitions against premarital sex and a relative absence of birth control decades ago, couples frequently married early and had large families; of course, children were also useful for farm or domestic chores. For example, Jeffrey Donnelly's mother married at fifteen; his father was nineteen. "Then a year and a half later or something my older brother was born," Donnelly continued; "then from there about every two years they had a kid!" The couple had a total of eight children. One of Claudia Alexander's sisters was sixteen when she got married; Mrs. Alexander was eighteen or nineteen. John Summers admitted that "when I first got married, you know, we didn't have nothing, just kids really; . . . she's sixteen, I's eighteen. We didn't have no car. The house rent was five dollars a month. And [Robert Davidson, a neighbor] had an old pickup that you had to wire the doors shut to. And he brought me that old pickup up there and told me to just drive that thing. . . . And I drove that old truck everywhere. And I never will forget it. You know, we didn't have nothing. And that sure helped us out."

As a girl raised in a conservative Christian household, Claudia Alexander remembered trying to overhear adult conversations after the children had been excused, and I asked what topics those forbidden conversations may have covered. She replied:

> Oh, probably about women having babies and stuff like that. That was not discussed. Back then, I think, I don't want to say that they were real private but that was just something you didn't talk about. I don't ever remember having that discussion with my momma to this day. I learned that from school out of a book. I think I checked one out at the library and brought it home and hid it, afraid Momma might find it, but she did not talk about – they didn't talk about sex. You didn't hear – when they would say a woman is pregnant, they would say they're "in the family way." If they got married they said they "got caught."

Brian Alexander also remembered the church ladies saying that his then-pregnant wife was "'in the family way.'"

Cynthia Niles married while still in high school and moved into the Jocassee Valley area to begin her married life. Like many other mountain inhabitants, Ms. Niles faced challenges during the early years of her married life:

> Would you believe it, I was in a twenty-four by twenty-four [square foot home]? And this is the first house I've had hot

> water in [her current home, built in the late 1960s]. And I don't feel sorry for kids today, girls today, that have babies. I had three children in two and a half years. . . . I had them in the hospital, but I had to carry water, and we didn't have no bathroom in the house. And today they have diapers, hot water, and all this. I don't feel sorry for them today because I know what I went through yesterday! But it wasn't that bad because where my parents live, where we was raised at we didn't have – we had a well. But [after marriage] I got water out of the creek! . . . You grow up fast. You get educated fast!

Because of cultural prohibitions on discussions of human sexuality to young adults, and also because of human sexual desires, sometimes children were born out of wedlock. For example, Robert Davidson remembered a family deep in a Pickens County valley where the mother was "half Indian," and despite the fact she was married to someone else (the boys took his last name), she had three sons "by an Indian," and that made these three boys "nearly full-blooded Indian." The man's daughter "had five children and never was married!" According to Mr. Davidson, the community knew who the father of three of these children was, but the woman "never would tell who these [other] two boys belonged to. She never would tell. Her daughter-in-law asked her on her death bed, and she would not tell who them boys' daddies was."

In a discussion with a woman and her cousin, one lady was describing life in their childhood rural neighborhood. In that community lived a married couple with a large family, including the narrator as the youngest daughter. Nearby lived a young unmarried woman with a small child. Trying to remember kin ties, the cousin asked who the father of that small child was, and the original narrator replied quietly that it was her own father.

Children without parents certainly needed quality homes, but rules about adoptions varied. Decades ago, regulations about working women who wanted to adopt children were fairly strict. In a poignant story, Josephine Chavis continued to teach after she married, first in the middle part of the state and then right back in her Oconee County mountain school. She and her husband considered adopting a little girl because her husband "loved children." The couple even had completed the home visit with social workers, to make sure they were an appropriate, caring home. But, in order to adopt at that time, Mrs. Chavis would have had to quit teaching and remain at home, because "they wouldn't let you adopt and then work on. And I thought about that a lot." Unfortunately, Mrs. Chavis was torn between a profession she had trained for and that she loved, and the possibility of becoming a loving mother to an orphaned child. "If they'd just let me taught," she sighed. Ultimately, she said softly, "we didn't get the little girl."

A common strategy used by couples to maintain their relationship is through the use of foods. Like in many traditional American households, wives most frequently cooked, typically following recipes they learned from their maternal relatives as they grew up. However, these recipes might not be familiar to their husbands, raised on their own maternally prepared foods. Thus, crafty wives must calculate strategies to blend traditions. For example, Donna Trask discovered that her husband "likes squash the way *his* grandmother made it [fried with flour, but] I like squash the way my grandmother made it [fried in cornmeal]. So, I had to compromise," she explained, by adding both flour and cornmeal to her own family's squash. On the other hand, Mrs. Trask's maternal grandmother made great biscuits, loved by her husband, and so, Mrs. Trask admitted, "I made a point to go over there and have her show me how she made them," just so she could cook them for her husband, which he greatly appreciated.

Like married couples everywhere, inhabitants described memorable arguments and disagreements. For example, Joshua Flowers discovered that he had ulcers, and so he bought a goat for the milk. Unfortunately, the goat "ran around here loose all the time," Anne Flowers recalled, and if it got into the house it would destroy everything in its path. One day, while the couple had gone to town, the goat butted open the door and scattered washing powder, flour, sugar, "and everything all over the place," Mrs. Flowers explained. Another time the goat had poked its head through a broken window pane and "chewed my curtain off just as far as it could go," Mrs. Flowers continued. "I was in the dog house!" Mr. Flowers ruefully added. One day a neighbor offered to buy the goat for a dollar; Mrs. Flowers immediately accepted the offer and her son captured it and sent if off. When Mr. Flowers came home, Anne told him she had sold his goat and then added: "'If you ever do bring another goat here,'" I said, "you're gonna live with it – you ain't gonna live with me!'" Several weeks later, Mrs. Flowers sent her son out to the woodpile for some stove wood and he heard a goat bleating in the woods. He reported this to his mother, who challenged her husband, who replied that he was going to slaughter it immediately for meat. "If you don't, I will!" Mrs. Flowers threatened sternly. In describing his long married life to friends, Mr. Flowers explained that he and his wife "never did fuss none, [but] we had a lot of loud explaining to do to one another!"

Another time Mrs. Flowers recalled that her husband and a neighbor had planned to go deer hunting one morning, but it was raining. Figuring that his neighbor would not come by, Joshua Flowers lay in bed and complained about his back pain; he asked his wife for a back massage, which she started to provide for him. "So I was laying there rubbing his back and he happened to hear that [neighbor's] Jeep pull up out there. He throwed that cover back and jumped clean out over me on the floor," Mrs. Flowers related. Joshua Flowers' back pain mysteriously disappeared, and the men went hunting.

With divorce nearly impossible socially, legally, and perhaps religiously, couples with irreconcilable differences adopted clever strategies for managing their separated lives. For example, Robert Davidson described an interesting solution developed by a couple in upper Pickens County:

> And there was an old man, and his wife lived in there, and they separated. And he moved across the river. And she was on this side and he was on that side. He had a boat and he'd come across in the boat part of the time. . . . He'd come over there and milk her cows and cut her wood and all that stuff but they still didn't live together!

In an earlier interview, Mr. Davidson described another solution he had heard from a common ancestor he shared with Douglas Edison. One grandfather "left them mountains up there. He just walked off and left his wife and [five] young'uns and just 'root hog or die,'[4] and gone. And nobody knows where he was at and nothing told about it. Never did know nothing." During the interview, another man asked him if his grandfather ever came back, and Mr. Davidson explained that he turned up years later in Walhalla [Oconee County seat], married to another woman with another "house full of young'uns." He had written to a son that he was dying of tuberculosis and asked his son to carry him back to his old homeplace in upper Pickens County, which he did. He asked his first wife if she would nurse him, she agreed, and she cared for him until he died.

Several individuals told romantic stories that emphasized spousal love and commitment. For example, Josephine Chavis, then a teacher in a small rural school, remembered one winter night when "it came a big snow, a big snow, and I had to stay with the lady that had the lunchroom" because the country roads were impassable. "And that night somebody knocked on our door and it was [my husband]." Under a full moon so bright "you could read a newspaper outside," Mr. Chavis had ridden a horse down to the school to bring his wife home.[5] According to Elizabeth Nelson, one of her neighbors turned down a significant promotion with a regional company and retired early rather than travel the country "because she said it was more important" to be with her husband that it was to be "traveling all over." Margaret York, reflecting on her long marriage, turned to her husband and said, "We didn't have a lot of money so we just made our own entertainment. And that was good to do – to get out and walk. And the kids enjoyed it." Suffering from emphysema and on oxygen,

---

4 The expression means the woman was left to fend for herself.

5 Jennifer Goree, a regional folk musician and a neighbor of Mrs. Chavis's, was so touched by the story that she composed a song about the incident: "Pauline," located on her 1998 album *Don't Be a Stranger*.

Mr. York faced his wife and asked quietly, "Wouldn't it be nice to do that again with me?" "Yes, it would be," Margaret replied with a smile; "I wish we were able to." As Claudia Alexander's mother aged, Claudia and her siblings wanted their mother to move into a mobile home near one of them, but she refused for the longest time, because her husband had built her four-room house for her, entirely by hand, when they first got married. "'I ain't a-moving out,'" Mrs. Alexander reported her mother saying adamantly, because "she loved this little house that he built for her. They were just young and in love, you know. What an adventure!"

Married life certainly can be an adventure, and for the inhabitants reporting in these pages, it almost unanimously was. While the stories may not express any significant moral teachings or provide important life lessons, they do offer another glimpse into the social conditions that added to life in the upper parts of South Carolina beginning in the early twentieth century. On the other hand, perhaps there are themes – of the vagaries of life, and how wonderful it is to have someone with whom to share those challenges. Love may take many forms, involve different types of people, and lead to various outcomes. But love, and someone with whom to share love, makes the journey of life much more pleasant.

Chapter Nine

"Now, You Talk About A Character!": Character Stories and Anecdotes

One of the questions I frequently asked my contributors was whether they recalled any eccentric characters, letting them decide for themselves the definition of "eccentric" or "character." Some of those stories are included in this chapter. In addition, I have placed into this chapter stories about local folks well known for their quirkiness or their unique sense of humor. I also include stories about individuals I thought were humorous or expressive within their times or places. While the stories may not offer morals, they do provide another glimpse into the social and physical settings of the area, and another window into the culture of the people in the southern Appalachians.

Stories of Famous People

Probably the best-known visitor to the South Carolina mountains (recalled by my inhabitants) was Lyndon Baines Johnson, the thirty-sixth president of the US. Charles Watson described a time probably in 1960, before Johnson was John F. Kennedy's vice president but already "some big politician" (a US senator from Texas). According to Watson, a helicopter carrying the senator had planned to land at the "4-H Camp" in upper Pickens County but instead landed at the baseball diamond at the Royal Ambassadors (RA) Baptist Camp.[1] A local man picked Johnson up (it is unknown whether he was traveling by himself) and gave him a ride. The narrator continued: "But going up the road [the man] asked him who and all he was and where he was from. Found out who he was, [the man] got scared and he couldn't hardly

1 Now Camp McCall Baptist Camp, founded in 1960.

drive when he found out who he was, but they made on!"

Two Hollywood movie stars, Burt Lancaster and Cameron Mitchell, happened to be in downtown Pickens one afternoon as they were in the area, probably in 1973, filming *Midnight Man* in and around Clemson (where the movie would premiere in March 1974). "They came to town and just dressed up in dungarees and all," Jesse Alexander (a retired Pickens barber) related, but "I wasn't in there [the shop] at the time." But his boss and co-owner was. Both Lancaster and Mitchell entered the shop, and the owner had no idea who they were. According to Alexander, the owner said to the two Hollywood stars, "'Fellas, watch the front; I want to go over across to the SCN [South Carolina National] Bank and make a deposit,' and they said, 'Yeah, we'll watch the place.' So they went in and set down on the benches, and then he came back and found out who they were. They were just out browsing around."

The most infamous movie shot in the southern Appalachians undoubtedly was *Deliverance*, filmed in 1971.[2] Since scenes from the film were shot on location as the Jocassee Dam was constructed and as Lake Jocassee filled, several of my informants remembered the film and the actors. For example, John Summers and a neighbor used to take their children up to the lake to go swimming as the waters backed over roads and trees. One evening they visited the lake, and they saw mailboxes "out in the water;" they assumed someone had stolen them. So the good citizens collected the mailboxes, carried them up the hill, stashed them in the woods, and called the sheriff. "Come to find out they was making a movie," and they had destroyed a movie set instead, Summers admitted.

John Summers remembered talking with both Jon Voight and Burt Reynolds, two stars from the film. Their car's chauffeur had stopped at a country store in upper Oconee County to buy some cigarettes, and as the driver smoked two of them, he invited the bystanders at the store to go out to the car and meet the stars, and they rolled their windows down and talked. However, Summers made it very clear that he did not appreciate the image of the southern Appalachian inhabitants portrayed in the film. Patrick O'Connell, then in construction, also met Burt Reynolds as O'Connell worked on the dam. "Did you ever see that bulldozer in there [in a scene in the film]? That's me!" O'Connell proudly exclaimed, perhaps describing the scene when graves were being moved. O'Connell added that after shooting for the day, Reynolds would "knock off" just like everybody else and come to the job site to watch the heavy earth-moving equipment, "you know, like a little kid." "You know, you could tell he was 'Mr. Reynolds,' you know – which he was!" John Summers related, "but he was all right. He

2 See John M. Coggeshall, *Something in These Hills: The Culture of Family Land in Southern Appalachia* (Chapel Hill: University of North Carolina Press, 2022).

was all right." On the other hand, "that old Jon Voight up there just as vulgar as he could be. Right in front of everybody," Summers admonished.

Harry Edison had met another character from the movie, Herbert "Cowboy" Coward. According to Wikipedia, as a young man Coward worked at a Wild West amusement park in Maggie Valley, North Carolina, where he met Burt Reynolds, who also worked there at one time early in his career. When the casting call for *Deliverance* went out, Reynolds remembered Coward, and he got the job as the "toothless man" who, along with character actor Bill McKinney, accosts the characters played by Jon Voight and Ned Beatty.[3] "Our company, we used to have a plant up at Enca, North Carolina," Harry Edison explained, "and one of the guys, one of these weirdos in the movie, he worked up there at the plant. He was an extra, but he was one of the main characters that violated the guy! . . . Now you talk about a character!"

Another character from the movie was "Lonnie the Banjo Boy," the young man with Down Syndrome who appeared to play the banjo in accompaniment with the character played by Ronnie Cox. John Summers believed that "the guy that picked the banjo – sat on the porch and picked the banjo? He's taking out carts up yonder at Food Lion [grocery store] at Cherokee," North Carolina. In fact, Summers related, "I talked to him – I talked to him Wednesday evening."

Preacher Billy Holcombe[4]

One of the better-known local characters was "Preacher" Billy Holcombe, related to many, including several people I had interviewed. Charles Watson narrated a very well-known local anecdote:

> And my Grandpa Holcombe, he used to, I told you he was a preacher. Back then, he walked wherever he went; didn't have no car, never owned one in his life. . . . And back then they had foot washings. . . . Grandmother, she'd always on Saturday evening lay his Sunday clothes out on the bed, you know, the next service and all. . . . But them older boys . . . they got into Grandpa's socks and pulled them up over their arm, reached up inside the "chimley" and rubbed them up in that smut. And took the socks back down and laid them back like they's supposed to be, so they looked good and clean. But Pa got up and everything and put them socks on and took off to church and they had a foot washing. Naturally, you know, he was one of the first to get up there. He pulled that

3 See also Burt Reynolds, *My Life* (New York: Hyperion, 1994), 156–57.

4 More information about "Preacher" Billy Holcombe may be found in Claudia Whitmire Hembree, *Jocassee Valley* (Pickens, SC: Hiott Printing Company, 2003), 52–54, 56 (foot-washing story).

> sock off, stuck that foot out and just as black as a colored man's! He knews [sic] what happened, them devilish boys! Ended up all of them, them boys turned out to be pretty good; . . . they just full of the devilment when they was young and all.

Rachel Edwards told the same story about "Uncle Billy Holcombe," adding "just everybody loved him and they called him that. And he had a son that was hilarious, too." Mrs. Edwards explained that Uncle Billy's son was also a preacher, pastoring at

> the Rocky Bottom Baptist Church, and the song director there was – he was a Broome, his last name was Broome, Kermit Broome. And [Preacher Holcombe] was up in the pulpit, and he says, "Mr. Songbook, would you please pass me a broom?" Then he would refer, back then it was customary for Christians to call each other "Brother" and "Sister," and he would, one night (I remember this quite well), he looked over at his dad (he was on the front pew there), and he says, "And now we'll ask Brother Pa to dismiss us."

A grandson of "Preacher Billy," Douglas Edison, told a story about two brothers who were always getting in trouble. The preacher (perhaps "Preacher Billy") asked to speak to each one separately. "Do you know where God is?" the preacher thundered at one boy. He replied that he did not know. He asked three times, and when the boy left and rejoined his brother, he exclaimed worriedly: "God's missing and they think we're to blame!" Another story Edison told was about a boy who always exaggerated the truth, and one time a preacher was going to catch him in a lie, so he asked him if he was in church last Sunday. "No, sir," the boy replied. "Well," the preacher said, "while I was preaching, a bear came running into church, chased by a dog nipping at his heels. The dog chased the bear all around the church, out into the yard, caught and killed the bear, skinned it, and buried it. What do you think about that?" The boy replied, "That was my dog."

J. D. Chappell

A character of a different sort was Julius D. Chappell, known locally as "J. D."[5] Many Eastatoee Valley residents knew him, and Harry Edison (a distant relative) provided some background. Born in 1924 in the Big Cane Break in the Carolina mountains, J. D. had been sent as a preteen by his father to live with his aunt and uncle in the upper portion of Eastatoee Valley after his mother had

5 Julius David Chappell, born November 18, 1924, died July 26, 1989. His father was Julius Chappell, mother unknown. He was given to live with his uncle Arthur Anderson Chappell and his wife, Emily; https://www.findagrave.com/memorial/220981426/julius-david-chappell, accessed June 25, 2024.

died. He never married; he drove an old car up and down the valley (without a driver's license) until the car failed, and then he walked everywhere, waiting for passers-by to pick him up and take him to his destination.

During his interview, Harry Edison tried to recall the wedding present J. D. had given him and his wife, and he thought the gift had been pillowcases, but his wife reminded him that it was "a set of sheets." "He was just a sweet person," Edison added; "everybody just thought the world of him." "J. D. didn't have a real high IQ, but that's okay. It didn't matter to us. He was great," Elizabeth Nelson (also a neighbor) concluded. While "some people didn't think he was that smart," Edison said in a separate interview, "J. D. really was a highly, he was an intelligent person, but he was just – I don't know if whether the word backward would be the right word, but he was just raised different."

Ryan and Donna Trask (also neighbors) remembered J. D., with Mrs. Trask exclaiming: "He was a really big – his hands! Do you remember how big his hands were? Just absolutely huge!" "Had a big wart on his tongue," Ryan added. According to Harry Edison, J. D. worked in a sawmill as a young man and "got so muscled up and everything; he was just so stout." "And a lot of people might be scared of him because he was just so big and bulky looking, you know, and everything," Edison added. Elizabeth Nelson observed that "he did a lot of handy work on people's farms and helped them out with their crops and such. And he was a big help and they always paid him."

Much of J. D.'s income came from Social Security, Elizabeth Nelson explained, and thus he was

> very frugal. Of course, he had to be. He didn't turn the lights on unless he had to. He didn't cook. Other people would bring him food. I think, when he took a bath, when he could he'd go down to the creek and take a bath. . . . It was a good life. I remember as a child, he would come out and help my dad in the fields. And he would be so shy that when Daddy would come in for lunch to eat he wouldn't come in and eat with us. He was so shy. He would sit on the doorsteps and my mother would take him a plate of food out there. And in later years, he became more outgoing, thanks to people, you know, taking him under their wing and doing things with him. And he would come in and sit down at the table and eat with us. But he was never totally comfortable, because he would sit with half of his behind on the chair and the other half hanging off – like that!

After J. D. lost his car because it had finally broken down, he walked everywhere, and, Harry Edison explained,

> he'd be walking down the road and you'd stop to pick him up, and he'd act like he didn't even see you; he'd be looking off in the ditch and you'd have to tell him, say "Get in the car, J. D.!"

> He'd come on get in then. And he had them big old thick hands. And I remember this one time in particular – I seen him do more than this but we were going fishing, that's back when we had Keowee River down in there [before Lakes Jocassee and Keowee were built]. We were going down the road and he said, "Stop!" So we had stopped the car. And here was this big wasp nest on the bank. He just walks up to that wasp nest and with all these wasps on it and just breaks it off and gets it and puts it in his pocket for fish bait. And always they'd pop [sting] him and he didn't pay them any attention; he just went on. . . . And this lady, she told me one time, . . . she always went out every morning going to work in Pickens, and he figured out what time she was going out. So he'd be coming up the best side of the bridge down here walking. He'd have it planned just right 'cause he knew she'd stop and pick him up.

Donna Trask, also raised in the valley, recalled a time when her younger sister had just gotten her driver's license and came home to announce proudly that she had just picked up J. D. and had taken him somewhere. Donna and her husband Ryan tried to help me imagine the scene of a young teenaged girl by herself on a country road picking up a hitchhiking huge, muscular, older, eccentric man. To a stranger, Ryan Trask explained, J. D. "would have been frightening."

"And I guess most people'd think that was just – would be an awful thing to do," Donna explained about her sister's decision, "but you know, we all knew him. And everybody picked him up." Ryan Trask then added that this incident best portrayed the community support that J. D. had.

Toward the end of his life, J. D. became more and more dependent on his surrounding community for care. According to Elizabeth Nelson, J. D. lived with a widow for many years, "and she just looked after him because he was like a child in a lot of respects." By the 1980s J. D. had been diagnosed with a brain tumor, but the community rallied to care for him in his own home, a small log cabin in Eastatoee Valley, "the ultimate picture of peace and rustic simplicity," journalist Dot Robertson wrote. For eleven weeks, each night a volunteer would stay with J. D. and provide personal nursing care while others brought food and cleaned the patient and the cabin. On July 26, 1989, during a thunderstorm, a neighbor lady held J. D.'s hand; a big clap of thunder came, his hand relaxed, and he died. He was buried in Holly Springs Baptist Church cemetery.[6]

6 For this information, see Dot Robertson, "Eastatoe Mourns Death of

Paul Bowie

Another well-known inhabitant of Eastatoee Valley was Paul Bowie.[7] Since I never interviewed him because he had passed away by the time of my research, I did not collect direct autobiographical information; instead, inhabitants told stories about him. Born and raised in Eastatoee Valley and the descendant of some of the first white settlers, Bowie had taught school in one-room schoolhouses and had walked miles through the mountains to get there. During his lifetime he raised cattle and crops on family land, and in retirement many locals sought him out for his storytelling ability. While his surviving daughter deferred to her brothers for examples of stories, she did remember when she and Dot Robertson/Jackson, a retired regional journalist with family ties to the area, sat on the front porch of the Bowie home one summer evening and Paul and Dot exchanged stories. The daughter remembered that they sat in rocking chairs "on the front porch for five hours while she and Daddy told funny stories. And finally at eleven o'clock, she [Dot] said, 'Paul, I have to go home. I don't want to, but I have to!'"

In an interview with Paul Bowie's daughter and a neighbor, Ryan Trask, Trask described the elder Bowie as "brilliant. He was wise; he was always several steps ahead of whoever he was talking to, and so his humor it was very dry, it was intelligent." Bowie's daughter agreed. Trask continued: "And it was in every conversation. . . . A part of his life, his character, was wit." "Now he was that way when he was talking with neighbors and friends and when family gathered together for special occasions," Bowie's daughter explained, but "on everyday basis, he was a very quiet man. . . . I especially appreciate a dry sense of humor now because of his wit being that way. A lot of people don't catch that!"

Ryan Trask then related a story about how Bowie had gotten "in trouble for making sausage in his later years." The daughter remembered the event, explaining that Bowie had butchered hogs all his life and had processed the meat for his family (as virtually every farmer had done), "and I think he did this . . . for two reasons," the daughter explained: "One, . . . it was a skill that he had known all of his life and he enjoyed doing it," and second, "we gathered in, you know, family and friends here in the kitchen to help him make the sausage and package it and everything and that was fun." But, Trask added, as commercially prepared meat became more commonplace, Bowie "would give it away; he would sell it for what he spent making it."

A worker at the Holly Springs General Store had obtained some of Bowie's homemade sausage and had stored it in the cooler at the store. The US

'Innocent' Friend, Neighbor," *Greenville News*, August 2, 1989.

7 See also Coggeshall, *Something in These Hills*, 97; and Hembree, *Jocassee Valley*, 66–68, for additional stories and further information.

Food and Drug inspector, visiting the store's restaurant, happened to notice the sausage and "here we go. So, I think they came to see your daddy," Trask stated, and the daughter agreed. Trask explained that "some young, aggressive inspector was going to take care of this problem." The inspector tried to get Paul Bowie to sign a form stating that he would never make any more sausage, but Bowie refused, further angering the inspector, who insisted he could not sell homemade sausage. According to Trask, Bowie patiently explained to the young government official: "'You're right; I don't have to sell sausage and I won't sell any sausage, but I'll make as much as I want and give it away!'" Trask explained that the inspector grew even more irate,

> but Paul the whole time was probably smiling and keeping his cool . . . because Paul knew something that the inspector didn't know, and that was that the inspector's boss bought sausage from Paul every year! And so, as the fella was leaving, Paul (and I can't recall the inspector's boss's name), but Paul said, "You know, be sure and tell such and such that I'll have his sausage ready for him next week." That was his closing remark! And they never bothered him again.

Robert Perry

Born in the North Carolina mountains, Robert Perry told me that he ran moonshine for his family in his earlier life, taking advantage of the state line between the Carolinas to avoid state police, who would not cross the line in pursuit. In his later years, Perry served the region as the epitome of a "mountain man," even winning the title of "Best Hillbilly" multiple times at the July 4 "Hillbilly Days" festival in Mountain Rest (Oconee County). He also operated a model still at the festival and at the folklife center at Hagood Mill (Pickens County), demonstrating the process (without actually producing alcohol) and telling stories to visitors. I had the opportunity to interview Robert Perry before he passed away in July 2018, but his stories remain behind a pseudonym in my previous books. Photos of Perry in his late adulthood may be found online.[8]

When I interviewed Mr. Perry I did so at his home, located in upper Pickens County near Hagood Mill. To find the house, I turned off the paved road onto a gravel driveway that became more rugged as I traveled uphill, drove past a side road and a trailer (residence of one of Perry's sons), and followed the hand-lettered signs for "Perryville." I emerged into an open field, facing a century-old two-story wood frame house with extensive porches

---

8 For example, Daniel J. Gross, "Known for Bluegrass and Moonshine, Pickens County's 'Mountain Man' Dies," *Greenville News*, July 28, 2018, https://www.greenvilleonline.com/story/news/local/greenville/2018/07/28/bluegrass-moonshine-pickens-county-mountain-man-robert-perry-dies/855686002/.

13. Perryville.
Photo by John M. Coggeshall.

upon which sat various kinds of chairs and benches. Metal tools and other items hung on the exterior walls. Firewood was stacked under the porch, and the house was propped up on stones and cement blocks. A grass-free yard surrounded the house. To the far right of the house were some cages and pens, probably holding chickens, dogs, or pigs; I did not walk over to look. A donkey brayed in the distance, chickens ranged freely near the house, and a small black dog nipped at a pig as it wandered by us while we sat on the side porch.

After our interview Mr. Perry then led me into his house, cool and just a little musty, looking neat but very well lived-in (he had lived there for forty-seven years). The wooden floor sloped in several places, and I noticed that the rug or floor covering had been worn through in several places, too. Through the little kitchen we walked and into a log room that he said he had built himself, cutting and splitting the timber from his land to build it. The logs were square and about a hand's length wide. Lining the room were several stuffed birds and a large wild boar head that Mr. Perry said he had killed in the area. The bed in his bedroom was covered with a beautiful quilt, made by his late wife, with bright red tulip squares on a white background. On the walls in the living room were numerous family photos, some faded and some relatively new. The hearth had a large iron pot suspended by irons, and he said he still cooked on that. Over the mantel was a black wooden shelf unit that he said had come from an organ that a church bought; they wanted the instrument but not the piece above it, so he took it for a mantelpiece.

Surrounding the house was a field full of randomly placed, rusting vehicles of various makes, including an old truck under a wooden shelter that Perry said his family had used to run moonshine years ago. At the crest of the hill was a long shed, open on the front and back, with about ten vehicles in various states of drivability – rusty trucks, a bright blue car he drove to church, and an old '20s car that he was trying to fix up. Out in another shed was a '40s coupe that he said had at one time run moonshine, and he was going to fix it up so that the trunk could carry jugs and the bumper could release oil to foil the law. We walked past what I thought was a kiln built into the ground, but he said he used it as an outdoor cooker. In another outbuilding he pointed out an old washboard and said his grandkids had sometimes demonstrated the old system of washing clothes at the Hagood Mill folk festivals.[9] He also had an old ice box and a very early refrigerator.

Bordering the field on two sides was what appeared to be a movie set of store fronts, all made of weathered wood, with signs indicating "Sherif's Office" [*sic*], "Opry," or "Barbershop." Mr. Perry had constructed the buildings himself, using mostly white oak lumber from old barns. Not all the buildings had actual rooms; some were only fronts, but he had plans to complete each one as a small four-walled structure. The completed rooms were about ten feet square, full of assorted artifacts (related to the building's function) and cobwebs and wasp nests. He first showed me the "Pharmacy," filled with old medicine bottles that either he had collected himself or others had given to him. Some were on shelves and others were stored in cardboard boxes on the floor. In the "Saloon" he had more bottles of all sorts, including some nice jugs he said had belonged to his grandfather. Others were contemporary beer or soft drink brands. The "Jail" had some iron bars blocking off about a third of the room, and two iron cots suspended above each other as a bunk bed. On the other wall was a hangman's noose, with thirteen loops (Perry said that was the traditional number; he also said the hanging platforms had thirteen steps). Mounted in frames were various photos, including one of four white men hung for some infraction, necks twisted and stretched at a grotesque angle. On the other wall were more photos, including one of Andy (Griffith) and Barney (Don Knotts), the sheriff and deputy characters from the TV series *Mayberry*. Perry wanted to show me his "Indian rocks" in the "Asay [*sic*] and Surveying" shop, but he could not open the padlock – it had rusted shut.

The "Church" was attached to the "Opry" building, and together they formed a twenty by sixty foot room, with chairs arranged in rows, and a large wood-burning stove he said had come from an old one-room school (Montvale). In the front of the room was a stage, and here he hosted picking and singing every Monday night. He said the wood stove in winter kept the

9 See the Mill's website for scheduled events: https://visithagoodmill.com/calendar/events-calendar-list/, accessed June 25, 2024.

place quite warm, and he had a large fan set in the wall to help cool the room during the summer. Outside the "Opry" was a small children's playground, a port-a-potty, and a gravel parking lot. Perry invited me to attend one of their jam sessions, and I did.

That next Monday I arrived at "Perryville" about seven thirty p.m.; several people sat outside the performance hall, but the musicians were already playing. The parking area was full (about fifteen cars). At the front of the hall, surrounded by a lot of equipment and several microphones, were four older men playing guitars, with another man on fiddle and Robert Perry on his self-described "hillbilly bass" (a washtub attached to a board, with strings), strumming along, while his little black dog sat at his feet. Off to one side was an older man who brought a small washboard and also played a spoons-like device and a harmonica for several songs. The musicians all played gospel songs, and the lead guitarist tried to get everyone to sing. On the stage was a lyrics book with a wide variety of songs - gospel, country, and popular (such as songs by John Denver and John Fogarty). People came and went all evening, but by the time I left (about nine p.m.), there were about eight people in the audience, along with a middle-aged woman serving soft drinks, bottled water, and a food item (perhaps cornbread).

Silas Butts

One of the more colorful Oconee County characters was Silas Butts, born in 1880 and described as a "typical mountain man."[10] Gambrell's oral history utilized contemporary interviews to describe Butts. For example, Clem Smith said that Butts "could stop blood and draw fire out of burns." He was also well known as a moonshiner, and customers would leave money under the highway sign for Brasstown Road (upper Oconee County) in exchange for liquor. Others remembered him driving through area mill towns, selling vegetables and moonshine from his truck.[11]

David and Marie Ellison, from Oconee County, knew Silas Butts. According to Mr. Ellison, Butts had adopted "about twenty children," and "he bootlegged for a living." Mrs. Ellison explained that, for these mountain children, "their parents, I guess, couldn't take care of them, and he just took them." One time, Mr. Ellison continued, Butts got caught moonshining and had to appear in court. With his children in tow, Butts stood before the judge and said, "Now children, if I have to go to prison, the judge is going to take good care of you; he'll look after you." According to Mr. Ellison, the judge

10 Nicholas Gambrell, "Sha' Hell . . . and Good Corn Liquor: The Legacy of Silas Butts" (MA thesis, Clemson University, 2003), 21; see also Piper Peters Aheron, *Images of America: Oconee County* (Charleston, SC: Arcadia, 1998), 62–63, for a photo of his house.

11 Statements are from Gambrell, "Sha' Hell," 21, 60, 65, 39, 88–89.

turned Butts loose. Another time, Mr. Ellison recalled, some deputies went to his house and declared, "'Silas, I cut [destroyed] your still.' He said, 'Which one?'"

At one time Marie Ellison worked at the Oconee County Courthouse, and Butts "used to come to the courthouse and . . . we just loved him to death and some of the things that he would say would just blow your mind!" When I asked Mrs. Ellison for examples, she explained that "he wasn't too polished." Mr. Ellison interrupted and asked his wife to tell me about the time Butts went to see the South Carolina governor. According to Mrs. Ellison, Butts wanted to complain about his muddy road, but county officials told him to travel to Columbia to talk with the governor. The governor's receptionist told Butts to wait because the governor already had a client in his office, but instead Butts declared: "'I'm going right back through there now' and just marched right on in! He was very country."

Another time, Marie Ellison recalled, Butts came to see the County Superintendent of Education, still seeking a paved road for his children to better attend school. "I was sitting in my office where I worked and he came down the street," Mrs. Ellison related, and "everybody in the building was hanging around to see what he said. He just kept a-saying 'I'm gonna cuss him out; I'm gonna cuss him out!'" She remembered that Butts eventually confronted the county superintendent and demanded, "'I want something done about my road, and I want it done now.' He says, 'All of my young'uns is a-walking in mud up to their *ass*, wet and dirty and have to go to stay in school that way.' And he says, 'I want something done about it.' And we all *laughed* at him but he got something done. He got that road fixed."

"Tom Smith"[12]

Another local character was a man I'll call "Tom Smith," from northern Pickens County. Charles Watson described him as "an old drunk" and said that "everybody was scared of him." Watson believed that Smith originally owned a number of stores in the area and may have been "well off at one time." But "his wife died, and I reckon he got where – that must undoubtedly have drove him nuts. And he got running through his money and the court appointed" someone his guardian, Watson recalled. According to Watson, Smith ventured down to Holly Springs Schoolhouse "and just watch us run 'cause everybody'd run just like a bunch of chickens running from a hawk. . . . Miss Pearl, she'd give two of the biggest boys ball bats and one'd stand at the front door and one at the back door and have them ball bats raised in case he come in!"

12 Although these stories are about the same person, I have created a pseudonym for him because of the less-than-flattering portrayals. There is a photo of this person in the Pickens County Library Historical Photos collection.

While Charles Watson acknowledged that Smith never entered the schoolhouse, he recalled a time when "Miss Pearl" let "some of the older kids" go to the nearest country store and buy candy and soft drinks for the pupils at the school. Watson continued:

> So they'd done had their stuff and headed back. And everybody was standing on the door steps looking there waiting for them to come, 'cause everybody was wanting their candies and co-colas. Meantime, we seen [Smith] coming up the highway and they said 'Uh-oh,' 'cause we didn't know what was going to happen. Well, [Smith], he . . . seen them kids coming in the other direction. He hid there in the bushes. When they sort of got even with him he jerked off his hat, jumped up and stood up and hollered 'Boo!' – or something o' other. Boy, they run just as hard as they could go and their paper bags busted and they scattered drinks and crackers and everything all the way up to here. It was an awful time, because back then, losing that co-cola or bar of candy was a big thing. It was.

While Tom Smith may have terrorized younger children, Charles Watson confessed that the "older boys liked to hang around [Smith] and aggravate him." Smith lived in Rocky Bottom, "in a little old one-room shack" without running water. He had to travel to a spring, fill a bucket of water, and then carry it back to his home. According to Watson, every time Smith would fill up his water bucket, the older boys would drink it empty, forcing him to travel back to the spring again. Eventually Smith tired of this, and "he decided he'd put a stop to that," Watson said, chuckling; "he took his false teeth and dropped them down in the bottom of that bucket so when they come get a drink of water and seen them teeth laying down in there that was the end of that!"

Rachel Edwards also remembered Tom Smith. When Edwards was a little girl, she recalled, "Momma would plait our hair." During revivals, since their older sisters got to sit in the back of the congregation, Edwards explained, the younger girls wanted to do so as well. Tom Smith would come to the revivals, sit in the back "and pull our ponytails or pigtails . . . and talk out loud and everything." "Well, they have this visiting preacher at Rocky Bottom, Preacher O'Dell Goode," Mrs. Edwards narrated, "and so Preacher Goode, after the service, he goes around and he's shaking hands with everybody, and got to [Tom Smith] and he said, 'Goode's my name, O'Dell Goode.' And [Tom Smith] said [in slurred speech] 'Ha! There ain't "airey" one of you O'Dells any good!'"

Tom Smith "was a hoot," Rachel Edwards continued:

> He hitchhiked everywhere. . . . He'd even lay out in the road! It's a wonder if he hadn't got run over, but he would lay down beside the road. If you were going down the mountain, he was

> trying to get a ride; if you were going up the mountain, he tried to get a ride. And one time he was right there at Scatterbrain's place [a local wayside bar[13]] somewhere there. Some people, some guys come up the road, they asked him, said, "You think maybe we can find us a drink of liquor anywhere around here?" [Tom] said, "Well, tell you. You don't go up the mountain there." Said, "You turn at Scatterbrains, turn at Scatters," said, "go down through there" [into Eastatoee Valley]. Said, "E'ry house down there you can get you a drink of liquor, all but the church house."

A friend of Charles Watson picked up a very drunk Tom Smith one time and asked him, "'Where we going, [Tom]?' Said, 'Anywhere! Just get out of here! Too many drunks around here to suit me!'"

Charles Watson recalled another time when he was in a small country store and Tom Smith came in and asked the proprietor for shoe polish. When the owner asked Smith what color he wanted, Smith replied, "'It don't matter; I'm gonna paint my insides.'" The owner did not understand, but he gave Smith a bottle of shoe polish that Watson said was virtually all alcohol. Smith turned the bottle upside down and drank it completely.

Other Mountain Characters

Alcohol also affected other mountain characters as well. As a child, Kayla Radcliffe remembered an older male relative who lived "like a mile down the road from us." Before the widespread use of motor scooters or golf carts, and after the era of horses and mules, this older man "would ride past our house on an old lawnmower because he got his license taken away for drinking. So he was about this eighty-year-old man driving down the road on a lawnmower to get to the store to buy like a Coke. So that's how I knew him," Radcliffe explained.

Eccentric characters abounded. As a girl, Rachel Edwards performed with her family at gospel sings held at churches in the Carolina mountains, and she remembered one old man who would appear at Homecoming, when church families brought enormous amounts of food:

> I'll never forget this character. . . . I can remember he looked scary. He was, he looked like a mountain man with a beard. He looked like he hadn't had a bath in a long time. But he would sit or stand out at the edge of the woods with his dog, and he had a tote sack on his back. And before the ladies at the end of the food, he would kind of wait till people got their food, he would go, and he had this cane, walking cane, and he would start with that stick and he'd start raking the food from the tables over into

13 See Coggeshall, *Something in These Hills*, 60, 91–94, and a photo at Figure 8 for stories about Scatterbrains.

> this tote sack. And then, by the time he got to the end of the table, he'd go through the woods back home. He did that *every* time.

Another form of eccentricity was handling problems on one's own. Robert Davidson told a story about a neighbor, eventually diagnosed with double pneumonia. A local country doctor advised an operation, and so friends carried the man to Greenville, where doctors "operated on him and drained that pus out of him and put a tube in him." But, Davidson admitted, as the man healed, his father "didn't have time to take him back and get that tube took out of his side. And he's about growed up and my mother and one of my aunts took that tube out of his side and he never did go back to Greenville!"

Although I have presented some moonshining stories in my previous books,[14] inhabitants told many others. During an interview arranged by Mable Clarke for the *Liberia* book, we met with the county sheriff and several deputies, all three raised locally. After a general discussion about moonshining, one of the deputies mentioned a local woman, "Ms. Bertha." "This is a true story, but it's funny," Deputy Jenn Grover related, and continued:

> We was gonna get old Ms. Bertha for some shine one night. So we all went out, we was gonna buy illegal liquor one night, . . . to get Ms. Bertha, and she was smart as a fox. Just smart like a fox. Well, some of us working Reserve was gonna hide under the porch and let somebody go to the door. That's the way you did it. And I – she wouldn't know me – and buy the liquor. Well, she knew they was there, hiding at [under] the back porch, and (where she'd go around there and get the liquor) and she went out there and pulled them drawers down and *peed* on 'em!

Joseph Yeats told of a time when a friend of his had a problem. The friend ran moonshine from the mountain distillers to mill village customers, but his car had broken down and he wanted Yeats to drive for him. Secret arrangements were made. "I was just to drive into a man's open-door garage," Yeats recalled, and so "I drove in, no lights or anything. Some man unloaded my six cases for me. I backed out and left. That's the only time I ever hauled any; I took six cases to Greenville." His wife Beth remembered that when she was a girl, the county sheriff (a friend of her family) would destroy stills, but if the liquor "was pure, they'd bring us a quart for 'medicinal purposes!'"

"Tell him about" another situation, Joseph Yeats implored his wife during our interview, but then told the story himself:

> I got stopped out at Pickens one day, and the deputy didn't know me that stopped me. And he pulled his weapon, you know. And he was just shaking; man, I – "Take me to the sheriff because I

14 Coggeshall, *Something in These Hills*, 94, and John M. Coggeshall, *Carolina Piedmont Country* (Jackson: University Press of Mississippi, 1996), 139–40.

> know him." "You're going to shake something out of that gun, you know" [accidentally shoot him]. And I told her daddy about it when I come on in, and he and the sheriff were good friends, you know, and [her daddy] went out and talked to him, the sheriff about it, you know. A few days [later] he brought a half gallon of liquor out here. Pure corn, you know. And I didn't drink, and her dad didn't drink then. We had it in the house. But I come in one day and [my wife] jumped all over me; said, "You're gonna have to get this liquor out of this house," you know. Well, we had a chicken lot over there. I went over with a post hole digger and I dug a hole, set the half gallon down in it and covered it up, you know. And after the chickens scratching over it, there was no sign, you know. Well, I had a friend come up a few days later that wanted it, you know. I told him, I says, "It's out there buried; if you can find it, you can have it." He dug all Sunday afternoon, never did find it. As far as I know, it's still over there!

In his slow, deliberate style, Robert Davidson told a story about some moonshiners he knew personally. Davidson remembered that the men had set up their still

> under a big waterfall. . . . And they was making liquor down there; they had to have a ladder. They had a ladder to go down. They'd go down in here and there's a big wide place in there. And there's a big hemlock tree, stood right in below these falls. Well, they was in there making liquor and the law come in. And the law was standing right at the top of that ladder before they knowed there was any where about. Well, [one man] said he knowed they's caught so far as that goes, and [another man] said he took a run and went out to the end of that rock and jumped into . . . this big hemlock, caught a hold of a limb and swung that limb down almost to the ground and he said he guessed it was thirty feet before he caught. And then he swung that hemlock limb down to the ground and he fell out of there onto the ground and got away! . . . He went off of that hemlock, off of that rock and caught on that hemlock limb like a squirrel and then from there he said he just knowed it killed him. And he went from there to the ground and turned loose, went on around the side of the mountain. But he never was caught!

As a child, Charles Watson remembered bootleggers trying to evade the law by racing past his home. "Sometimes on Saturday night you'd hear a car go by," Watson described; "back then, you know, they'd have it souped up and everything, hear one go by just wide open and just a second or two here'd come another one wide open and it'd usually be [the sheriff or a deputy] chasing somebody. In fact, one man got killed right there, running from the law, and wrecked and went off in that field and hit a tree," Watson stated. Another time, Watson continued,

> the law got this feller – he had a load of whiskey and the law got him hemmed up, had him cut off on this end [of a road] and on the other end too. And there was a post oak stump – it was that big around. I don't know why they'd sawed that stump off, but it was as high as your head. And they had that road blocked, and the only way to get around it was to run over that post oak stump. And he [the fugitive] knocked that thing out of the ground and . . . kept a-going! I don't know what kind of shape his car was in when he got through, but Lord a' mercy! Next morning, went to school, you could smell whiskey before you got half a mile to the schoolhouse. I reckon all that stuff busted and all, that collision and all, but he knocked that stump out of the ground and kept going.

Women would help in their family's bootlegging business, as Robert Davidson explained. "And, now, that woman I was talking about awhile ago," Davidson began,

> she was old man George [Edison's] daughter. And after her old man got killed she stayed down there and she toted liquor for my granddaddy. She'd tote liquor from over there at the [Taylor] Place come right up that mountain there where there's – there used to be a trail right behind [Taylor's] house and she'd come straight up the mountain there. . . . And she'd tote five gallons of liquor in a stone jug over there. And maybe her girls that was with her, they's about fourteen or fifteen years old and they'd have a gallon or two apiece. And they'd tote that liquor over there with my granddaddy. He lived there in the Cane Break. And they'd come over there and go to town. Grandpa'd probably bring them to town and let them buy groceries and stuff. Then they'd go back and tote it in.

While children might be involved in "toting" liquor or guarding stills, adults typically did not share the alcohol with them – at least, most of the time. Elizabeth Nelson told a story she heard from a neighbor lady in her valley when she was a little girl:

> She said that she and her brother, . . . her dad had asked them to go out and find the cows one afternoon because the cows didn't come home out of the woods in time to be milked like they usually did. And they went up into the woods, up into the hills and they were along a stream and they came across a moonshine still. . . . And her uncle was there at the still with

> some other people. They were making moonshine and she said they offered each of them a cup of what they called "backings." Said, "I've never heard that term. What does it mean?" She said, "Well, it's before they finish making the moonshine and it's not completely ready, but it's still alcoholic." And she said, "Ooh, it tasted so good! And I remember it." And she said, "Then they gave us another cup and then they gave us a third cup." And she said, "We got drunk and then we came home and we forgot all about the cows!" Said, "Daddy was so mad because they gave us that and got us drunk." But she said, "That's one of my favorite memories."

Once county officials confiscated moonshine, the actual disposal presented ethical dilemmas for some people. Wasting a perfectly good and valuable commodity seemed illogical, and some folks succumbed to the temptation. For example, John Summers remembered that a county deputy would confiscate illegal whiskey and, instead of taking it to the courthouse, would take it home and his "wife was taking it to Tennessee. She had a wreck up there in the Caddy [Cadillac] and had a little whiskey in it, his wife did! Yeah. They got her in Tennessee with it!" Rachel Edwards remembered a story from her father, a county official and a friend of the sheriff. One time, after busting up a still, the sheriff brought gallons of moonshine into the basement of the courthouse to dispose of it in a "big, long sink." The sheriff asked Mrs. Edwards's father if he had problems with dandruff, and the sheriff replied that "there ain't nothing like moonshine" to cure dandruff. And so the sheriff instructed Edwards's father to cup his hands into the liquor as the sheriff poured out the moonshine, and then to rub the moonshine onto his scalp. Her father complied but quickly choked and coughed and "lost his breath and he thought he was going to die" because the fumes were so strong.

Occasionally, over-consumption of alcohol did kill. Robert Davidson told a story from the 1940s, of a State Park ranger who "got drunk and'd been on a drunk about a week and went over there in the Number Five cabin and laid down and went to sleep and died. And when they got to hunting for him and that's where they found him." On the other hand, Jesse Alexander remembered a country store proprietor who lived well into his nineties despite the fact that he drank heavily. As the man lay in his casket, Mr. Alexander related, two old ladies approached a friend of the deceased and asked what killed him. Sardonically, Alexander's friend replied, "'Liquor!'" Then Alexander said that his friend added: "'I wouldn't have told them that if they hadn't been nosey.'"

While most often not life-threatening, alcohol consumption might trigger pugnacity. One afternoon, as I listened to Douglas Edison and Robert Davidson tell stories, the latter narrated a tale in his special melodic voice. Davidson began:

> Old [Cal Riley] down here, he used to get drunk and want to start a fight. Well, this old [John Miller] fellow lived over there above him up around Salem and he was about half crazy. [Cal] was supposed to have good sense and old [Miller], everybody knowed him – and stout as a bull. He was about half crazy and stout as he could be. . . . So they's all went over there at Shallowford Bridge . . . one Sunday and [Bob Rands] was with [Cal Riley]. They'd walk over there to get a drink of liquor and they went over there and got the liquor and come back out there at the bridge. . . . They's down there around the bridge hanging out. . . . [Cal] – he got mouthy, said he got to yah – yah, yah, yah around, mouthy. Said that old [John], he could tell ol' [John] wasn't liking it too good and said he kept on. Said directly they got into it, sure enough. [Cal] was a big old fellow, too; old [Cal Riley] was a big fellow, pretty big fella. He said directly old [John] hauled off and hit old [Cal] and said he hit the ground and he said about the time he got up he hit him again; back down he'd go. And he said every time [Cal'd] hit him [John] would jump straight up, just jump straight up and pop his feet together and fart! And he said he'd jump up and pop his feet together and fart! And said directly he reached down and jerked up a big old root about that big in the ground, sitting out there in the road, said he grabbed up a big old root, said he didn't know how in the world he got that thing out of the ground. Said he jerked that thing up and he hit [Cal Riley] and said that was the end of it.

During that same interview, Robert Davidson told another story about stubborn or cantankerous mountain dwellers. "My great-granddaddy on the [Davidson] side," he began, and then added, "I'll just tell it like it is – he was mean as a stripe-ed snake!"[15] We all laughed, and Davidson explained: "All of them [old-time mountain] people would catch hogs and mark them, cut their ears and mark them[16] so they'd know which hog was theirs and which wasn't. But they said old man [Davidson] didn't care what mark. He'd catch one and he'd mark it with his mark, and most of the time he'd be killing somebody else's hog!"

Women also could be cantankerous. Patrick O'Connell told several stories about his mother, who had been forced out of her Jocassee Valley home because of lake construction and had moved into a neighborhood that allowed small livestock (goats and chickens) but not vegetable gardens. Nevertheless, she planted a garden despite her neighbors' complaints. But the neighbors' goats began to eat her garden, and so O'Connell's mother "went

---

15 See also Joseph S. Hall, *Smokey Mountain Folks and Their Lore* (Asheville, NC: Cataloochee Press, 1960), 63.

16 A common practice that gave rise to the word "earmark" as an indicator of something.

up town, bought her a twenty-gauge shot gun, . . . and she's putting the lead to them. . . . Never did see the goats no more." Then, O'Connell continued, "the chickens started eating her garden up." So she called the county animal control officer and requested "'the worst chicken-eating dog that you got.'. . . Killed them chickens like that."

Another time, Patrick O'Connell decided to play a practical joke on his mother. One evening O'Connell came home from work and called his mother, disguising his voice and pretending to be the county sheriff. "I told her, I says, 'I got papers here on you for where you owe on some furniture.' (She didn't owe nobody nothing.) She said, 'I'll tell you right now, I don't owe nobody nothing.' . . . I said, 'Well, I got a paper here that say you do.' 'Well, I don't.' I said, 'Well, I'm coming to get it, now.' 'I'll tell you right now, you come down here, you get some lead in your hind end!'" We all laughed.

Gregory Clayton told a story about his grandparents that parallels an anecdote widespread in popular culture. According to Clayton, his grandfather and "his oldest boy" were incarcerated in the Ashe (North Carolina) County jail for making moonshine. "And it was coming wintertime," and his grandmother became concerned about how she would feed her family during wintertime. So, Clayton continued,

> she made a cake and went about seventeen mile on a mule and buggy to take it to the jail where he was at. Had a hacksaw in the cake. Then before that old jailer took it up to him, he cut him a slice and missed that hacksaw blade! And then my granddad and his oldest boy, too, was little [thin] like me and so they just had to saw one bar in two and raised up. They went out and took bed sheets and went down on the other building until they got to the ground, and they headed off to Georgia then. . . . And they lived there until the [statute of] limitation run out . . . and then they went back to the North Carolina mountains. I always liked that story about her making that cake. She could've been in jail, too!

As a teenager, Donna Trask worked in her family's country store, and she described many characters who came in, including a woman who "still wore a dress, and a[n] apron and boots every day. It sounds like something off of *Little House on the Prairie*[17] or something but not quite like that. But every day she'd come [and I would ask her]: 'How are you doing today?' 'I'm not fishing; [so] I'm not doing too good.' That's what she'd say. If she wasn't fishing, she wasn't doing too good."

17 A television show that aired from 1974 to 1982, based on characters originally from the book of that title by Laura Ingalls Wilder.

As a teenager in her church, Kayla Radcliffe remembered a large family who had ten children, and eight of them were females. Unmarried and now in their seventies or eighties, the ladies all sat together in church. One of the sisters, Radcliffe continued, would get a fancy new hat every Easter, "and that was her big thing. And she was a little bit too much into music, so whenever anyone got up to sing, she'd be trying to sing along with them, even though it was a solo, and that got annoying! . . . They knew her reputation and they knew what she was going to do. . . . And if you were watching really closely you'd notice, like if she got loud, they'd glare at her for a bit. She didn't care; she would just keep on singing."

Practical Jokes, Pranks, and Anecdotes

While today "blackface" is seen as racist and humorless, among Euro-Americans in past generations the practice served different functions. The following story reflects racist overtones by making a "monster" out of a supposedly African American person. The audience and the tellers of the story are all Euro-Americans. As I interviewed Garvin Bradshaw, his wife, and his sister, Mr. Bradshaw told a story from his childhood about when his father was cutting cross ties by hand with an axe, and Bradshaw and some of his siblings were pestering him as he tried to work. Bradshaw continued:

> Well, Daddy hollered and told Momma to come down and get us and take us out of his way. Well, she went over and got us, and we come to the house up there, and thirty minutes later we was back down there. Well, she took and put on an old pair of overalls on, put her flop hat on, and she got in the heater, wood heater, took soot, smutted her face all over and everything. She hollered for us to come to the house; she had something she wanted to give us. Well, we stepped in the house, she stepped out behind the door. Well, we didn't know what a n----- was. But that black person? Buddy, we left you [sentence unclear]. One went one way, the other went the other way, and some went that way. She had to clean up and put us young'uns up. She scared us.

Charles Watson, a distant relative of Douglas Edison, shared their extended family's reputation for practical jokes. Watson stated that "if a feller can't take a joke, he ain't no good much anyway. . . . I just don't like a man like that who can't take a joke, laugh and go on. I don't fool with him." Watson then told a story about one of his distant relatives playing a joke on all the cousins, when they were about ten years old. Watson explained that Edison

> took his dad's old hunting horn, filled that thing about half full of water. And you can blow that thing and that water start dripping – oh Lord, it'd make the hair on your head stand up. Lord, you

> ain't never heard such an awful sounding booger[18] in your life! Lord o' mercy! And we was all out in the yard playing over there; . . . [Douglas Edison], he'd be a teenager. He just knew we was all out there playing, he'd hear us, I guess. Getting almost dark. He cut loose blowing that hunting horn and we didn't know what it was – we thought it was a varmint. Boy, everybody took off towards the house as hard as they could go!

John Summers used the same device for another practical joke. In his neighborhood, Summers explained, a man owned a dog called "Little Man." And the man frequently bragged that everything he owned was better than everyone else's – including Little Man, who "'wasn't scared of nothing.'" So one night Summers had an old hunting horn, and filled it about half full with water. He went over to the house, blew the horn, and frightened Little Man so much that the dog dove under the house and ran, bumping his head on the floor over and over again – "bump, bump, bump, bump! Oh, Lord, we pulled all kind of pranks like that," Summers concluded, as his friend George Tanner and I laughed along with him.

Charles Watson also described a contraption he called a "dumb bull," which must have sounded very similar. According to Watson, the device consisted of "a gallon bucket, I guess, and had a cat skin, like a banjo head stretched over it, and had a waxed string, waxed real heavy. And they'd pull that string through that dumb bull and that was an awful sounding thing too, Lord o' mercy." One time, Watson related, "Chill" (the "tower man" at a forest fire station) thought he had heard panthers in the surrounding wilderness, but his friends did not believe him. So they all agreed to spend the night at the fire tower, to see if they could all hear the panther. Secretly, "Tom" [pseudonym] took the dumb bull along with him. Watson continued:

> Here all of them's in there, waiting around, started getting dark. [Tom], he slipped out (told everybody "too much tension"). He slipped out and got that dumb bull and got up there on the ridge out from the house aways. He started pulling that string, and ooh that thing, it was awful. Some looked and said, "Chill, is that it?" "Yeah, that's it! That's it! That's it! No doubt about it, that's it!" . . . They finally talked Chill into going outside. Well, he had to got his butcher knife before he went – he wouldn't go out without something. He had his butcher knife. Just as he opened the door someone shouted, "Look out – here he come!" He dropped his butcher knife and went back in the house. But they never would tell. [Tom] went on for a long, long time before they ever told Chill what it was – that it was that dumb bull.

---

18 A monster of some kind. See Appendix Two.

Charles Watson told another story of one of Douglas Edison's relatives. He and another man went hunting in the mountains, and since it was getting late, they both lay down to rest, one on each side of a log. One man "tunneled a way through that log . . . to where . . . he could see [the other man's] big old fat foot sticking out. He whittled him off a stick and got it real sharp and stuck it in [the man's] foot and he thought a snake bit him. [The man] about died on him; he's getting sick. Finally he told him what he'd done. . . . Found out wasn't nothing to it, just a puncture wound."

Mac "Houn' Dawg" Erwin told a story about a well-known game warden, Franklin Gravely.[19] At the time, Gravely was training two younger game wardens, who wanted to determine who was the faster draw, as they had seen in old Western movies. Gravely knew this was dangerous, but he wanted to teach them this lesson in a more subtle way. As the two young men emptied their revolvers, pocketing the bullets and showing each other they had done so, Gravely quietly took a seat on a nearby log and slowly removed his own pistol from its holster, keeping it behind him. As the two men paced off and turned to draw on each other, Gravely fired his own pistol behind him. Immediately both men clutched desperately at their bodies, looking for a wound. They learned their lesson and never did anything like that again.

John Summers played a practical joke on some fundamentalist Christians in his neighborhood on the upper Keowee River. He remembered a group came into the valley one time, claiming that with God's help they could walk on water. The group would gather by the river on moonlit nights. According to Summers, "some boys" investigated and found a flat board just beneath the water's surface upon which the believers stepped, giving the appearance of walking on water. The boys secretly sawed the board almost in two, so that the next time the believers gathered and started "walking on water," the board cracked and broke, and "they all got wet!"

Jeffrey Donnelly told a similar story. He recalled a time local pranksters knew that some neighbors might "be drinking and they had an old foot log they had to walk across, a log with it hewn off on the top. And they'd get out there with a saw and saw underneath it. They'd get out over the creek, the log would break, and into the creek he would go! . . . Yeah, they didn't have anything else to do, any outlets anyway. I guess they had to do something."

On another occasion, Donnelly recalled, his uncle had been making moonshine with his father back in the woods, and the uncle

> knew about what time they would be coming out that night. It would be after dark. So he goes up there along the trail and

19 Franklin Gravely (1927–2000) was a game warden in upper South Carolina, and Erwin served under him. The story comes from a video, "Franklin Gravely Remembrance 2021," produced by the South Carolina Department of Natural Resources and loaned to me by Greg Lucas of the department.

> back then they used to have those "haints," you know. . . . He got a sheet and tied a rope to it – threw the rope over a limb and pulled the sheet up and when he heard them coming talking, then he'd start lowering that sheet down when they went by!

Some stories involve local folks who appear in the stories as "country bumpkins" or somewhat unsophisticated rural residents. For example, Ryan Trask told a story of a man born and raised in Rocky Bottom (upper Pickens County) and who had never been anywhere else. One day someone asked him if he would like to ride into Pickens (the county seat), about sixteen miles away, and "he got excited and he got in the back of that old truck. I mean it was just like somebody else going to the moon." "People were kind of gathered around, watching him leave," Trask continued, "and he stood up in the back of the truck and he said, 'Goodbye, old South Carolina; I'm going to Pickens!' He thought he was leaving the state. That was, I mean, that was how big his world was."

Harry Edison told a story about one of his father's brothers, working in Chattanooga, Tennessee, during World War II. A group of friends decided to attend the "Chattanooga Lookouts" football game,[20] and Edison's uncle wanted to go, too, explaining that he had never seen a football game before. So the men attended, and Edison remarked that his uncle was "sitting up there and he said, 'Boy, it was cold,' he says. He sits up there awhile, he said, 'Boy, when's this thing going to get started?' And he said, 'Get started? It's half over with.' He said, 'Half over with nothing – it's over with me!' And he left!"

Jeffrey Donnelly remembered a prank pulled on him when he was "probably five years old, I guess." He had been spending a few days with his uncle in Eastatoee Valley, and the two men and the boy sat on the front porch and watched county highway gravel trucks spreading gravel on the roads – "entertainment," Mr. Donnelly said wryly. And Donnelly's uncle told the little boy that "they were going to make me go out there and pick up all of that gravel and put it up into one pile, and I believed it. And I was worried to death; I thought, 'I will never get all of that done!'"

Donna Trask remembered a character who used to patronize her family's country store, but he did not want to pay the state tax on soft drinks. At that time, South Carolina levied a sales tax on soft drinks sold over the counter but not on drinks purchased through vending machines. So, to avoid the tax, the man would ask Trask and her fellow clerks for change, go outside to the soft drink dispenser, feed the money in for one drink at a time, and purchase his soft drinks that way. "I mean he'd want dollars of change and then he'd brag about what he was doing," Donna Trask observed.

20 A search of the internet did not find a Lookouts football team but instead a minor league baseball team by that name. Perhaps Edison meant the football team of the University of Tennessee.

Ryan Trask told a story from his grandfather's generation, about a neighbor who had a terrible toothache. He got a ride into Pickens to see a dentist, who pulled the tooth. The man asked to keep the tooth, and when the dentist asked him why, he replied, "'I want to take that tooth home with me.' And the dentist said, you know, 'Why? It's pretty bad. You know, it's not something you'd want.' He said, 'I want to take it home and pour molasses on it and watch it explode.' That was his mindset, 'cause every time he ate something sweet, it was – and so he thought he could take that tooth home, pour molasses on it and he wanted to watch it explode."

I heard a story from a man in Pickens about two brothers living way back in the Horsepasture area. Their father had died, and they were bringing him out on a sled because there were no roads back in there. The undertaker (the father of the storyteller) was going to meet them at the road with the hearse. When they arrived, the man said, "Boys, I'm sorry to see you lost your daddy." "Yep," they said, "but he had a good life." "No," the undertaker replied, "I mean you lost your daddy!" The boys turned around and said, "Damn – he must have fallen off the sled somewhere back up the trail!"

Peter Abney had been a volunteer firefighter for the state forest service before his retirement, and he told a story about himself. One time he was helping to fight a fire in Reedy Cove (Pickens County) and was driving a tractor to cut a firebreak through the woods. Abney reported that the smoke was so thick he could hardly see what he was doing. The pilot of a spotter plane above him radioed and said, "'Boy, you making a beautiful line!' I think, 'Well.' He says, 'They's only one thing wrong with it; you putting it in on the wrong mountain!'"

Margaret and James York, friends of Brian and Claudia Alexander, told stories of Claudia's parents (and those of her brother Garvin Bradshaw). The Bradshaw children were raised in a four-room house built by their father (see Chapter Six), with no indoor plumbing. Margaret York described the family as "*real*, real country. I'm not quite as bad as they were." Mrs. York explained that the senior Bradshaw called his wife "old lady." Mr. Bradshaw had suspended a long pull cord from the overhead light bulb to the head of the bed, so that one could lie in the bed and pull the cord. Mrs. York described a story she heard from Claudia when she was a little girl:

> She said when she was little one night, she said, she slept with her mommy and daddy. Said he had a pair of old long johns and he slept in these long johns. She was in the bed. Said [laughing; pause] all of a sudden her daddy said, "Old lady, pull the light!" Said they had the string up on the woman's side of the bed, you know, tied to the bed post. [Claudia] said, she turned that light on and seen her daddy, looked down there and there was a cat's

> head sticking out of his pants! Said he took that cat and slung it up against the wall. She said, "That's the truth – I seen that!"

Mrs. York added that she told Claudia that she would know "'every time he said that [sentence] there was action gonna start?' And she said, 'You better believe it!'"

Despite the fact that the Cherokee as a cultural group had been removed from South Carolina by the late eighteenth century,[21] it is very likely that Native American families, or individuals, remained in the mountainous counties well into the nineteenth century. Several inhabitants told stories involving Native Americans. For example, as Stephanie Jamison spoke with her aunt Alice Flowers, they recalled a story from Anne Flowers's girlhood. Ms. Jamison recalled that

> when Grandma was a little girl, . . . she was doing laundry and she had folded it up and put it in the basket and had it sitting on the side porch or something. And some drunken Indian came wandering by and sat down in the basket and passed out and Grandma was like, trying to wake him up and he couldn't wake up. So she got his tomahawk from the side of his pants 'cause he had on trousers, took the tomahawk from his trousers and held his braid up and axed it to the wall so he wouldn't lean over and drool on her nice clean laundry. And finally when he come to she told him, "You get out of here and don't you ever come back or I'm going to cut your braid off!" I mean, that was Grandma for you.

Fitting the pattern of similar American treasure tales,[22] Ralph Glenn related a legend about lost Cherokee treasure somewhere up in Eastatoee Valley:

> There's a story about a party [of Indians] coming through here in those years in the early 1800s, and they were looking for a rock on one of these hills up here with a carving of a squirrel on it. And the story is that they said that's where, that squirrel looked at the place where they had buried their gold and their things that they thought were culturally significant, spiritually significant, and they were back here to pick those up. And a friend of mine tells a story of one of his uncles being up here drunk coon hunting one night and they set the lantern down on this rock and there's this squirrel carved in it. . . . And they got back down the next morning and couldn't go back there if they had to. A year or so later, just in passing conversation, they

21 John M. Coggeshall, *Liberia, South Carolina: An African American Appalachian Community* (Chapel Hill: University of North Carolina Press, 2018), 25–26.

22 See Gerald Hurley, "Buried Treasure Tales in America," *Western Folklore* 10, no. 3 (1951): 197–216.

> were talking about that squirrel they saw on that rock and they said one girl asked, leaned over and said, "You saw a squirrel on a rock?" And they said, "Yeah." She said, "Boys, you need to find that rock." She said, "That's where them Indians come through here, seventy-five years ago, and talked to Grandma and wanted to know if they'd seen that rock 'cause that's where all the gold is!" So, if you ever see a rock up here with a squirrel carved on it, you need to pay attention.

Stories of local characters and personal anecdotes about family members, or even of oneself, add another dimension to life in the South Carolina foothills of the Blue Ridge Mountains. The stories add context and humor to the descriptions of daily life and daily activities from earlier chapters, and they also demonstrate the sense of humility, or the consequences of pride, for many mountain folks. Finally, the stories add to the collective sense of humor characteristic of the region.

Chapter Ten

Conclusion

This collection of stories, elicited from inhabitants of the three northwesternmost counties in South Carolina about a decade ago, illustrates several points. First, the stories demonstrate changes to general American culture as well as to the social life of South Carolina over more than a century. Second, the stories are entertaining. Third, the stories demonstrate the commonality of all of us as humans, regardless of time or space.

In this book, the third one produced through my Jocassee Gorges Cultural History project,[1] I can still hear the voices and recall the times spent with the wonderful people who told these stories. For example, I can recall sitting in the comfortable living room of Joshua and Anne Flowers, and the true enjoyment they reflected as they talked about their decades of married life and their adventures together. I can recall laughing with Robert Davidson and Douglas Edison as Mr. Davidson regaled us with stories from his mountain past. I panted with exhaustion while I climbed the mountain behind Harry Edison's home as we walked up his favorite trail and he pointed out his favorite wild azaleas. And I remember sitting in my university office and talking with Jason Taylor about his high school adventures, and his rather sheepish expression as he thought back on some of his earlier escapades. All of these folks, and those described in Appendix One, are human beings who volunteered to share their lives with all of us,

1 John M. Coggeshall, *Something in These Hills: The Culture of Family Land in Southern Appalachia* (Chapel Hill: University of North Carolina Press, 2022); and John M. Coggeshall, *Liberia, South Carolina: An African American Appalachian Community* (Chapel Hill: University of North Carolina Press, 2018).

and it has been a highlight of my life to meet all of these people and to listen to all of these stories.

It seems difficult to imagine the changes in American society that have occurred during the lives of some of these people. I have spoken with folks who attended one-room schoolhouses, who walked miles over mountain trails to attend school or church, and who grew up in homes without running water. Older inhabitants remember their grandparents seeing their first automobile or hearing their first airplane; others recall their first moments of electrified lights or televised pictures. Also included are stories about ways of life that have mostly vanished: cake walks and wood choppings, for example. On the other hand, Friday night football games, church homecomings, and Sunday family dinners are still quite commonplace (albeit changed), and parents still restrict younger ears from certain types of stories.

As I reflect on these stories and their tellers, I can also think about types of stories that I did not collect. For example, what were the first video games people played, and how did those change the traditional games of childhood? When was letter writing replaced by emails and then by texting? How have these new forms of media and communication platforms modified human communication and mate selection? How have air conditioning and television transformed family gatherings and children's play activities? What has been the social and economic impact of the transformation of visiting at crossroads stores into shopping at large supermarkets and now into scrolling by phone to elicit home deliveries? How has the shift from walking long distances to driving even greater ones changed American perspectives and general health? As sexual identities and nonbinary rights have become more commonplace in general American culture, how have these alternatives affected the people in these categories and those with whom they interact? These questions could be topics for future exploration by other authors.

Desegregation was another topic I did not pursue in this book.[2] By the late 1960s, schools in South Carolina finally were desegregating, and teachers faced new students and new colleagues while students faced new classmates and new buildings. Sports teams desegregated locker rooms, and cheerleaders now touched the bodies of those of other ethnicities. African Americans and Euro-Americans now mingled in entirely new ways. Just recently Allen Hill shared with me a life-threatening experience he faced as a black teenage school bus driver in northern Pickens County. How did parents, teachers, and students respond to the challenges of desegregation? How did these responses vary by generation, gender, ethnicity, region,

2 Although see Coggeshall, *Liberia*, 121–22, 149–51.

neighborhood, or individual? What lessons were learned? What lessons might still be learned?

It is also sad to realize that approximately one-third of the people whose stories were told in the preceding pages have passed away. One of the more somber duties I feel a responsibility for is trying to attend as many funerals as I can for those whom I have interviewed. I distinctly remember that the families of both Douglas Edison and Garvin Bradshaw thanked me for attending their memorial services. It is a serious reminder for all of us to document the stories and life experiences of our loved ones in order to help them preserve their stories for all to enjoy.

Another theme of the stories is that (I hope) they are entertaining. The banter between longtime friends Robert Davidson and Douglas Edison, or Cynthia Niles and Patrick O'Connell, was engaging and amusing. Jason Taylor provided an insider's view of early twenty-first-century high school social life – stories I could have listened to for hours. Mesmerized, I sat outside Garvin Bradshaw's modest home in northern Oconee County one summer evening as he narrated stories of witchcraft, of boogers, and of ghosts, supported by additions from his wife and his youngest sister.[3] Donna Trask met many characters as she worked at her family's snack bar in a crossroads service station, and she enjoyed reflecting on their eccentricities. Gregory Clayton's colorful past provided tales of adventure, and he readily shared them with me with a twinkle in his blue eyes. Peter Abney told self-deprecating anecdotes about his life, punctuated with expectorations of tobacco juice into a nearby cup. These and other stories still entertain extended families at reunions and church homecomings, and children still strain to eavesdrop on restricted adult conversations. Quick wits, and a propensity to take oneself not too seriously, seem to be characteristic of the area.

Above all else, to me the stories remind me of a fundamental concept in anthropology – that despite significant differences in cultures across time and space, we are all equally human. We all celebrate the arrivals of newborns, we all relish the camaraderie of childhood friends, we all love and share that love with our intimate partners, and we all mourn the passing of loved ones. For some reason, we take pleasure in seeing the proud humbled (bombastic preachers having blackened feet), or the tables turned (a moonshiner urinating on entrapping deputies), or ironic episodes ("Kick a Freshman" Day thwarted by an insightful principal). We empathize with the knowing glances of long-married spouses as they confess earlier romances with others or remember their first thoughts of each other as

3 Tales of the supernatural may be found in Coggeshall, *Something in These Hills*, 101–8.

potential mates. Despite the fact that the people in these stories may have been raised with different values than my readers, may have been raised in a different place, and may have been raised in different generations, there are common threads in these stories to which we can all connect. That is what makes us human, and that is what makes these stories worth documenting. I hope it also makes them worth reading.

Appendix One

Informant Biographies

These biographies are in alphabetical order by pseudonym.
Biographical details were current at the time of interviews, but I have inserted death notices to demonstrate the fragility of life.

Peter Abney – Born and raised in upper Pickens County, Mr. Abney lived on family land surrounded by his in-laws. He worked for the state as a career. Active in his local church, Mr. Abney was friends with the family of Shirley Patterson. Mr. Abney was of European descent, and he has passed away.

Claudia and Brian Alexander – A married couple from upper Pickens County. Mr. Alexander was in his fifties and was a friend of James York. He worked as a laborer. Claudia Bradshaw Alexander (sister of Garvin Bradshaw) was born and raised in upper Oconee County in the early 1960s, and she worked as an administrative assistant for a local governmental agency. Both are of European descent; Mr. Alexander has passed away.

Jesse Alexander – Father of Brian Alexander. Born about 1930, Mr. Alexander moved out of the Jocassee Valley and later owned a small business in downtown Pickens for decades. He is of European descent, and has passed away.

Bruce Anderson – Born and raised in upper Oconee County around 1950, he owns an agriculturally based family business there. He had obtained a college education. He is of European descent.

Marsha and Dennis Baird – A married couple in their seventies living in upper Pickens County. Mr. Baird was born and raised in mill towns in Greenville County, but his ancestors were from the mountains. Mrs. Baird had been raised on farms in Pickens County. Both had graduated from college, and Mr. Baird had worked for a regional company until his retirement. Both are of European descent.

Andrea Bowers – Daughter of Adam and Beth Yeats, she was born and raised in upper Pickens County but now lives downstate. She is in her late forties, married, and of European descent.

Garvin and Cheryl Bradshaw – A married couple living in upper Oconee County. Mr. Bradshaw was a lifelong resident of Oconee County and was interviewed when he was in his seventies. He was the brother of Claudia Bradshaw Alexander and lived on family land in the county. A laborer all his life, he had a high school education. He was of European descent and has passed away.

Pamela Charles – Neighbor of Shirley Patterson, she has spent her life in upper Pickens County and manages a small business. She is in her late fifties and of European descent.

Josephine Chavis – Born and raised in upper Oconee County in the 1920s, she was college educated and taught school. In her younger years she traveled extensively to other continents. Her husband had a successful family business and had recently passed away. Mrs. Chavis still lived in her own home near her birthplace. She was of European descent and has passed away.

Gregory Clayton – Born and raised in the mountains between North and South Carolina in the 1930s, Mr. Clayton eventually settled in upper Pickens County with his family. A laborer for most of his life, Mr. Clayton lived on his late wife's property in upper Pickens County. Of European descent, Mr. Clayton has passed away.

Norman Cleveland – In his seventies, Mr. Cleveland lived in upper Pickens County. During his life he did many things, including moonshining (sometimes with Robert Davidson). He was of European descent and has passed away.

Denise and Benjamin Craig – A retired married couple in their late sixties, they live in upper Pickens County on Mrs. Craig's family land. Mrs. Craig, with a college education, is from the middle part of the state, but her family is from upper Pickens County; she is related to the Davidson, Edison, and Flowers families. Both are of European descent.

Nancy Abney Daniels and Edward Daniels – Nancy Daniels is the married daughter of Peter Abney, and Edward Daniels is her college-aged resident son. Mrs. Daniels is a college-educated grade- school teacher in her fifties, born and raised in upper Pickens County and living on family land. She is of European descent.

Mike Davidson – Born in the early 1950s and raised in upper Pickens County, he is the son of Robert Davidson and still lives near his extended family in upper Oconee County. A master of many trades with a high school education, he has traveled overseas several times and has worked for several Upstate companies. He is of European descent.

Robert Davidson – Born and raised in the upper valleys of Pickens County, Mr. Davidson was in his late eighties. He worked at many trades, including moonshining, and probably had not graduated from grade school. He was good friends with Douglas Edison, nephew of Anne Flowers, and the father of Mike Davidson. Of European descent, Mr. Davidson has passed away.

Jeff Donnelly – Mr. Donnelly was born and raised in a valley in upper Pickens County, but after high school he enlisted in the military and worked on the West Coast for decades, only to return to his upper Pickens County valley in the 1990s. He and his wife are in their seventies and are both of European descent.

Amy Driver – A whitewater guide living in upper Oconee County, she is in her early forties. Originally from the Northeast, she and her family moved to Oconee County in the early 1970s to develop a river rafting company, and she has been here ever since. She is of European descent.

Douglas Edison – Born and raised in upper Pickens County, he grew up in the upper Keowee Valley. He was in his seventies for the interviews. He had worked for a state agency for much of his life and was a good friend of Robert Davidson's. Of European descent, Mr. Edison has passed away.

Harry Edison – Cousin to Douglas Edison, Henry was born, raised, and still lived in upper Pickens County. Married to his high school sweetheart (who has passed away), Mr. Edison is in his early sixties and works at a textile plant in the same county. He is of European descent.

Rachel and James Edwards – Both born and raised in upper Pickens County, the married couple is in their late sixties. Mr. Edwards operated a small store, and Mrs. Edwards had been a professional gospel singer in her youth and still enjoyed playing and singing music. Both are of European descent. Mr. Edwards has passed away.

David and Marie Ellison – Born and raised in upper Oconee County, Mr. Ellison was a retired farmer. He and his wife owned her family's land in the county, and they lived near their children. He was probably in his seventies at the time of the interview. Both are of European descent. Mr. Ellison has passed away.

Alice Flowers – Youngest daughter of Anne and Joshua Flowers, she was born and raised in upper Pickens County and is now in her seventies. She is of European descent.

Anne and Joshua Flowers – Married for over seventy-five years, both were in their nineties at the time of the interview. Neither had graduated from high school, and they had spent almost all their lives in upper Pickens County. Anne Flowers is the aunt of Robert Davidson. Both were of European descent, and both have passed away.

Theodore Franklin – Born and raised in upper Pickens County, he currently lives there on his wife's family land. Retired and perhaps in his seventies, he is friends with Rachel and James Edwards and is of European descent.

Ralph Glenn – Spent his childhood and some retirement years in upper Pickens County. Mr. Glenn also had a long military career. He was in his mid-fifties at the time of the interviews and was married with children. He is of European descent.

Jenn Grover – A county employee in her early fifties, Ms. Grover was born and raised in the Oolenoy Valley near Pumpkintown, upper Pickens County. She is friends with Shirley Patterson and is of European descent.

Daniel Hall – A retired physician in his late seventies, Mr. Hall lived on the South Carolina coast but vacationed in a house in upper Pickens County on his wife's family's land. Mr. Hall had spent his childhood vacationing in upper Pickens County. He is of European descent and has passed away.

Allen Hill – Raised in Pickens County, Mr. Hill as a boy spent many days in the Liberia Community visiting his friend, a younger brother of Shirley Valentine Patterson. Today he is a Christian minister and still lives in Pickens County. He is of African American descent.

Carrie Jackson – Born about 1920, Mrs. Jackson grew up in the Oolenoy Valley in upper Pickens County and still lived near her family's ancestral land when I interviewed her with her two married adult children, Chris and Julie. She is of European descent and has passed away.

Julie Jackson – Born in upper Pickens County, she graduated from Pickens High School. She spent part of her life working in Texas only to move back to the family land. She is in her mid-sixties. Daughter of Carrie Jackson, she is of European descent.

Stephanie Jamison – Niece of Alice Flowers and granddaughter of Anne and Joshua Flowers, she is in her forties. She was born and raised in Pickens County and is of European descent.

Brenda Kendrick – Born and raised in Oconee County, she was in her seventies at the time of the interview and was married. While she does not live on family land, members of her extended family still own the homeplace. She is of European descent.

Beth Lepre – Born and raised in upper Pickens County, she and her family vacationed frequently in Jocassee Valley before it was flooded. In her late forties, she worked for the county until she retired to care for her aging parents. She lives in her family's homeplace in upper Pickens County. Cousin to Elizabeth Nelson, she is of European descent.

Deborah Tanner Mitchell – Born and raised in upper Pickens County, Mrs. Mitchell is in her seventies and is widowed. She has an advanced college education and taught school for a career. Having lost her family home to the flooding of the lakes, Mrs. Mitchell now lives in Greenville County. She is a sister of George Tanner, related to Elizabeth Nelson, and is of European descent.

David Nelson – Born in 1913 and raised in upper Pickens County, Mr. Nelson was in his nineties during the interviews. He is Elizabeth Nelson's father's brother; their family has been in their valley for centuries. Of European descent, Mr. Nelson has passed away.

Elizabeth Nelson – College educated and in her late fifties, Ms. Nelson lived in the same upper Pickens County valley where she has spent most of her life. She is the niece of David Nelson, and at the time of the interview lived in her family's homeplace. She is a cousin to Beth Lepre and also related to Deborah Mitchell. She is of European descent.

Cynthia Niles – Born in upper Oconee County but (after marriage) moved into upper Pickens County, where she spent the rest of her life. Members of her family worked for the federal government. In her late sixties at the time of the interview, she married as a teenager and may not have finished high school. She is related by marriage to Robert Davidson and directly to Douglas Edison, although distantly. She is of European descent, and has passed away.

Patrick O'Connell – Former neighbor and long-time friend to Cynthia Niles and her late husband, Mr. O'Connell is in his sixties, and was born and raised in upper Pickens County. His family home is now under the lakes. He is of European descent.

Elaine and Robert Parker – A married couple in their eighties living in northern Greenville County. Mr. Parker, a minister in a conservative Christian denomination, bore the name of a prominent Confederate politician. He was related to Shirley Valentine, and both Parkers were of African American descent. Mr. Parker has passed away.

Shirley Valentine Patterson – Born and raised in upper Pickens County, Mrs. Patterson (in her mid-sixties) had spent several decades in the north before moving back to her family land. Mrs. Patterson worked at various jobs, and her husband was a professional in a nearby city. She is the sister of Michael Valentine and friends with Peter Abney. She is of African American descent.

Kayla Radcliffe – Born and raised in upper Pickens County, Ms. Radcliffe was about twenty and a college student during the interviews. She is a graduate of Pickens County High School. She is of European descent.

Joan Randall – Born in the upper parts of Oconee County, she moved with her family to a larger village in the county so that she could attend high school regularly. Her father ran a business in Jocassee Valley for years. In her eighties at the time of the interview, she lived in a comfortable home in a town in Pickens County. Mrs. Randall has passed away.

Forrest Sanders – A friend of Kayla Radcliffe, Mr. Sanders is a college student about twenty years old and a graduate of Pickens High School. He was born and raised in Pickens County and is of European descent.

John Summers – Born and raised in upper Oconee County and in his seventies, he lives on his family land surrounded by his extended family. He had a high school education and had worked for a regional company but is now retired. He is of European descent.

George Tanner – Boyhood friend of John Summers and brother to Deborah Mitchell, Mr. Tanner had been born and raised in Jocassee Valley but was forced to move out with his family in the late 1960s. Now retired, he is of European descent.

Jason Taylor – A friend of Kayla Radcliffe, Mr. Taylor is a college student about twenty years old and a graduate of Pickens High School. He was born and raised in Pickens County and is of European descent.

Donna and Ryan Trask – A married couple in their forties and both college educated. Mrs. Trask was raised in upper Pickens County and teaches school. Mr. Trask, born and raised in Pickens County, was an administrator for a higher education institution in the area. They lived on land they purchased in upper Pickens County, near Mrs. Trask's parents. Both are of European descent.

Helen Urban – Girlhood friend of Denise Voight, born in the 1950s. Raised in Oconee County, Mrs. Urban is of European descent.

Philip Valentine – Born and raised on a farm in upper Pickens County, Mr. Valentine married and left the area for the Northeast but still visited his homeplace frequently. He was an older brother to Shirley Patterson. Of African American descent, Mr. Valentine has passed away.

Denise Voight – Girlhood friend of Helen Urban, born in the 1950s. Raised in Oconee County, Ms. Voight is of European descent.

Charles Watson – Born and raised in upper Pickens County, Mr. Watson worked for a state agency and is now retired and living on family land in upper Pickens County. Mr. Watson is related directly to Douglas Edison and Robert Davidson, and by marriage to Peter Abney. He is in his mid-sixties and is of European descent.

Joseph and Beth Yeats – A married couple in their eighties, friends and neighbors to Colleen Zimmerman. Mr. Yeats was born in a Pickens County mill village and married into the Arnold family who lived in upper Pickens County; the couple spent their married life farming Arnold family land. Mr. Yeats served in the military, and they were friends to Shirley Patterson's family. Both are of European descent, and both have passed away.

Margaret and James York – Born and raised in upper Pickens County, the couple (late sixties and early seventies) had met originally in grade school. Mr. York had been a laborer all his life, moving throughout the county, and his wife worked for the county; in retirement, Mr. York collected and sold all sorts of materials. Of European descent, Mr. York has passed away.

Colleen Zimmerman – Friend and neighbor to Joseph and Beth Yeats, she married into a family in upper Pickens County in the mid-1950s and lived there ever since. She was in her seventies, and originally came from the northeastern U.S. She was of European descent and has passed away.

Appendix Two

Curious Words in Appalachian Dialects

While many studies of the Appalachian dialects provide word lists of characteristic or unusual words (such as "yonder" or "mash" [rather than "press"]), I will provide a list of some (but certainly not all) curiosities, along with their use in a sentence or several sentences. For convenience, the list is alphabetized, and I include mostly one example of each case, but these usages are not unique to a particular individual.

Acorn
Pronounced "akern" by many inhabitants.

Bad (tendency to do something)
One of her siblings had a childhood nickname of "tar heel," "and to this day we're still bad to call him that." *Brenda Kendrick*

Behold (to see)
Talking about a rock outcrop near her home: "Lordy, behold one day I was going to work, and I glanced at the rock. I said, 'Somebody done turned a rock upside down, sticking up.' And I looked again, I said, 'Oh, my goodness, that's a bear sitting on that rock!'" *Shirley Valentine Patterson*

Blackguard
"My daddy'd say, 'We can't blackguard.' They'd say 'blackguard;' blackguard means you saying dirty stuff in front of a woman." *Claudia Alexander*

Book (go quickly)
"Went on up there and got in sight of it [a treed raccoon], and he booked plumb to the end of the limb." *Joshua Flowers*

Boot (car trunk)
In speaking about a moonshiner apprehended by the law: "And they had big, half a gallon fruit jars, had their car boot full of half a gallon fruit jars." *Anne Flowers*

Borrow (to loan or rent)
"Buck's daddy borrowed that place [a residence] in nineteen and eleven" to another neighbor. *Norman Cleveland*

Bunt (bundle)
"My daddy, he worked the woods all the time; he'd dig ginseng. And he'd cut a bunt of it up and put it in a little fruit jar, you know." *John Summers*

But (just about to a place)
"And it's amazing how these people survived that [a flood] 'cause it [flood waters] came right down but where those people had their homes." *Harry Edison*

Come (alternate past tense, used with third person neuter)
"In the late '60s, early '70s it just come a blizzard." *Brian Alexander*
About a fishing spot in the mountains: "It come up a cloud while we was up there." *Mike Davidson*

Dog bread (corn bread)
"He'd get up every morning and build him [personal dative] a fire, go to the cupboard when he got ready to start, got his clothes on, go to the stubbard and have dog bread on the stove." *Joshua Flowers*

Dusky dark (twilight)
"My dad was a lot of fun. He would, when we were kids I mean, he'd work all day and just at dusky dark he'd want us to get us out and we'd play hide and seek." When asked to explain the term, she offered: "When it's that little area between not quite dark but daylight's about gone." *Brenda Kendrick*

(Stove) Eye
As her grandmother healed, "her hands felt like an eye, like she had laid them on a burner, or the eye of the stove." *Stephanie Jamison*

Invade (to intrude upon)
In describing watching her grandmother milk cows: "I stood right beside her. I invaded her, I guess." *Marie Ellison*

Lamm/Lamb (to beat or thrash)
"And this goat turned around and he lammed me straight into my leg with his horn and picked me straight up from the ground and took me back down." *Shirley Valentine Patterson*

Long (gone for a time)
"Said he thought somebody took some deer guts or something in there. But I believed he knowed 'cause they's long." *Garvin Bradshaw*

Look to (to consider, attend)
"Now when his [her husband's] mother was living, she looked to [her husband] every Saturday night, and we'd take her out." *Josephine Chavis*

Manor/Manner (a tract of land)
In talking about her shift from a small grade school to a larger middle school: "You know, we knew kids from church and from other manors, but that was – that's kind of neat." *Donna Trask*

Mess (quantity sufficient to make a meal)
"I wouldn't bring back a load of fish. But I'd bring back a mess." *Joshua Flowers*

Mislick (poorly aimed blow)
In speaking about a water snake striking him: "That thing was getting them fish scraps. I reckon he's hungry. He made a mislick; got my hand!" *John Summers*

Mule
"Mr. McJunkin always told us, 'If you get a mule (he called it – that means a heavy stick) – so everybody has to get a mule" to walk the land. *Pamela Williams, relative of Shirley Patterson*

One (in comparison)
A building "got burned down in about, 1939 or '40, one, and they built back about the same place, so we didn't have to walk but just a short distance." *Joan Randall*

Over-doubled
"And he sold it [a house] for twenty something thousand. He over-doubled his money on it." *Robert Davidson*

Paid (spoiled)
Her father loved his grandchildren, but barely knew his first great-grandchild. "She was born in May and my daddy died that December. He would have had her paid rotten had he lived long enough." *Brenda Kendrick*

Pillow (verb)
"You put God first and you do what's right because when you pillow your head, you gotta answer to God." *Claudia Alexander*

Plunder (verb) (to rummage)
In describing her mother's visits back to the home place: "We'd let her go down there and she'd sit. . . . And she could plunder in her doo-dads and see all her stuff and she had that feeling of 'I still have my home.'" *Claudia Alexander*

Quare (queer)
"My husband's quare and [chuckles] that means that he has ways that are different, I guess. The term quare – odd – is what that means." *Claudia Alexander*

Satisfied (to be certain)
"He went to school some'ere's, I'm satisfied, in there because he had about as much education as any of them did." *Robert Davidson*
My question: "Did some people die pretty quickly after they sold the land" [to development]? "I'm satisfied they did." *Norman Cleveland*

Shah (exclamation)
My grandfather "was in his late seventies then . . . and he'd be sitting there . . . watching TV; the next thing they say [is] 'This is Channel 7 Spartanburg.' . . . He said 'Shah! Turn that thing [off], I don't want to watch that!'" *Harry Edison*

Sorry (not highly thought of)
"There were families [in the area] that had reputations of being sorry, and they were sorry." *Beth Lepre*
"This state legislature we have is a sorry bunch, because this [law change] should have been done years ago." *Harry Edison*

Spring Lizard (salamander)
A waterline from a spring to her house might freeze, "and then we'd have to walk the line and see where the water, where the ground was wet. Or a spring lizard would get in there and get turned." *Beth Lepre*

Stob (noun and verb)
"Momma always said she wanted to be buried beside her babies, and she took an iron stob – remember, they put a stob out there and stob Momma and Daddy's spot." *Claudia Alexander*

Stout (strong)
"Nobody done pick on this boy [bullied as a child]. 'Cause we had never done nothing but hard work, you know – stout. We were strong." *Patrick O'Connell*

Streak-ed Meat (striped like bacon)
At his mother-in-law's house, "I couldn't wait to get to the table. There'd be cornbread and beans and corn and streak-ed meat and pork chops and just everything you could think of." *Brian Alexander*

Suck Eggs (to be worthless)
After shooting at a thief on his property: "That broke him sucking eggs! [both chuckle] I didn't kill him, but I fixed him good." *John Summers*

Summerset (somersault)
“Them boys was cutting summersets on the cane pullings, . . . and [a man] broke his neck.” *Robert Davidson*

Sweet Bread
A neighbor offered, “‘Don’t you want some sweet bread?’ And I looked at my mom like, ‘What is sweet bread?’ And Momma says . . . ‘That’s cake.’” *Elizabeth Nelson*

Trim
“The house we lived in was a[n] old house. Had a big hallway trimming through there with two twenty-foot rooms on each side.” *Joan Randall*

Wonderful (amazing)
“And we had homemade sleds and Daddy’d hook ’em behind the car, and you know that’d scare everyone to death, anybody doing something like that today. It’s wonderful nobody got hurt.” *Harry Edison*

Yield (serving)
“And she [her mother] would make like a blackberry cobbler, a yield of that.” *Shirley Valentine Patterson*

Index

www.ingramcontent.com/pod-product-compliance
Lightning Source LLC
La Vergne TN
LVHW091126080826
845145LV00008B/2059

* 9 7 8 1 6 3 8 0 4 1 9 6 2 *